Libertarian Capitalism

A Journey to the Austrian School of Economics

LUIS TEJADA

INDEX

Introduction

In the vast landscape of economic theories, the Austrian School emerges as a beacon of thought that challenges conventional currents and embraces individual freedom as a fundamental principle. This book aims to be an enlightening guide to the foundations and applications of the Austrian School of Economics, unraveling its key principles and exploring its relevance in the contemporary world.

On the horizon of this intellectual journey, we encounter figures such as Ludwig von Mises, Carl Menger, and other pioneers who, in the early 20th century, laid the groundwork for a unique economic perspective. Their focus on human action, the theory of subjective value, and the critique of centralized planning marked a milestone in understanding how the economy operates.

As we delve into these pages, it is impossible to ignore the contemporary relevance of the Austrian School, particularly its impact on the economic discourse in Argentina. The potential election of a new president, known for his affinity towards Austrian School ideas, as is the case with Javier Gerardo Milei in Argentina, underscores the enduring influence of these principles on public policies and in the minds of leaders.

Milei's journey to political leadership and his passionate advocacy of Austrian ideas add an intriguing nuance to our analysis. How do these principles translate into concrete political decisions? Can the Austrian School offer practical solutions to modern economic challenges?

We are at a crucial moment where understanding these principles can have a significant impact on the direction of policies and on people's lives.

Prepare for a journey that not only seeks to illuminate the complexities of the Austrian School of Economics but also invites reflection on its relevance in political decision-making in Argentina and beyond. In a world constantly seeking answers, the Austrian School provides a unique, challenging, and at times, radically libertarian perspective.

1.Founders of the Austrian School

The Austrian School of Economics originated in the late 19th and early 20th centuries, with several key thinkers who made significant contributions to its development. Here are some of the most prominent founders:

Carl Menger (1840-1921): Considered the founder of the Austrian School, Menger published "Principles of Economics" in 1871, introducing the theory of subjective value and laying the groundwork for the Austrian School. Born on February 23, 1840, in Galicia (present-day Ukraine), and passing away on February 26, 1921, in Vienna, Austria, Menger is recognized as the founder and a major architect of the Austrian School of Economics. His seminal work, "Principles of Economics" ("Grundsätze der Volkswirtschaftslehre"), published in 1871, marked a fundamental milestone in economic theory. In this influential work, Menger revolutionized the understanding of economic value by introducing the notion of subjective value theory. In contrast to value theories based on objective costs, Menger argued that the value of a good or service is not derived from its production costs but is intrinsically linked to individuals' subjective preferences.

This concept laid the foundation for Austrian theory, emphasizing the importance of human action and subjectivity in price formation and economic values. Menger also addressed the issue of exchange and the origin of money, providing a perspective that would become an essential pillar of the Austrian School. His focus on the individualistic method, analyzing human action at the individual level, influenced future generations of Austrian economists. Menger's contribution not only lies in his revolutionary ideas but also in the lasting impact they had on economic thought. His legacy endures through generations, solidifying his position as the founder and intellectual visionary of the Austrian School of Economics.

Eugen von Böhm-Bawerk (1851-1914): A disciple of Menger, Böhm-Bawerk developed the theory of capital and interest. His work "Kapital und Kapitalzins" (Capital and Interest) is a significant contribution to economic theory. Born on February 12, 1851, in Brünn (present-day Brno, Czech Republic), and passing away on August 27, 1914, in

Vienna, Austria, Böhm-Bawerk was a prominent economist of the Austrian School and a close disciple of Carl Menger.

His contribution to economic theory, especially regarding the theory of capital and interest, has left a lasting mark on economic thought. Böhm-Bawerk elaborated and expanded Menger's ideas, extending subjective value theory to the realms of capital and interest. His most influential work, "Kapital und Kapitalzins" (Capital and Interest), published in three volumes between 1884 and 1912, thoroughly examines the nature of capital and interest formation.

In this monumental work, Böhm-Bawerk addressed the issues of time and time preference as key factors in determining interest rates. He argued that people value present goods more than future goods, and this phenomenon has profound implications for understanding why interest exists. Additionally, he developed the theory of capital, explaining how it is structured and how its use in the productive process has implications for income generation and interest formation. Böhm-Bawerk's work not only influenced Austrian theory but also had an impact on economics in general.

His ideas on interest and capital continued to be discussed and debated by economists from various schools throughout the 20th century. Böhm-Bawerk is remembered as a crucial thinker in the evolution and consolidation of the Austrian School of Economics.

Ludwig von Mises (1881-1973): One of the most influential thinkers of the Austrian School, Mises developed the theory of the business cycle and is known for his work "Human Action," where he delves into the importance of individual action in the economy. Born on September 29, 1881, in Lemberg (present-day Lviv, Ukraine), and passing away on October 10, 1973, in New York, Mises was one of the most prominent and prolific thinkers of the Austrian School of Economics. His work significantly influenced the development of economic theory and the defense of classical liberal principles.

Mises is known for his meticulous approach and his contribution to the theory of the business cycle. In his magnum opus, "Human Action," first published in 1949, Mises comprehensively articulates the fundamental principles of the Austrian School. This extensive treatise explores economic theory from the perspective of human action, emphasizing the importance of individual decisions and the role of the entrepreneur in market coordination.

In "Human Action," Mises addresses key issues such as value theory, the role of money, central planning, and the critique of socialism. Additionally, he presents his theory of the business cycle, explaining how government interventions and credit expansion can trigger cycles of boom and recession in the economy. Mises was also a passionate advocate of classical liberalism and the free-market economy. His work and teachings influenced numerous economists and thinkers, contributing to the resurgence of liberalism in the second half of the 20th century. His emphasis on the importance of individual action as the engine of the economy and his critique of state intervention have left a lasting impact on economic theory and political thought.

Friedrich von Wieser (1851-1926): Another disciple of Menger, Wieser made significant contributions to value theory and the theory of opportunity cost. Born on July 10, 1851, in Vienna, Austria, and passing away on July 22, 1926, in Hinterstoder, Wieser was another distinguished disciple of Carl Menger and a key figure in the development of the Austrian School of Economics. Wieser made significant contributions, particularly to value theory and the theory of opportunity cost. His most notable work, "Der Ursprung der Volkswirtschaft" ("The Origin of Economic Value"), published in 1884, addressed fundamental questions about value formation and the relationship between value and costs.

Regarding the theory of value, Wieser expanded on Menger's ideas, introducing the concepts of "use value" and "exchange value," and exploring how these concepts relate to price formation in the market. He also worked on the theory of opportunity cost, emphasizing the importance of considering the benefits forgone when making an economic decision.

Wieser's theory of value and analysis of opportunity cost contributed to the broader development of the Austrian School and complemented the works of other economists of the time. Although his influence may have been overshadowed at times by more prominent contemporaries, Wieser played a crucial role in consolidating and expanding the ideas of the Austrian School in the realms of value theory and costs.

Joseph Schumpeter (1883-1950): While later diverging in certain aspects from the Austrian School, Schumpeter was initially influenced by it. He is known for his theory of creative destruction and his work "The Theory of Economic Development." Joseph Schumpeter, born on February 8, 1883, in Triesch, Moravia (now in the Czech Republic), and passing away on January 8, 1950, in Connecticut, United States, was an Austro-American economist who played a prominent role in 20th-century economic theory. Although Schumpeter distanced himself in certain aspects from the more traditional ideas of the Austrian School, he was initially influenced by thinkers of this school, especially his mentor Eugen von Böhm-Bawerk.

His most well-known work, "The Theory of Economic Development," published in 1911, reflects that initial influence. Schumpeter is famous for his concept of "creative destruction," describing how innovation and the introduction of new technologies can displace and replace old business practices, leading to the creation of new industries and forms of production.

While this concept is recognized as a valuable contribution, it marked a substantial departure from some aspects of traditional Austrian theory. In addition to his theory of economic development, Schumpeter is also known for his work on economic cycles, entrepreneurship, and the theory of the entrepreneur.

His focus on the role of the entrepreneur as a key agent in innovation and economic change had a lasting impact on economic theory and the understanding of dynamic processes in the economy. Overall, Schumpeter represented a bridge between the Austrian School and new currents of economic thought, and his legacy has influenced many areas of economics and entrepreneurial innovation.

These thinkers, along with other followers and contributors, laid the intellectual foundations of the Austrian School of Economics. Over time, the school has evolved and has had prominent figures in different eras, but these founders were essential in formulating its fundamental principles.

2.Principles of the Austrian School

The Austrian School of Economics is characterized by a set of fundamental principles that distinguish it from other economic thought currents. Here are some of the main principles of the Austrian School:

Subjective Value Theory: The Austrian theory asserts that the value of goods and services is subjective and depends on individual preferences. It is the utility that individuals assign to a good that determines its value.

The Subjectivity of Value: The value of a good or service is not determined by any inherent characteristic of the object itself but is subjective and depends on individual preferences.

Marginal Utility: Marginal utility is a key concept. This theory argues that the value of a good or service is based on marginal utility, i.e., the additional utility or satisfaction a person gains from consuming an additional unit of that good or service.

Individual Preferences: Individual preferences and choices are central to value formation. Each person assigns subjective value to a good based on how much it satisfies or pleases them relative to other available options.

Changes in Preferences: The value of a good can change as individual preferences change. There is no objective measure of value; it is dynamic and adjusts according to circumstances and changing preferences.

This subjective approach to value was developed by Carl Menger, the founder of the Austrian School, and has influenced economic theory in general. The Subjective Value Theory is essential for understanding how prices are formed in a free market and how individual interactions influence economic decisions.

Methodological Individualism: The Austrian School advocates for methodological individualism, which focuses on the study of individual actions as the basic unit of analysis in economics. It examines how individual decisions and actions affect economic outcomes.

Focus on Individual Actions: Methodological individualism emphasizes that economic analysis should focus on the individual actions of economic agents, such as consumers, producers, and entrepreneurs. It considers these individual actions as the basic unit of analysis that determines economic outcomes.

Rejection of Abstract Aggregates: The Austrian School criticizes the use of abstract aggregates in economic analysis, such as averages or totals of variables. It prefers to break down the economy into individual actions and decisions to better understand economic processes.

Emphasis on Diversity of Preferences: It recognizes the diversity of preferences, abilities, and circumstances among individuals. Each person acts according to their own goals and knowledge, contributing to the complexity and dynamism of the economy.

Non-Homogeneity of Individuals: Methodological individualism addresses the non-homogeneity of individuals, arguing that people have different knowledge, experiences, and goals, influencing their economic choices and actions.

Rejection of Rigorous Predictive Models: The Austrian School tends to be skeptical about the possibility of developing rigorous predictive economic models due to the complexity of individual interactions and limitations in predictive capacity.

Emphasis on Human Action: This methodological approach is closely related to the overall view of the Austrian School on the importance of human action as the engine of the economy. Ludwig von Mises, in his work "Human Action," explores how individual decisions and actions shape economic outcomes.

Methodological Individualism of the Austrian School highlights the importance of understanding the economy from the perspective of individual action, recognizing the complexity and uniqueness of human choices in economic analysis.

Theory of the Business Cycle: The Austrian School has a unique theory of the business cycle that emphasizes the importance of credit expansions and contractions in the economy. It argues that interventions in the monetary and credit system can generate cycles of boom and recession.

Origin in Credit Expansion: The Austrian Theory of the Business Cycle posits that economic cycles originate in expansions and contractions of credit in the banking system. During a credit expansion, banks tend to lend excessively, inflating the money supply and causing an economic boom.

Boom Cycle: During the boom phase, credit expansion results in increased investment and spending on capital goods. This leads to an apparent growth in economic activity, with interest rates seemingly low due to readily available credit.

Distortion of the Production Structure: The abundance of credit during the boom phase distorts the production structure of the economy. Investments are directed toward long-term projects that, under normal conditions, would not be economically viable.

Recession Cycle: The boom phase is followed by a recession phase. During this stage, the distortions caused by credit expansion become apparent. Unsustainable investment projects cannot be sustained, leading to an economic adjustment.

Discoordination and Bankruptcies: The Austrian Theory of the Business Cycle contends that discoordination between supply and demand, especially in specific sectors of the economy, leads to business bankruptcies and an overall decline in economic activity.

Avoiding Government Interventions: The Austrian School argues that government interventions, such as attempts to stabilize the economy through monetary and fiscal policies, can prolong and worsen the business cycle, rather than solve it.**

Ludwig von Mises and Friedrich Hayek were two prominent Austrian economists who significantly contributed to the development and formulation of the Theory of the Business Cycle. The Austrian perspective emphasizes the importance of freedom in markets and cautions against the artificial manipulation of the monetary and credit system to avoid harmful economic cycles.

Emphasis on Human Action: Ludwig von Mises, a key figure in the Austrian School, underscores the importance of human action in economic decision-making. His work "Human Action" emphasizes that the economy is the result of rational decisions and actions by individuals.

Action as a Fundamental Element: Mises considers human action as the fundamental element of economic theory. He argues that the economy is not merely a mechanical or impersonal system but the result of deliberate actions by individuals seeking to achieve their objectives.

Individuals as Rational Actors: In "Human Action," Mises starts from the assumption that individuals act rationally to maximize their goals and satisfy their preferences. This perspective aligns with the homo economicus approach, a behavioral model assuming the rationality of economic actors.

Importance of Individual Decisions: According to Mises, the economy is built upon the individual decisions people make in their efforts to improve their well-being. He examines how these decisions affect the allocation of resources and the production structure in society.

Knowledge and Entrepreneurship: Mises highlights the importance of knowledge dispersed among individuals and the role of the entrepreneur in the economy. Entrepreneurs, according to Mises, are those who take risks and use dispersed knowledge to undertake new ventures, thereby driving innovation and economic progress.

Critique of Socialism: Mises' work also includes a detailed critique of socialism, arguing that centralized planning is inherently flawed due to the impossibility of efficiently collecting and utilizing dispersed information in society.

The emphasis on human action in Ludwig von Mises' work highlights the centrality of individual decisions and rationality in shaping economic activity and provides a solid foundation for understanding the economy from an Austrian perspective.

Entrepreneurship Theory: It recognizes the crucial role of the entrepreneur in the economic process. Entrepreneurs are viewed as agents who take risks and seek profit opportunities, thus driving innovation and economic improvement.

Role of the Entrepreneur: The Austrian School recognizes the entrepreneur as a central actor in the economic process. Entrepreneurs play a crucial role in coordinating resources and taking risks in the pursuit of profit opportunities.

Assumption of Risks: The entrepreneurship theory highlights the entrepreneur's willingness to take risks. By investing capital in entrepreneurial projects, entrepreneurs face the possibility of loss but also seek to obtain significant benefits.

Innovation and Change: The Austrian School argues that the entrepreneurial function goes beyond merely managing existing resources; it involves actively seeking opportunities for innovation and improvement. Entrepreneurs introduce changes in the production structure and aim to satisfy changing consumer preferences.

Conditions of Uncertainty: The entrepreneurship theory emphasizes that entrepreneurs operate in an environment of uncertainty. Entrepreneurial decision-making involves facing the unknown, as the future is inherently uncertain. The entrepreneur's ability to anticipate and adapt to changing conditions is essential.

Decentralization of Knowledge: The Austrian School emphasizes the idea that knowledge is decentralized and dispersed among individuals. Entrepreneurs, by acting in response to market signals, use their particular and unique knowledge to make decisions.

Critique of Perfect Competition: The entrepreneurship theory questions the idea of perfect competition and general equilibrium, arguing that economic reality is dynamic and subject to changes driven by entrepreneurial action.

Resource Coordination: Entrepreneurs play a crucial role in coordinating resources in the economy. By seeking profit opportunities, they help allocate resources efficiently and contribute to the overall improvement of economic well-being.

The entrepreneurship theory in the Austrian School highlights the entrepreneurial nature of the economy and underscores the importance of individual action and risk-taking in economic dynamics.

Critique of Central Planning: The Austrian School strongly criticizes the effectiveness of centrally planned economies, arguing that the knowledge dispersed among individuals cannot be centralized or fully understood by central authorities.

Problem of Decentralized Knowledge: The Austrian School contends that relevant knowledge for economic decision-making is dispersed among individuals and businesses. It argues that this knowledge is time- and place-specific and cannot be fully grasped or utilized by central planning authorities.

Impossibility of Economic Calculation: Ludwig von Mises, in his work "Economic Calculation in the Socialist Commonwealth," argues that centralized planning cannot efficiently replicate the economic calculation process that naturally occurs in a market system. The lack of genuine market prices in a planned economy hinders the efficient allocation of resources.

Dynamic and Changing Conditions: The Austrian critique points out that the economic environment is dynamic and constantly changing. Information about preferences, technologies, and scarcity is too fluid and variable to be accurately captured by central planning.

Incentives and Motivations: The Austrian School argues that the absence of clear incentives and motivations in a centrally planned system can lead to a lack of initiative, innovation, and economic efficiency. Without the possibility of gaining profits or incurring losses based on entrepreneurial decisions, incentives for efficiency decrease.

Market Adaptability: The critique also highlights the market's ability to adapt to changing conditions and effectively coordinate resources in response to supply and demand signals. Central planning, being static and inflexible, may not efficiently respond to changes.

Historical Experiences: Historical evidence, especially observed in countries that have implemented centrally planned systems, has partly supported the concerns of the Austrian School. Issues of scarcity, inefficiency, and a lack of innovation have been cited as common outcomes in planned economies.

The Austrian School's critique of central planning is based on the idea that dispersed information and market dynamism are intrinsic aspects that make centralized planning impractical and prone to failures.

Marginal Utility Theory: Proposes that the value of a good or service is determined by marginal utility, i.e., the utility of the last increment or unit consumed. This principle influences consumption and production decision-making.

Subjective Value: The Marginal Utility Theory is based on the idea that the value of a good or service is not derived from its total utility but from marginal utility, i.e., the additional utility provided by the last unit consumed.

Rational Consumption Decision: Individuals make rational consumption decisions by evaluating the marginal utility of each additional unit of a good or service in relation to its price. If the marginal utility is greater than the price, it is expected that the individual will consume more.

Law of Diminishing Marginal Utility: The theory postulates the "Law of Diminishing Marginal Utility," suggesting that as a person consumes more units of a good in a given period, the marginal utility tends to decrease. This reflects the idea that individuals tend to satisfy their most urgent needs first.

Production Decision-Making: The Marginal Utility Theory also applies to production decisions. Entrepreneurs assess the marginal utility of each additional unit of a production factor (such as labor or capital) in relation to its cost.

Price Formation: This theory influences price formation in a market. Prices tend to reflect the perceived marginal utility for consumers and the productive marginal utility for producers.

Concept of Value and Scarcity: The Marginal Utility Theory is linked to the concept of subjective value and the notion that scarcity is a key determinant of relative values. Goods that are scarcer and have higher marginal utility tend to have higher value in the market.

Influence on Economic Policy: This theory has influenced economic policy formulation, especially in understanding how government interventions can affect consumption and production decisions by altering incentives and the relationship between prices and marginal utility.

The Marginal Utility Theory is essential for understanding consumer behavior, price formation, and production decisions in the economy.

Opportunity Cost Theory: Introduces the notion of opportunity cost, which involves giving up the best available alternative when making an economic decision. This concept is fundamental to understanding individual economic decisions.

Forgoing the Best Alternative: The Opportunity Cost Theory asserts that when making an economic decision, the real cost is not simply the expenditure in terms of money but the forgoing of the best available alternative. It is the value of what is sacrificed.

Scarcity of Resources: This concept is related to the scarcity of resources. Since resources are limited, decisions on how to allocate them involve giving up other options. Opportunity cost reflects the value of those foregone alternatives.

Rational Decision-Making: The Opportunity Cost Theory is essential for understanding the rational decision-making of individuals and firms. Economic agents tend to make rational decisions by evaluating not only explicit costs but also implicit opportunity costs.

Production and Consumption: In production, opportunity cost is related to the best alternative use of resources. In consumption, it is linked to forgoing the best use of resources to obtain a good or service.

Benefit and Cost Evaluation: Individuals constantly evaluate the benefits and costs of their actions, taking into account opportunity costs. This evaluation influences decisions regarding consumption, production, and investment.

Intertemporal Comparison: The Opportunity Cost Theory is also relevant in decisions involving time. Intertemporal comparison involves evaluating opportunity costs over time, considering benefits and costs across different periods.

Economic Calculation: This concept is related to the ability to make efficient economic calculations. Entrepreneurs, when considering different production options, must take into account opportunity costs to make informed decisions.

Critique of Central Planning: The Opportunity Cost Theory supports the Austrian School's critique of centrally planned economies. It argues that central authorities cannot effectively know or consider opportunity costs due to the dispersion of knowledge and individual preferences.

The Opportunity Cost Theory is essential for understanding how individuals make decisions in a world of limited resources and how these costs affect resource allocations in the economy.

Critique of Inflation and Monetary Manipulation: The Austrian School warns of the dangers of inflation and monetary manipulation, arguing that they can distort market signals and lead to economic imbalances.

Distortion of Market Signals: The Austrian School argues that inflation and monetary manipulation distort market signals. An increase in the money supply can lead to higher prices, making it difficult for economic agents to discern between relative price changes due to real supply and demand.

Poor Investment Decisions: Distortion in market signals can lead to poor investment decisions. Entrepreneurs may be induced to believe that there is more savings available than there actually is, resulting in unsustainable investments and imbalances in the production structure.

Economic Cycles: The Austrian critique of monetary manipulation is closely related to its theory of economic cycles. They contend that interventions in the money supply, especially through credit expansion, can be a fundamental cause of economic boom and bust cycles.

Production Discoordination: Monetary manipulation can discoordinate production by inducing entrepreneurs to undertake investment projects not backed by real savings. This can lead to misallocation of resources and imbalances in the economy.

Ineffective Wealth Redistribution: Inflation may have redistributive effects, but the Austrian School argues that it does not result in effective wealth redistribution. Often, those closer to the point of origin of newly created money benefit more than those farther away, generating inequalities not based on economic merit.

Critique of Activist Monetary Policy: The Austrian School criticizes the idea of activist monetary policy that seeks to manipulate the money supply to achieve short-term goals. They argue that these interventions can have unintended consequences and create more problems in the long run.

Emphasis on Market Self-Regulation: Instead of monetary interventions, the Austrian School advocates for market self-regulation and argues that economic imbalances will naturally be corrected through adjustment processes in a system free from interference.

The Austrian School's critique of inflation and monetary manipulation is based on the idea that these practices can trigger market distortions, generate economic imbalances, and contribute to economic cycles.

Emphasis on Private Property and Individual Rights: The Austrian School upholds private property and individual rights as essential foundations for a functional and ethical economic system.

Property Rights as Fundamental: The Austrian School asserts that private property and individual rights are fundamental to the efficient and ethical functioning of an economic system. Private property is considered an essential human right.

Incentives for Productivity: Private property provides individuals with incentives to be productive and careful in the use of resources. When people have property rights over goods and resources, they have a personal interest in maximizing their value and ensuring efficient use.

Decentralized Coordination: Private property facilitates decentralized coordination of resources in an economy. Owners, in seeking to maximize their own interests, automatically contribute to the efficient coordination of supply and demand in the market.

Protection against Arbitrariness: Private property acts as a mechanism for protection against arbitrariness and abuse of power. Individuals have the ability to control and decide on the use of their own property, and respect for private property limits the possibility of unjust confiscation.

Stability and Social Peace: The Austrian School argues that protecting private property contributes to stability and social peace. When people feel that their property rights are secure, they are more likely to engage in economic transactions and maintain a peaceful social order.

Critique of Socialism and Central Planning: The defense of private property is linked to the Austrian School's critique of socialism and central planning. It argues that private property and free enterprise are more efficient and ethical than collective ownership and centralized planning.

Justice and Individual Freedom: Private property is considered an essential component of justice and individual freedom. Property rights protect autonomy and individuals' ability to make decisions about their own resources.

Fair Distribution: The Austrian School argues that private property allows for a fair distribution of resources, reflecting individual choices and efforts. Any attempt at forced redistribution may be seen as a violation of property rights.

The defense of private property and individual rights is a fundamental pillar in the Austrian School and is considered essential for economic prosperity and the preservation of individual freedom.

3.Theory of Subjective Value

Subjective Value Theory is a central principle in the Austrian School of Economics. This theory posits that the value of a good or service is not inherent to the thing itself but is subjective and depends on individual preferences. Here are some key aspects of Subjective Value Theory from the Austrian perspective:

Value as a Product of the Human Mind: The Austrian School argues that value is not an objective property of a good or service but is the result of the human mind valuing and preferring. Each individual assigns value according to their needs, desires, and personal circumstances.

Individualism and Diversity: Subjective Value Theory embraces methodological individualism, asserting that economic analysis should focus on the actions and decisions of specific individuals. It recognizes the diversity of preferences and circumstances among people.

Utility and Preferences: Value, according to the Austrian School, is derived from individual utility and preferences. Utility is subjective and depends on the ability to satisfy the specific needs and desires of a person at a given time.

Changes in Preferences: The theory acknowledges that individual preferences can change over time and circumstances. What is valuable at one moment may not be at another, contributing to market dynamics and the adaptability of the economy to changing needs and desires.

Influence of Psychological Factors: Subjective Value Theory also considers psychological factors in the formation of value. Emotions, perceptions, and personal experiences can affect how people value different goods and services.

Subjective valuation involves comparisons between different available options. An individual chooses between alternatives based on their subjective perception of which will best satisfy their needs or desires.

Critique of Objectivism: The Austrian School criticizes the idea that value is an objective property inherent to a good. It argues that approaches attempting to measure value objectively, such as the Labor Theory of Value, are insufficient to explain the reality of economic behavior.

Market Interaction: In a free market, the subjective valuations of individuals interact through supply and demand. Prices are formed based on consumer preferences and entrepreneurial production decisions.

Economic Calculation: Subjective Value Theory is essential for economic calculation in a market system. Subjective valuations provide the necessary information for entrepreneurs to efficiently allocate resources and make production decisions.

The Austrian School emphasizes that value is not an intrinsic property of goods but arises from the human mind and individual preferences, which is essential for understanding how economic decisions are made in a dynamic and diverse environment.

Marginalism: Subjective Value Theory is closely linked to marginalism, which posits that value is formed at the margin, i.e., in the utility of the last unit consumed of a good or service. Marginal utility determines perceived value.

Concept of the Margin: Marginalism focuses on the concept of the margin, referring to the last unit of a good or service consumed or produced. The idea is that the value of that last unit is crucial in determining the total value.

Marginal Utility: In the consumer context, marginalism manifests through marginal utility, which is the additional satisfaction or utility gained from consuming one additional unit of a good. Marginal utility is specific to each individual and can change with circumstances.

Price Formation: In a free market, prices are determined at the margin, where supply and demand meet. The perceived marginal utility by consumers and the marginal costs incurred by producers are key factors in price formation.

Rational Decision-Making: Decision-making based on marginalism is considered rational. Individuals tend to allocate resources efficiently by comparing marginal benefits with marginal costs. If marginal utility exceeds marginal cost, the action is considered beneficial.

Law of Diminishing Marginal Utility: The Austrian School recognizes the Law of Diminishing Marginal Utility, stating that, generally, as a person consumes more units of a good or service, the marginal utility tends to decrease. This reflects the idea that more urgent needs are satisfied first.

Microeconomic Analysis: Marginalism is a central tool in microeconomic analysis. It is applied in evaluating individual decisions, price formation in specific markets, and efficiency in resource allocation.

Critique of Socialism: Subjective Value Theory and marginalism also support the Austrian School's critique of socialism. It argues that efficient resource allocation and price formation based on individual preferences are challenging to achieve in a centrally planned system.

Marginalism, in the context of Subjective Value Theory, highlights the importance of evaluating economic decisions in terms of marginal benefits and costs, contributing to efficiency and understanding market dynamics.

Individual Preferences: The theory acknowledges the diversity of individual preferences. What is valuable to one person may not be to another, and vice versa. Individual preferences change over time. Personal circumstances, life experiences, and other factors can influence what a person values at different times in their life.

Market Adaptability: The diversity of preferences is fundamental to market adaptability. In a free-market system, producers have incentives to adjust their supply of goods and services in response to changes in consumer preferences.

Innovation and Entrepreneurship: Variability in individual preferences fosters innovation and entrepreneurship. Entrepreneurs seek to identify new ways to satisfy the changing needs and desires of consumers to succeed in the market.

Freedom of Choice: The defense of freedom of choice is intrinsically linked to the valuation of individual preferences. The ability to choose freely allows people to seek and acquire goods and services that best align with their preferences.

Decentralization of Decisions: The Austrian School advocates for the decentralization of economic decisions, emphasizing that efficient coordination between supply and demand occurs when decisions are made at the individual level rather than centrally planned.

Economic Pluralism: The diversity of preferences contributes to economic pluralism. In a free market, there is room for a variety of goods and services that can satisfy a wide range of individual preferences, thus fostering competition and economic diversity.

Subjective Valuation of Resources: The Subjective Value Theory extends to the valuation of resources in production. Entrepreneurs subjectively evaluate which combination of resources will maximize their utility and satisfy the changing preferences of consumers.

Recognizing individual preferences and their variability is essential to understanding how values are formed and how a market-based economic system operates efficiently.

Value and Scarcity: Subjective Value Theory is related to the concept of scarcity. Value increases when a good is scarce and desired by individuals. Scarcity and subjective utility interact to determine value.

The relationship between value and scarcity is a key aspect of Subjective Value Theory in the Austrian School of Economics. Here is an in-depth exploration of how scarcity and subjective utility interact to determine value:

Scarcity as an Essential Condition: The Austrian School argues that scarcity is an essential condition for a good to have economic value. If a good or service is abundantly available and not scarce, it is likely to have little or no value in economic terms.

Subjective Utility in the Context of Scarcity: Subjective utility of a good is emphasized even more in situations of scarcity. When resources are limited, and a good is scarce, the subjective utility that individuals assign to that good becomes a determining factor in its economic valuation.

Choice and Prioritization: Due to scarcity, individuals are forced to make decisions and prioritize their choices. Subjective utility influences these decisions by guiding people toward acquiring goods they perceive as more valuable given their specific preferences and needs.

Relation to the Law of Supply and Demand: The interaction between scarcity, subjective utility, and value is reflected in the law of supply and demand. When a good is scarce and in demand, its value tends to increase. On the other hand, if a good is abundant and in low demand, its value tends to decrease.

Changes in Availability: Changes in the availability of a good can alter its value. If a previously abundant good becomes scarce due to some change in supply or demand, its value may increase significantly.

Relative Value: Subjective Value Theory emphasizes that value is relative and depends on circumstances and individual preferences. Two people may value the same good differently based on their needs and perceptions.

Market Coordination: Scarcity and subjective utility operate in a coordinated manner in the market. Competition and free interaction in a free market allow prices to reflect the subjective valuations of consumers and the relative availability of goods.

Economic Calculation: Considering scarcity and subjective utility is fundamental to economic calculation. Entrepreneurs evaluate how to efficiently allocate scarce resources to meet the changing demands of consumers.

The Subjective Value Theory in the Austrian School highlights the inseparable relationship between scarcity, subjective utility, and economic value, providing a conceptual framework for understanding how resources are allocated in a market-based economic system.

Critique of Labor Theory of Value: The Austrian School criticizes the Labor Theory of Value, which suggests that the value of a good is determined by the amount of labor embodied in it. Subjective Value Theory argues that value is not an objective property based on labor but a subjective assessment based on perceived utility.

Value as a Subjective Property: The Austrian School argues that value is not an objective property based on the amount of labor embodied in a good. Instead, value is considered subjective and derived from individual valuations based on perceived utility.

Diversity of Preferences: The critique highlights the diversity of individual preferences and how these affect the valuation of goods. Two goods may require the same amount of labor to produce, but their value can differ significantly based on individuals' subjective preferences.

Changes in Productivity: Labor productivity does not necessarily translate directly into economic value. Technological advancements that increase productivity can reduce the amount of labor needed to produce a good, but its value will still depend on subjective preferences and perceived utility.

Context of Supply and Demand: Subjective Value Theory emphasizes the interaction between supply and demand in determining prices and, therefore, value. The amount of labor invested in production is a factor, but not the sole or most determinative one.

Marginal Valuation: The Austrian School emphasizes the importance of marginal valuation, where the value of the last unit of a consumed good becomes the most relevant determinant of its value. This perspective contrasts with the idea that value is determined by the total amount of embodied labor.

Critique of Objective Measurement: The critique is directed at the idea that value can be objectively measured by the amount of labor. It argues that individuals' subjective valuations cannot be reduced to a universal objective measure.

Market Flexibility: The Subjective Value Theory supports the flexibility of the market to assign values to goods and services based on changing consumer preferences. An approach based on labor might not adjust as efficiently to these variations.

Emphasis on Individual Decisions: The critique reflects the Austrian School's emphasis on individual decisions as the determining factor in the formation of economic values, rather than an objective measure like the amount of labor. The critique of the Labor Theory of Value highlights the importance of recognizing the subjective nature of value and how it forms in the context of individual preferences and market interactions.

Market Dynamism: The Subjective Value Theory highlights the dynamism of the market. As individual preferences and market conditions change, the perceived value of goods and services also changes.

Adaptability: The Subjective Value Theory recognizes the market's ability to adapt and adjust to changes in individual preferences and economic conditions. This adaptability is crucial for efficiency and effectiveness in resource allocation.

Changes in Preferences: Market dynamism reflects the reality that individual preferences are not static; they change over time due to factors such as fashion, innovation, and personal experiences. These changes directly affect the perceived value of goods and services.

Innovation and Entrepreneurship: The dynamic market provides a conducive environment for innovation and entrepreneurship. Entrepreneurs constantly seek new ways to satisfy changing consumer needs and desires, potentially resulting in the introduction of new products and services.

Creative Competition: Competition in a dynamic market extends beyond price competition to include creative competition. Companies compete to offer unique products and services that stand out in the market, stimulating continuous improvement.

Product Life Cycles: Market dynamism is reflected in product life cycles. Products experience stages of introduction, growth, maturity, and decline, and their perceived value may change at each stage.

Response to Market Signals: The dynamic market allows participants to respond quickly to market signals. Changes in demand, prices, and economic conditions generate automatic adjustments in the production and supply of goods and services.

Price Flexibility: In a dynamic market, prices can adjust quickly and efficiently in response to changes in supply and demand. This contributes to the efficient coordination of resources.

Decentralization of Decisions: Decentralized decision-making in a dynamic market allows individuals and companies to make autonomous decisions based on the most up-to-date information. This contrasts with centralized models that may be less agile in adapting.

Continuous Marginal Valuation: Market dynamism also involves continuous marginal valuation by consumers. As new options arise, consumers constantly evaluate whether an additional unit of a good or service remains valuable in relation to its price.

In summary, the Subjective Value Theory highlights that market dynamism is essential for understanding how the perceived value of goods and services evolves in response to changes in individual preferences and market conditions.

Price Formation: In a free market, prices are determined by the interaction of supply and demand, reflecting the subjective valuations of consumers and the production costs of producers.

Supply and Demand: The interaction between supply and demand is the key mechanism for price formation in a free market. Demand reflects the subjective valuations of consumers, while supply is determined by production costs and producers' willingness to sell.

Market Equilibrium: The point where supply and demand meet determines the equilibrium price. At this point, the quantity demanded is equal to the quantity offered. This price reflects the subjective valuation of consumers and the production costs of producers.

Price Flexibility: In a free market, prices can freely adjust in response to changes in supply and demand. Changes in consumer preferences, resource availability, and other factors can influence the direction and magnitude of these adjustments.

Competition: Competition among producers and the free entry and exit of companies contribute to efficient price formation. Producers seek to maximize profits, and competition fosters efficiency and continuous improvement in the supply of goods and services.

Marginal Valuation: The Subjective Value Theory highlights the importance of marginal valuation in price formation. The perceived marginal utility by consumers and the marginal production costs are fundamental factors in buying and selling decisions.

Changes in Preferences: When consumer preferences change, the demand for certain goods and services may change, affecting prices. Producers respond by adjusting their supply accordingly.

Innovation and Entrepreneurship: The free market encourages innovation and entrepreneurship by allowing new ideas and products to enter the market. This can influence supply and demand, thus affecting the prices of existing goods and services.

Market Signals: Prices act as market signals, conveying information about the scarcity or abundance of a good and stimulating adjustments in production and consumption. Changes in prices indicate changes in market conditions.

Economic Calculation: Price formation is essential for economic calculation. Prices provide valuable information for entrepreneurs to make decisions about efficiently allocating resources and producing goods and services.

Price formation in a free market reflects the dynamics of supply and demand, as well as the subjective valuations of consumers and the production costs of producers, being a crucial component of efficient resource coordination in the economy.

The Subjective Value Theory of the Austrian School underscores the importance of individual preferences and subjectivity in determining economic value, providing a crucial conceptual foundation for understanding economic behavior and market interactions.

4.Critique of Positivism and Empiricism

Deductive Approach: The Austrian School criticizes the positivist and empiricist emphasis on the inductive method, advocating for a deductive approach. It argues that economic theory should be derived from fundamental principles and logical reasoning, rather than relying exclusively on empirical observation.

Complexity of Human Actions: Austrians criticize the excessive simplification of human actions by positivist approaches. They argue that human actions are complex and motivated by subjective factors that are difficult to capture through purely empirical methods.

Subjective Motivations: Austrians assert that human actions are motivated by subjective factors, including preferences, expectations, and individual values. These motivations are hard to quantify and can vary significantly among individuals.

Historical and Cultural Context: They argue that the diversity of historical and cultural contexts influences human actions. Understanding these influences requires an approach that considers subjectivity rather than merely observing empirical patterns.

Tacit Knowledge: Austrians acknowledge the existence of tacit knowledge, i.e., knowledge that cannot be easily articulated or expressed explicitly. This type of knowledge is crucial for individual decisions but may escape traditional empirical observation methods.

Methodological Individualism: The Austrian School advocates for methodological individualism, focusing on the study of individual actions as the basic unit of analysis in economics. This approach recognizes the uniqueness of each individual and their ability to make decisions based on their unique and subjective knowledge.

Dynamics of Preferences: Individual preferences can change over time and circumstances. A purely empirical approach may not capture the dynamics and evolution of these preferences, as human actions respond to a variety of stimuli and experiences.

Critique of Rigorous Models: Austrians criticize rigorous models that overly simplify reality. They argue that excessive simplification can lose sight of the richness and complexity of human interactions, leading to conclusions that do not accurately reflect reality.

Limitations of Prediction: The complexity of human actions is also reflected in the limitations of precise prediction. Since knowledge is distributed among individuals and is subjective, accurately foreseeing how people will respond to different stimuli can be challenging.

Emphasis on Human Action: Ludwig von Mises, a prominent representative of the Austrian School, emphasizes the importance of human action in shaping economic reality. He argues that economics is the result of the conscious actions of individuals, and understanding it goes beyond superficial empirical observation.

The Austrian critique highlights the need to address the complexity of human actions through an approach that values subjectivity, tacit knowledge, and the diversity of individual motivations. This approach contrasts with the often-present simplification in positivist approaches that seek to objectively find observable regularities.

Subjective Motivations: Austrians assert that human actions are motivated by subjective factors, including preferences, expectations, and individual values. These motivations are difficult to quantify and can vary significantly among individuals.

Individual Preferences: Individual preferences are subjective and vary among people. What one person values and seeks in a particular situation may differ significantly from another person's preferences in the same situation. These subjective differences influence individual decisions and actions.

Expectations and Perceptions: The expectations and perceptions of individuals are fundamental subjective motivators. Economic decisions are based on how individuals perceive the future, their expectations about events that may occur, and how they evaluate those expectations in terms of their personal goals.

Individual Values: Personal, ethical, and moral values influence economic decisions. The Austrian School recognizes the diversity of values among individuals and how these values impact decision-making, especially in situations involving ethical or moral choices.

Personal Context: The response to external stimuli and economic situations is influenced by each individual's personal context. Family, educational, cultural, and social circumstances shape subjective motivations and affect economic decisions.

Complexity of Human Action: Ludwig von Mises, a prominent representative of the Austrian School, emphasizes the complexity of human action. He argues that human action is intentional and goal-oriented, and that subjective motivations are fundamental to understanding economic decisions.

Tacit Knowledge: In addition to conscious preferences and expectations, the Austrian School also highlights the importance of tacit knowledge. This knowledge, which cannot be easily expressed, plays a crucial role in subjective motivations and significantly affects economic decisions.

Free Will: The Austrian perspective acknowledges the role of free will in human actions. It argues that individuals have the ability to make rational decisions based on their own subjective motivations, rather than being merely deterministic products of external forces.

The Austrian School emphasizes the importance of understanding subjective motivations in economic decision-making. It recognizes the diversity and complexity of these motivations, arguing that any comprehensive economic analysis must take into account the richness of subjective factors influencing human behavior.

Historical and Cultural Context: They argue that the diversity of historical and cultural contexts influences human actions. Understanding these influences requires an approach that considers subjectivity and not simply the observation of empirical patterns.

Influence of History: The Austrian School acknowledges that human actions and economic decisions are influenced by past events and historical evolution. Understanding how institutions and economic structures have evolved over time is crucial to understanding the context in which decisions are made.

Changes in Institutions: The evolution of institutions plays a significant role in shaping preferences and economic decision-making. Austrians argue that institutions and economic structures emerge from historical processes and affect how people interact in the present.

Culture and Values: Cultural diversity and variation in individual values are considered fundamental elements. Cultural differences affect people's preferences, expectations, and perceptions, influencing their economic decisions in ways that may not be easily captured by purely empirical approaches.

Localized Knowledge: The Austrian perspective emphasizes the localized and dispersed nature of knowledge. It argues that knowledge relevant to economic decision-making is distributed among individuals and cannot be fully centralized or captured by general empirical observations.

Learning Over Time: Historical experiences and lessons learned over time influence economic behavior. The Austrian School maintains that people learn from past experiences and adjust their actions accordingly, affecting economic dynamics.

Changes in Preferences: Individual preferences can change as historical and cultural circumstances evolve. An approach that does not consider these changes might overlook the variability and complexity of economic decisions in specific contexts.

Critique of Generalizations: The Austrian School criticizes simplistic generalizations about economic behaviors based solely on empirical observations. It argues that these generalizations may overlook the richness of contextualized details that influence economic decisions.

Emphasis on Human Action: Ludwig von Mises, in particular, highlights that understanding human action involves considering historical and cultural context. He insists that economics cannot be separated from the conscious actions of individuals and their historical and cultural environment.

Consideration of historical and cultural context is essential for the Austrian School, as it argues that human actions and economic decisions are inherently influenced by past events, the evolution of institutions, and cultural diversity. This approach brings a more comprehensive and contextualized perspective to understanding the economy.

Tacit Knowledge: They acknowledge the existence of tacit knowledge, i.e., knowledge that cannot be easily articulated or expressed explicitly.

This type of knowledge is crucial for individual decisions but may escape traditional empirical observation methods.

Definition of Tacit Knowledge: Tacit knowledge refers to forms of knowledge that people possess but cannot be easily articulated or expressed explicitly. It includes practical skills, intuitions, subjective understandings, and experiences that influence decision-making.

Inability to Fully Articulate: Austrians argue that tacit knowledge cannot be completely expressed in words or fully codified. This type of knowledge is often personal, contextual, and based on individual experience, making its complete transmission through formal means challenging.

Role in Decision-Making: According to the Austrian School, tacit knowledge plays a crucial role in economic decision-making. People use this implicit knowledge to assess situations, anticipate outcomes, and make decisions that align with their specific circumstances.

Limitations of Empirical Observation: Traditional methods of empirical observation may not adequately capture tacit knowledge. Since this type of knowledge is subjective and personal, it is not always evident in external observations and cannot be fully unraveled through quantitative data.

Diversity of Tacit Knowledge: Tacit knowledge can span a wide range of areas, from specific practical skills to intuitive understandings of complex situations. It may include knowledge about interpersonal relationships, local contexts, and other aspects significant for individual decision-making.

Implicit Learning: The acquisition of tacit knowledge often occurs through experience and implicit learning. People develop intuitions and practical skills as they interact with their environment and face diverse situations over time.

Critique of Simplistic Models: The Austrian School criticizes economic models that overly simplify reality and do not account for the complexity of tacit knowledge. They argue that people's ability to use this knowledge effectively is essential for understanding human action.

Emphasis on Human Action: Ludwig von Mises, one of the leading representatives of the Austrian School, emphasizes that human action is always guided by tacit knowledge, as individuals respond to stimuli and situations based on their unique experience.

In summary, the recognition of tacit knowledge by the Austrian School highlights the importance of subjective and not fully articulated dimensions in economic decision-making, underscoring the inherent complexity of human action.

Methodological Individualism: The Austrian School advocates for methodological individualism, which focuses on the study of individual actions as the basic unit of analysis in economics. This approach recognizes the uniqueness of each individual and their ability to make decisions based on their unique and subjective knowledge.

Focus on Individual Actions: Methodological individualism involves centering economic analysis on individual actions as the basic unit of study. Instead of considering aggregates or abstract groups, attention is directed toward how individual decisions and actions contribute to economic phenomena.

Singularity of Each Individual: The Austrian School acknowledges that each individual is unique and possesses distinctive circumstances, experiences, knowledge, and preferences. This recognition of singularity highlights the impossibility of applying universal laws to all individuals uniformly.

Capacity for Rational Decision-Making: Methodological individualism assumes that individuals are capable of making rational decisions based on their own knowledge and subjective perspective. The importance of understanding the reasons and motivations behind individual actions is emphasized.

Decentralized Knowledge: The Austrian perspective maintains that knowledge relevant to decision-making is decentralized among individuals. Each person has unique and local information that contributes to their decision-making, and this diversity of knowledge cannot be fully centralized.

Interaction of Individual Preferences: Methodological individualism considers the interaction of individual preferences in the formation of economic outcomes. The market is viewed as the result of millions of interconnected individual decisions, rather than a centralized design.

Critique of Homogeneous Generalizations: The Austrian School criticizes the application of homogeneous economic laws to all individuals. It argues that generalizations may overlook the diversity of individual preferences and circumstances, leading to inadequate analyses.

Free Will and Individual Responsibility: Methodological individualism is in line with the idea of free will and individual responsibility. It posits that individuals have the capacity to make conscious decisions and should be accountable for the consequences of their actions.

Emphasis on Human Action: Ludwig von Mises, a prominent representative of the Austrian School, emphasizes that the economy is the result of individual human actions. His work "Human Action" underscores the importance of understanding individual decisions to comprehend economics.

The methodological individualism of the Austrian School acknowledges the significance of individual actions and decisions as the driving force behind economic phenomena, highlighting the diversity and uniqueness of each individual in economic analysis.

Dynamics of Preferences: Individual preferences can change over time and circumstances. A purely empirical approach may not capture the dynamics and evolution of these preferences, as human actions respond to a variety of stimuli and experiences.

Change in Circumstances: The Austrian School recognizes that individual preferences can change as a person's life circumstances evolve. Factors such as changes in income, family situations, or personal experiences can influence what a person values at different times.

Adaptation to Experiences: People tend to adapt their preferences as they accumulate experiences. Interactions with the environment, feedback from past decisions, and exposure to new ideas can influence the evolution of individual preferences over time.

Impact of Innovation: The introduction of new products, technologies, or ways of life can affect people's preferences. The Austrian School emphasizes that innovation and change are inherent to the economic process and can alter consumer preferences in unpredictable ways.

Social and Cultural Context: Individual preferences are also influenced by social and cultural context. Changes in social norms, cultural values, or general trends can have a significant impact on what people consider valuable or desirable.

Limitations of Empirical Data: A purely empirical approach may struggle to capture the complexity and dynamics of individual preferences. The Austrian School argues that preferences are subjective and contextual, and empirical data may not fully reflect the variety of factors influencing individual decisions.

Actions as Responses to Stimuli: The dynamics of preferences imply that human actions are responses to a variety of stimuli. Understanding these responses requires considering how preferences evolve based on experiences and interactions with the environment.

Importance of Entrepreneurship: The Austrian School highlights the role of entrepreneurship in the economic process. Entrepreneurs, by identifying opportunities and creating new products or services, can influence consumer preferences and contribute to the dynamic evolution of the market.

Emphasis on Human Action: Ludwig von Mises and other representatives of the Austrian School emphasize that the economy is the result of human action. Understanding the dynamics of preferences involves recognizing that people are not static in their choices but actively respond to their changing environment.

The Austrian School underscores the importance of understanding the dynamics of preferences as an evolutionary and complex phenomenon that goes beyond simple static empirical observations. This highlights the need for a broader and more contextualized approach in economic analysis.

Critique of Rigorous Models: Austrians criticize rigorous models that oversimplify reality. They argue that excessive simplification may lose sight of the richness and complexity of human interactions and lead to conclusions that do not accurately reflect reality.

Complexity of Human Interactions: The Austrian School contends that economic reality is inherently complex due to human interactions, which are difficult to fully capture and model. Economic relationships cannot be reduced to simple mathematical equations.

Methodological Individualism: The critique of rigorous models aligns with the principle of methodological individualism. It argues that individual human action and decisions cannot be adequately represented by models that oversimplify and do not consider the diversity of individual preferences and circumstances.

Decentralized Knowledge: The Austrian School highlights the decentralized nature of knowledge, meaning that relevant information for decision-making is dispersed among individuals. Rigorous models may overlook this dispersion of knowledge and fail to reflect the reality of how decisions are made in practice.

Critique of Centralized Planning: In connection with the critique of rigorous models, the Austrian School also criticizes the effectiveness of centralized planning in the economy. It argues that central planning cannot account for the diversity and complexity of human actions and tends to oversimplify economic reality.

Emphasis on Human Action: Ludwig von Mises, one of the prominent representatives of the Austrian School, emphasizes that the economy is the result of individual human actions. Rigorous models often overlook the inherent complexity of human decisions and actions by oversimplifying variables and relationships.

Critique of Positivism and Empiricism: Austrians criticize positivist and empiricist approaches that seek to reduce economics to objective and observable laws. They argue that economics involves subjective and contingent factors that cannot be fully captured through purely empirical methods.

Importance of Creativity and Innovation: Rigorous models may not be able to adequately incorporate creativity and innovation, which are fundamental aspects of the economic process according to the Austrian

School. The creation of value and adaptation to new circumstances cannot be fully anticipated through highly simplified models.

Limitations in Prediction: Criticism of rigorous models also relates to limitations in the ability to predict human behavior. The complexity of human interactions makes predictions based on simplified models inherently limited.

The Austrian School advocates for an approach that recognizes the complexity and richness of human interactions in the economy and criticizes the excessive simplification that characterizes some rigorous models that do not fully reflect economic reality.

Limitations of Prediction: The complexity of human actions is also reflected in the limitations of precise prediction. Since knowledge is distributed among individuals and is subjective, accurately foreseeing how people will respond to different stimuli can be difficult.

Complexity of Human Interactions: The Austrian School argues that economic reality is inherently complex due to human interactions, which are difficult to capture and model comprehensively. Economic relationships cannot be reduced to simple mathematical equations.

Methodological Individualism: Criticism of rigorous models aligns with the principle of methodological individualism. It argues that individual human action and decisions cannot be adequately represented by models that oversimplify and do not consider the diversity of preferences and individual circumstances.

Decentralized Knowledge: The Austrian School highlights the decentralized nature of knowledge, meaning that relevant information for decision-making is dispersed among individuals. Rigorous models may overlook this dispersion of knowledge and not reflect the reality of how decisions are made in practice.

Critique of Centralized Planning: In connection with the criticism of rigorous models, the Austrian School also criticizes the effectiveness of centralized planning in the economy. It argues that central planning cannot account for the diversity and complexity of human actions and tends to overly simplify economic reality.

Emphasis on Human Action: Ludwig von Mises, one of the prominent representatives of the Austrian School, emphasizes that economics is the result of individual human actions. Rigorous models often overlook the inherent complexity of human decisions and actions by oversimplifying variables and relationships.

Critique of Positivism and Empiricism: Austrians criticize positivist and empiricist approaches that seek to reduce economics to objective and observable laws. They argue that economics involves subjective and contingent factors that cannot be fully captured through purely empirical methods.

Importance of Creativity and Innovation: Rigorous models may not be able to adequately incorporate creativity and innovation, which are fundamental aspects of the economic process according to the Austrian School. The creation of value and adaptation to new circumstances cannot be fully predicted by highly simplified models.

Limitations in Prediction: Criticism of rigorous models also relates to limitations in the ability to predict human behavior. The complexity of human interactions makes predictions based on simplified models inherently limited.

The Austrian School advocates for an approach that recognizes the complexity and richness of human interactions in the economy and criticizes the excessive simplification that characterizes some rigorous models that do not fully reflect economic reality.

Emphasis on Human Action: Ludwig von Mises, a prominent representative of the Austrian School, emphasizes the importance of human action in shaping economic reality. He argues that economics is the result of the conscious actions of individuals, and its understanding goes beyond superficial empirical observation.

This principle is known as the "principle of human action" or "axiom of action," and it is a central concept in Austrian economic theory.

According to von Mises, human action is the foundation of economics and the formation of economic reality. This principle is outlined in his magnum opus "Human Action," first published in 1949. Von Mises argues that economics cannot be understood simply through the observation of empirical data or through natural scientific methods but requires a deductive approach from human action.

Some key points related to this principle are:

Axiom of Human Action: Human action, according to von Mises, is the only irreducible reality. Assuming otherwise would be self-contradictory, as even the denial of action implies some form of action.

Subjectivity of Values: Von Mises emphasizes the subjective nature of economic values. Individuals assign values to goods and services based on their personal preferences and circumstances.

Praxeology: Von Mises develops a methodology called praxeology to study human action. Praxeology is the science of action and is based on logical and deductive reasoning rather than empirical methods.

Market and Price Theory: Through praxeology, von Mises develops a theory of the market and prices based on human action. He argues that prices are the result of individuals' subjective valuations and interaction in the market.

Ludwig von Mises's emphasis on human action is a distinctive feature of the Austrian School. It provides a philosophical foundation for understanding economics from an individualistic, subjective, and action-conscious perspective.

Austrian criticism highlights the need to address the complexity of human actions through an approach that values subjectivity, tacit knowledge, and the diversity of individual motivations. This approach contrasts with the often-present simplification in positivist approaches that seek to find objectively observable regularities.

Emphasis on Human Action: The Austrian School highlights the importance of human action as the central point of study in economics. While positivist approaches tend to focus on quantifiable data, Austrians emphasize that true economic understanding requires a deeper appreciation of human decisions and choices.

Subjective Methodology: The Austrian School argues that economic reality cannot be fully understood without considering the subjectivity of individual decisions. While positivist approaches often rely on the observation of quantifiable data and mathematical modeling, Austrians argue that this can lose sight of the subjective nature of human preferences and valuations.

Tacit Knowledge: Austrians also emphasize the importance of tacit or unarticulated knowledge in economic decisions. This type of knowledge is difficult to quantify or express but plays a crucial role in individual choices and the coordination of economic activities.

Theory of the Business Cycle: The Austrian School has also developed a unique theory of the economic cycle, highlighting how economic expansions and contractions can result from distortions in interest rates, which in turn affect individuals' investment decisions.

Emphasis on Entrepreneurial Action: Great importance is given to entrepreneurial action and the role of the entrepreneur in the Austrian School. Entrepreneurs, according to this perspective, play a crucial role in anticipating changes in market conditions and taking risks to seek profit opportunities.

Critique of Central Planning: The Austrian School also criticizes the effectiveness of central planning in the economy, arguing that decentralized and dispersed information in the hands of individuals is difficult to coordinate effectively through centralized planning. The Austrian School emphasizes human action, subjectivity, and the importance of tacit knowledge as fundamental elements for understanding economic reality, in contrast to more positivist approaches that focus on quantifiable data and mathematical modeling.

Tacit and Subjective Knowledge: They criticize the idea that all knowledge can be explicitly articulated and measured. The Austrian School acknowledges the existence of tacit and subjective knowledge, which is difficult to quantify but plays a crucial role in economic decision-making.

Tacit Knowledge: This type of knowledge refers to information that people possess but cannot easily express in formal or quantifiable terms. It can include practical skills, intuitions, personal experiences, and unarticulated understandings. The Austrian School argues that this tacit knowledge is essential for decision-making and cannot be fully captured by mathematical models or objective measures.

Subjectivity of Preferences: Austrians highlight the inherent subjectivity in human preferences and valuations. Each individual has their own preferences and goals, and these subjective choices are fundamental to understanding economic outcomes. While more positivist approaches tend to seek objective patterns, Austrians argue that the diversity of individual preferences is a central aspect of economic reality.

Entrepreneurship and Discovery: The Austrian School emphasizes the role of the entrepreneur as someone who uses tacit knowledge to discover profit opportunities in the market. Entrepreneurial decision-making often involves the use of information that is not fully articulated or quantified.

Competition as a Discovery Process: Instead of viewing competition simply as a process of efficiently allocating resources, Austrians see competition as a continuous discovery process. Market participants are constantly learning, adapting, and adjusting their decisions in response to changes in economic conditions and new subjective information.

In general, the Austrian School advocates for a more holistic and qualitative approach, recognizing the limitation of purely quantitative approaches to capture the complexity of human action and economic decision-making. This perspective highlights the importance of tacit and subjective knowledge that cannot always be easily measured or formally expressed.

Issues with Centralized Prediction: Austrians criticize the idea that accurate prediction and centralized planning are feasible. They argue that the information necessary to foresee market behavior is scattered and locally known by individuals, making centralized planning inefficient.

Decentralized Knowledge: The Austrian School argues that the information necessary for efficient economic decision-making is decentralized. Each individual possesses specific knowledge about their circumstances, preferences, and skills, and this local knowledge is difficult to effectively transmit to a central entity.

Knowledge Problem: Friedrich Hayek, another prominent economist of the Austrian School, developed the concept of the "knowledge problem" to explain why centralized planning is inherently inefficient. He argues that information about local conditions and individual preferences is dispersed and largely unarticulated, making it impossible for a central authority to fully know and understand this information.

Incentives and Coordination: Austrians contend that, due to the lack of complete information and the impossibility of centrally calculating individual preferences, centralized planning cannot efficiently coordinate the production and allocation of resources. Additionally, they argue that competition and market prices, reflecting individuals' subjective valuations, are better mechanisms for efficiently coordinating economic activities.

Theory of Economic Calculation: Ludwig von Mises developed the "theory of economic calculation" to explain how prices in a free market system allow people to make informed calculations and decisions regarding resource allocation. He argues that without market prices based on the decentralized interaction of supply and demand, there is no effective way to calculate the relative costs and benefits of various production options.

The Austrian School's criticism of centralized planning is based on the idea that the information necessary for efficient economic decision-making is dispersed among individuals and cannot be fully known or calculated by a central authority. They argue in favor of decentralized systems based on competition and market prices as more effective mechanisms for coordinating economic activity.

Knowledge of Particular Circumstances: The Austrian School emphasizes the importance of decentralized knowledge of particular circumstances. They argue that individuals, when acting in their own interest, effectively use this knowledge, while centralized measures lack this specific information.

Tacit and Specific Knowledge: The Austrian School emphasizes that knowledge relevant to economic decision-making is often tacit, difficult to articulate, and specific to an individual's particular circumstances. This knowledge includes details about personal preferences, skills, local opportunities, and changes in market conditions.

Human Action, according to the Austrian School, implies that individuals are constantly adapting to new circumstances and opportunities. Adaptability and responsiveness to change are fundamental to economic efficiency. Individuals, when acting in their own interest, use their specific knowledge to make decisions that best suit their unique circumstances.

Entrepreneurs and Discovery: The figure of the entrepreneur in Austrian theory plays a crucial role in utilizing this decentralized knowledge. Entrepreneurs are seen as agents who discover profit opportunities by combining resources innovatively, leveraging their specific knowledge of market circumstances.

Market Dynamism: The Austrian School argues that market dynamism, with competition and the entry and exit of firms, is essential for adaptability and economic efficiency. Market prices, determined by the decentralized interaction of supply and demand, reflect the dispersed knowledge of market participants.

Critique of Central Planning: The criticism of socialism and other forms of centralized planning is based on the idea that information about particular circumstances is so vast and specific that a central entity cannot access or process it efficiently. The Austrian School emphasizes that decentralized knowledge of particular circumstances is crucial for effective decision-making and argues that individual action in a free market environment allows for better utilization of this knowledge than centralized measures.

Critique of Mathematical Modeling. The Austrian School criticizes the positivist emphasis on complex mathematical modeling. They argue that mathematical complexity does not guarantee greater precision or understanding of economic phenomena and often oversimplifies reality.

Limitations of Quantification: Austrians argue that the economy involves complex and variable phenomena that cannot always be reduced to mathematical formulas. Excessive quantification can lead to simplifications that do not capture the richness and diversity of human actions and economic interactions.

Subjectivity and Diversity: The Austrian School emphasizes the subjectivity inherent in human preferences and decisions. Each individual has their own subjective valuations, and these cannot always be accurately represented through mathematical equations.

Furthermore, the diversity of individual preferences and circumstances complicates the possibility of accurately modeling economic reality.

Tacit and Non-articulated Knowledge: As mentioned earlier, the Austrian School emphasizes tacit and non-articulated knowledge that is crucial for economic decision-making. This type of knowledge is difficult to quantify and, therefore, cannot be easily incorporated into mathematical models.

Dynamism and Constant Change: The economy is a dynamic system subject to constant changes due to factors such as innovation, shifting preferences, and market conditions. Austrians argue that mathematical models often cannot adequately capture this dynamism, thus providing a static and simplified understanding of economic reality.

Emphasis on Praxeology: In contrast, the Austrian School advocates for praxeology, a methodology based on deductive logic and verbal reasoning rather than mathematical quantification. They argue that this approach provides a deeper understanding of human action and economic interactions.

In summary, the Austrian criticism of mathematical modeling focuses on the limitations in capturing the complexity, subjectivity, and dynamism of human and economic behavior through mathematical formulas. Instead, they advocate for more qualitative approaches based on deductive logic.

Emphasis on Praxeology: Praxeology, a methodological approach of the Austrian School, criticizes empiricism by asserting that human action and deducible logic are the foundations of economic theory, and controlled experiments are not applicable to the social sciences.

Definition of Praxeology: Praxeology is the methodology used by the Austrian School to study human action. Ludwig von Mises, a leading figure in the Austrian School, defined praxeology as the science of human action, focusing on deductive logical reasoning as a method to understand economics.

Human Action as Axiom: In praxeology, human action is considered an irrefutable and self-evident axiom. Mises argues that any attempt to deny human action would itself be an act of action, demonstrating the impossibility of refuting this principle.

Critique of Empiricism: Praxeology criticizes empiricism, the idea that knowledge is primarily derived from observation and experience. Austrians argue that human action and decision-making cannot be simply reduced to empirical observations or controlled experiments, as these methods are inapplicable to the social sciences due to the complexity and variability of human behavior.

Aprioristic Theory: Praxeology is aprioristic, meaning it is based on a priori or self-evident principles, rather than relying solely on empirical observation. Austrians argue that certain principles, such as time preference (the idea that people value present goods more than future ones), can be understood through logical reflection without the need for empirical evidence.

Limits of Empirical Method in Social Sciences: Austrians argue that social sciences, including economics, cannot follow the same empirical method as the natural sciences due to the unique nature of human actions and the impossibility of conducting controlled experiments in complex societies.

In summary, praxeology is a methodology that highlights human action as a starting point for understanding economics, using deductive logical reasoning instead of relying solely on empirical observation or controlled experiments, which, according to Austrians, are not suitable for the social sciences.

The Austrian School criticizes the positivist and empiricist view that seeks to find universal laws through direct observation and measurement, advocating instead for an approach based on human action, deductive logic, and recognition of the complexity of economic interactions.

5.Critique of Mathematization of Economics

Critique of the Mathematization of Economics: The critique of the mathematization of economics is a common perspective in the Austrian School and other heterodox schools of thought in economics.

Excessive Simplification: Mathematization often involves formulating economic models using mathematical equations and formulas. The Austrian critique suggests that these models may overly simplify economic reality by reducing complex phenomena to quantifiable relationships, ignoring the richness of human action and the specific conditions of the real world.

Limitation of Quantification: The Austrian critique emphasizes that not all aspects of human action and economic interactions can be easily quantified. Economic reality is nuanced and complex, and attempting to reduce everything to mathematical equations may overlook essential aspects of human action and economic interactions.

Diversity of Individual Actions: The Austrian economics highlights the diversity of human actions and individual preferences. Each person has their own goals, values, and unique circumstances, making it challenging to represent this diversity of behaviors through general mathematical models.

Specific Conditions of the Real World: Austrian economics argues that mathematical models often ignore the specific conditions of the real world, such as uncertainty, asymmetric information, and dynamic changes in preferences and technologies. These conditions are crucial for fully understanding economic action.

Not Always Rational Behavior: Mathematical models often assume rational and utility-maximizing behavior, but the Austrian critique points out that people do not always make decisions entirely rationally. Emotional, psychological, and social factors can influence economic decisions in ways that mathematical models may not fully capture.

Lack of Adaptability to Changes: Austrian economics emphasizes the dynamic and adaptable nature of the economic system. Mathematical models may not be flexible enough to adjust to unexpected changes or the evolution of economic conditions over time.

The Austrian critique of mathematization focuses on the concern that mathematical models may overly simplify economic reality by attempting to quantify complex phenomena, ignoring the diversity and specific conditions of the real world that are crucial for understanding human action and economic interactions.

Models without a Solid Empirical Basis: Critics argue that some mathematical models in economics are developed without a solid empirical foundation. Model construction often involves introducing simplifying assumptions, and the results may not be easily applicable or generalizable in the real world.

Simplifying Assumptions: The construction of mathematical models often involves introducing simplifying assumptions to make calculations more manageable. However, critics argue that these assumptions can be unrealistic and may not fully reflect the complexity of economic reality.

Lack of Consideration of External Factors: Some mathematical models may overlook external or contextual factors that are important in the real economy. This could include changes in market conditions, unexpected events, or social dynamics that are not adequately captured in the model.

Difficulty of Generalization: The results of some mathematical models may not be easily generalizable to different contexts or populations. The critique holds that a lack of a solid empirical basis can limit the applicability and external validity of results obtained through mathematical models.

Limitations of Data and Measurements: In some cases, the lack of availability of precise data or the difficulty in measuring certain economic phenomena can affect the construction of robust mathematical models. This can lead to the formulation of models that do not fully align with reality.

Causality vs. Correlation: Some mathematical models may identify correlative relationships without establishing causality. This can lead to erroneous or simplified interpretations of economic relationships, as models often cannot fully capture the complexities of cause and effect.

Ideological Bias: Critics also point out that some mathematical models may be influenced by ideological or theoretical biases, which can affect the objectivity and validity of the results.

The critique of the lack of a solid empirical basis in some mathematical models underscores the importance of ensuring that assumptions, simplifications, and results adequately align with economic reality for models to be useful and applicable in the real world.

Subjectivity and Heterogeneity: Mathematization sometimes struggles to capture the subjectivity of preferences and the heterogeneity of individual actions. Austrian economics emphasizes that each person has their own valuations and goals, making it challenging to accurately represent them with mathematical equations.

Subjectivity of Preferences: The Austrian School highlights that preferences and valuations are inherently subjective, varying between individuals and situations. Mathematization often seeks to establish objective and quantifiable relationships, but the subjectivity of human preferences may elude precise representation through mathematical equations.

Difficulty in Quantifying Subjective Variables: Subjective elements, such as personal preferences, perceptions, and emotional valuations, are challenging to quantify objectively. Mathematization, relying on quantification, may struggle to effectively incorporate these subjective variables.

Heterogeneity of Individual Actions: Mathematization tends to seek models that describe behaviors in a generalized manner. However, Austrian economics emphasizes that each individual is unique, and their actions are influenced by a unique combination of factors, making it difficult to create mathematical models that capture the complete heterogeneity of individual actions.

Social and Cultural Context: Preferences and economic decisions are also shaped by social and cultural context. Mathematization may struggle to incorporate these aspects, as social and cultural variables are often complex and qualitative.

Dynamic Changes in Preferences: Individual preferences can change over time due to factors such as personal experiences, changes in circumstances, and cultural evolution. Mathematization, with its tendency toward static models, may not be flexible enough to capture these dynamic changes.

Lack of Access to Individual Consciousness: Mathematization cannot directly access individual consciousness and subjectivity. Since preferences are often rooted in subjective aspects of human experience, some critics argue that mathematical equations may not be the most suitable means to represent such phenomena.

In summary, Austrian criticism emphasizes that mathematization may struggle to address the subjectivity of preferences and the heterogeneity of individual actions, fundamental aspects of human action that are central in Austrian economic theory.

Lack of Adaptability to Changes: Mathematical models, being inherently static, may face challenges in adapting to dynamic changes in the economic environment. Austrian criticism suggests that the economy is a constantly evolving system, and mathematical models may not be flexible enough to capture these changes effectively.

Dynamism of the Economic Environment: Austrian criticism highlights that the economy is a dynamic system subject to constant changes, such as technological innovations, fluctuations in consumer demand, and shifts in macroeconomic conditions. Static mathematical models may not be able to effectively capture this dynamic and evolving nature.

Unforeseen Incidents: Unexpected events, such as financial crises, significant political changes, or natural disasters, can have a significant impact on the economy. Mathematical models that do not consider these events or rely on historical data may struggle to adapt to unforeseen situations.

Limitations in Prediction: Adaptability to changes is linked to the ability to foresee and anticipate future events. Austrian criticism suggests that the complex and nonlinear nature of the economy makes accurate prediction difficult, and mathematical models heavily reliant on projections may be unreliable in dynamic environments.

Uncertainty and Complexity: Adaptability is also affected by the inherent uncertainty in economic decision-making. Austrian criticism emphasizes that the complexity of economic interactions and incomplete information may render mathematical models insufficiently flexible to handle real-world uncertainty and complexity.

Entrepreneurial Focus: The Austrian School often emphasizes the role of the entrepreneur and entrepreneurial action in the economy. Entrepreneurs, in seeking profit opportunities and responding to changes in the environment, introduce an element of adaptability that may be challenging to precisely model mathematically.

In summary, Austrian criticism underscores that mathematical models, being static and based on predefined functional relationships, may not be adaptable enough to capture the dynamic and changing nature of the economy, especially in the presence of unforeseen events and systemic complexities.

Uncaptured Tacit Knowledge: Mathematization often fails to capture the tacit and unarticulated knowledge individuals use in economic decision-making. This type of knowledge, fundamental to the Austrian School, is difficult to quantify and express through mathematical equations.

Unarticulated Nature of Tacit Knowledge: Tacit knowledge refers to information that people possess but cannot easily express in formal or quantifiable terms. It may include practical skills, intuitions, personal experiences, and unarticulated understandings. Mathematization, relying on formalization and quantification, may struggle to effectively capture this type of knowledge.

Importance in Decision-Making: The Austrian School argues that tacit knowledge plays a crucial role in economic decision-making. Individuals, acting in their own interests, use this implicit knowledge to adapt to changing situations and make informed decisions that may not be easily translatable into mathematical terms.

Contextuality and Singularity: Tacit knowledge is often highly contextual and specific to particular situations. Each individual may have their own unique set of implicit knowledge based on their experiences and personal circumstances. Mathematization, in seeking generalizations and abstractions, may overlook these singularities.

Entrepreneurial Discovery Process: The Austrian School highlights the role of the entrepreneur as a key actor in market opportunity discovery. Tacit knowledge plays a fundamental role in this discovery process, where entrepreneurs use non-fully articulated information to identify and seize profit opportunities.

Limits of Quantification: Quantification, an integral part of mathematization, has limitations in capturing the complexity and subjectivity of tacit knowledge. This type of knowledge often involves intuitive judgments and subjective evaluations that may not easily translate into numbers and equations.

In summary, Austrian criticism emphasizes that mathematization may overlook tacit knowledge, which is crucial in economic decision-making. This unarticulated and difficult-to-quantify knowledge is better understood through more qualitative and contextualized approaches.

Qualitative Alternatives: Austrians advocate for qualitative approaches based on deductive logic and a deep understanding of human actions. They argue that these approaches provide a richer and more comprehensive view of the economy, without relying exclusively on mathematization.

Emphasis on Human Action: The Austrian School highlights the importance of understanding human action in the economic context. They advocate for an approach that recognizes the complexity and diversity of individual actions, asserting that deductive logic is more suitable for understanding human action than mathematical quantification.

Praxeology as Methodology: Praxeology, as a methodology of the Austrian School, relies on deductive logic and verbal reasoning to understand human action. By considering action as a fundamental axiom and using logic to derive conclusions, praxeology seeks to provide a deep and a priori understanding of the economy.

Emphasis on Economic Calculation Theory: Ludwig von Mises, a prominent representative of the Austrian School, developed the economic calculation theory to explain how prices in a free-market system enable efficient resource allocation. This theory is based on the idea that understanding the market process is more effective through qualitative analysis of economic decisions rather than simply mathematical models.

Entrepreneurial Focus and Discovery: The Austrian School emphasizes the role of the entrepreneur as a key actor in the economic process. Entrepreneurial decision-making, involving the discovery of profit opportunities, is better understood through a qualitative approach that recognizes entrepreneurial creativity, judgment, and adaptability.

Critique of Excessive Formalization: Austrians criticize the tendency to excessively formalize economic theory through mathematical models. They argue that this approach often oversimplifies economic reality, overlooking the richness of human actions and the complexities of the market process.

In summary, the Austrian preference for qualitative approaches is based on the idea that human action and the economy itself are phenomena too complex to be fully captured by mathematical quantification. They advocate for methods that allow a richer and contextualized understanding of the economy, using deductive logic and an appreciation for the diversity of human actions.

Critique of the Mathematization of Economics is based on the concern that mathematical formulation may overly simplify economic reality, ignoring crucial aspects of human action and the complexity of the real world.

6.Theory of the Business Cycle

The Theory of Economic Cycles (TEC) is an important part of Austrian economic theory, focusing on explaining economic fluctuations over time.

Causes of Economic Cycles: Austrian TEC asserts that economic cycles result from distortions in the production structure caused by interventions in the economic system, especially by monetary and banking authorities.

Monetary Interventions: Austrian TEC points out that interventions in the monetary system, particularly by monetary authorities, play a crucial role in generating economic cycles. This refers to changes in money supply and interest rates that are not the natural outcome of market supply and demand.

Manipulation of Interest Rates: The most common intervention is the manipulation of interest rates. When monetary authorities artificially lower interest rates below the level that would be set in a free market, borrowing and investment are encouraged. However, this investment is based on interest rates that do not reflect the society's actual savings preferences.

Malinvestment and Distortions in Production Structure: The artificial reduction of interest rates leads to malinvestments, where businesses undertake investment projects that are not sustainable in the long term. This creates distortions in the economy's production structure as investments focus on areas that wouldn't be justified without intervention in interest rates.

Boom and Bust Cycle: The initial phase of low-interest rates leads to an economic boom, marked by increased investment and spending. However, these conditions are unsustainable and eventually result in a recession phase when malinvestments become apparent and interest rates return to more realistic levels.

Discoordination Among Economic Sectors: TEC emphasizes that interest rate manipulation causes discoordination among different economic sectors. Some sectors may experience an artificial boom while others contract, contributing to distortions and imbalances.

Role of the Banking System: TEC underscores the role of the banking system in credit expansion during the boom phase and how this process contributes to malinvestment. The creation of fiduciary money by banks triggers an increase in credit that drives investment, but this expansion is not supported by a corresponding increase in real savings.

According to Austrian TEC, economic cycles result from distortions in the production structure induced by interventions in the economic system, especially those related to money supply and interest rates.

Expansion Phase: The theory begins with an expansion phase of the cycle. During this phase, monetary authorities tend to expand the money and credit supply, artificially lowering interest rates below their market equilibrium level. This leads to increased investment and spending, stimulating economic activity.

Monetary Expansion: During the expansion phase, monetary authorities, often through central bank policies, increase the money supply in the economy. This is achieved by lowering interest rates and implementing policies that encourage credit and liquidity in the financial system.

Artificial Reduction of Interest Rates: A key feature of the expansion phase is the artificial reduction of interest rates. Monetary authorities intervene to set interest rates below what would be determined by market forces. This lower level of interest rates aims to stimulate borrowing and investment.

Stimulus to Investment and Spending: Lower interest rates make borrowing more attractive and accessible to businesses and consumers. This drives investment in projects that, under higher and unmanipulated interest rates, might not be considered profitable. Additionally, consumers, with easier access to credit, tend to increase spending.

Increased Economic Activity: The combination of business investment and increased consumer spending stimulates economic activity in various sectors. There is seemingly robust economic growth during this phase, with indicators such as employment and production showing improvements.

Malinvestment and Distortions: However, the key to the Austrian theory is that this growth is based on artificially low-interest rates, leading to malinvestments. Companies invest in projects that are only profitable in the short term due to reduced interest rates but are not sustainable in the long run.

Misalignment of Production Structure: Monetary expansion and manipulated interest rates cause a misalignment in the economy's production structure. Distortions occur in resource allocation and investment distribution among economic sectors.

It is important to note that, according to Austrian TEC, this apparent prosperity during the expansion phase is unsustainable and eventually leads to the contraction or recession phase when malinvestments become apparent, requiring a correction in the economy's production structure.

Distortions in Production Structure: The artificial reduction of interest rates leads to investment decisions that are not sustainable in the long term. Companies, perceiving lower interest rates, undertake investment projects that would not be economically viable otherwise. This leads to distortions in the economy's production structure.

Unsustainable Investments: Artificially low-interest rates induce companies to make investment decisions that, under conditions of unmanipulated interest rates, would not be economically viable or sustainable in the long term. Projects that seem profitable at lower interest rates may become unviable when rates return to realistic levels.

Focus on the Short Term: Interest rate manipulation leads to a greater preference for short-term investment projects, as they are more sensitive to interest rate fluctuations. This can result in a production infrastructure biased toward sectors that temporarily benefit from reduced interest rates but lack a solid foundation for sustained growth.

Discoordination Among Economic Sectors: Manipulated interest rates can generate discoordination among different sectors of the economy. Some sectors may experience an artificial boom while others, which might be more economically viable under normal conditions, may be neglected.

Overinvestment in Specific Assets: Distortions in the production structure can also manifest as overinvestment in specific assets, such as capital goods or properties. Companies may be incentivized to invest in these assets due to reduced interest rates, leading to saturation and eventually a market correction.

Necessary Correction: The subsequent contraction phase, following the expansion phase, involves a necessary correction of these malinvestments and distortions in the production structure. Unsustainable projects may face financial difficulties, and the economy seeks to readjust to a more appropriate allocation of resources.

In summary, Austrian TEC highlights how the manipulation of interest rates during the expansion phase can generate unsustainable investment decisions and distortions in the production structure, eventually requiring correction in the form of an economic recession.

Boom Phase: The economy experiences a boom in economic activity during the expansion phase. However, these conditions are unsustainable due to the mentioned distortions. Investments that seemed profitable at artificially low interest rates turn out to be unprofitable when interest rates return to more realistic levels.

Apparent Economic Growth: During the boom phase, the economy undergoes seemingly robust growth. Monetary expansion and artificially low interest rates lead to an increase in investment and spending, translating into higher employment, production, and overall economic activity.

Development of Misunderstandings: Lower interest rates during the expansion phase generate misunderstandings in the market. Companies interpret easy access to credit as a signal of higher savings rates and, therefore, view projects as more profitable that, under normal conditions, would not be.

Overinvestment and Overcapitalization: This boom period is often characterized by overinvestment in investment projects and overcapitalization in certain sectors. Companies, influenced by manipulated interest rates, may undertake projects that would not be economically viable without interest rate distortion.

Illusion of Prosperity: The economy may experience a temporary illusion of prosperity during this phase, as growth and expansion seem to indicate a genuine increase in wealth and economic efficiency.

Revelation of Mispresentations: However, these conditions are unsustainable. When interest rates return to more realistic levels, misinvestments and market misunderstandings are revealed. Projects that seemed profitable during the expansion phase now prove to be unprofitable, and companies may face financial difficulties.

Adjustment in Production Structure: The boom phase is followed by a contraction or recession phase. During this phase, the economy adjusts to correct distortions in the production structure. Misinvestments and unsustainable investments face difficulties, and resources are reallocated to sectors more in line with consumers' true preferences.

In summary, the boom phase in the Austrian Business Cycle Theory represents a period of apparent economic prosperity but is based on misunderstandings and misinvestments that become evident when monetary conditions return to normal, triggering the contraction phase of the economic cycle.

Contraction Phase: The contraction phase, or recession, follows the boom. Distortions in the production structure become evident, and unprofitable investments begin to fail. Companies face financial difficulties, and a market correction occurs. Recession is seen by the Austrian Business Cycle Theory (ABCT) as a necessary process to correct bad investments and restore the economy's production structure.

Revelation of Bad Investments: During the contraction phase, distortions in the production structure created during the boom phase become evident. Investment projects undertaken due to artificially low interest rates and that were not economically viable under normal conditions begin to fail.

Business Financial Difficulties: Companies that engaged in bad investments face financial difficulties. Projects that seemed promising during the boom phase and received easy financing now face the challenge of being unsustainable in the long term.

Unemployment and Economic Contraction: Recession is often accompanied by an increase in unemployment rates as companies, affected by lack of profitability and financial difficulties, may reduce production and, in some cases, close operations. Economic contraction is reflected in various indicators, such as declining GDP and economic activity.

Market Adjustment: ABCT sees the recession as a necessary market adjustment process. During this phase, bad investments are liquidated, and resources are reallocated to sectors more in line with consumers' true preferences and needs.

Correction of Coordinations: The recession also acts as a correction mechanism for the coordinations generated during the boom phase. Economic sectors that experienced artificial booms and were misaligned with market preferences contract, while other sectors may see a more realistic correction and adjustment.

Importance of Natural Adjustment: From the Austrian perspective, recession is not inherently negative but a necessary process to correct distortions and imbalances created during the expansion phase. This natural adjustment in the production structure is crucial to restoring a stronger and more sustainable economic foundation.

In summary, the contraction phase in the Austrian Business Cycle Theory is viewed as a necessary and healthy phase that allows for the correction of bad investments, the realignment of the production structure, and the restoration of more realistic and sustainable economic conditions.

Role of the Banking System: ABCT attributes a crucial role to the banking system in the creation of economic cycles. Artificial credit expansion by banks contributes to malinvestment and distortions in the production structure. When these distortions become evident, the banking system often faces crises and bankruptcies.

Artificial Credit Expansion: In the expansion phase, the banking system plays a fundamental role in artificially expanding credit. Monetary authorities, through policies including interest rate reduction, provide incentives for banks to increase credit supply to businesses and consumers.

Creation of Fiat Money: Banks not only lend the money they already have deposited but also create fiat money by granting loans. This money creation process is amplified during the expansion phase when the demand for credit increases due to artificially low interest rates.

Malinvestment and Distortions: Artificial credit expansion directly contributes to malinvestment and distortions in the production structure. Companies, influenced by the availability of easy credit, undertake investment projects that would not be economically viable without credit intervention.

Overcapitalization Process: During the boom phase, the banking system may also experience an overcapitalization process. Banks may appear healthy and well-capitalized due to apparent economic prosperity, but this situation can change rapidly when malinvestments and financial difficulties of companies are revealed.

Crisis and Banking Failures: When distortions in the production structure become evident and malinvestments begin to fail, the banking system faces the possibility of crises and failures. Loans that once seemed secure and profitable now result in significant losses for banks, leading to a financial crisis.

Credit Contraction: The contraction phase, following the boom, is often characterized by a credit contraction. Banks, affected by losses and perceived risk, may become more cautious in granting new loans. This contributes to economic contraction and correction in the production structure.

Importance of Liquidation: From the Austrian perspective, crises and bankruptcies in the banking system should not be artificially avoided, as they are part of the necessary process of liquidation and adjustment that allows for the long-term health and strength of the economic system.

The Austrian Business Cycle Theory highlights how artificial credit expansion by the banking system contributes to the generation of economic cycles, creating malinvestments and distortions that must eventually be corrected through crisis and market adjustment processes.

Critique of Active Monetary Policies: The Austrian Business Cycle Theory criticizes active monetary policies that seek to manipulate interest rates and money supply as a means to stabilize the economy. It argues that these interventions are, in themselves, generators of economic cycles and can exacerbate problems rather than solve them.

Manipulation of Interest Rates: ABCT maintains that the manipulation of interest rates by monetary authorities, with the aim of influencing economic activity, is a harmful intervention. When interest rates are artificially set below their market level, this distorts economic signals and leads to poor investment decisions.

Misallocation Generation: Active monetary policies, such as interest rate reduction to stimulate investment and spending, can lead to misallocations. Companies, influenced by artificial interest rates, may undertake projects that would not be economically viable under normal conditions.

Economic Cycles as a Result of Interventions: The Austrian Business Cycle Theory (ABCT) argues that economic cycles are largely the result of interventions in the economic system, especially those related to monetary policies. Manipulating interest rates and the money supply creates imbalances in the economy that must eventually be corrected, leading to cycles of boom and recession.

Lack of Accurate Information: The Austrian critique highlights the difficulty faced by monetary authorities in accurately determining the "correct" level of interest rates. By intervening to manipulate rates, there is a risk of creating imbalances in the economy, as authorities may lack the complete and up-to-date information needed.

Creation of Bubbles and Excesses: Active intervention in interest rates and the money supply can lead to the formation of asset bubbles and excesses in certain sectors of the economy. When easy credit is promoted and interest rates artificially drop, asset prices, such as real estate or stocks, may experience unsustainable increases.

Need for Natural Adjustment: From the Austrian perspective, active interventions in the economic system often prevent the natural adjustment process that would occur in the absence of manipulation. The ABCT advocates allowing natural adjustments, such as recession, to occur to correct distortions in the economy.

In summary, the Austrian critique of active monetary policies focuses on the argument that these interventions not only fail to prevent economic cycles but also contribute to their generation and can exacerbate long-term problems rather than resolving them.

The Austrian Business Cycle Theory provides an explanation of economic cycles based on the consequences of monetary and credit manipulation, highlighting how distortions in the production structure during expansion phases eventually lead to corrections and recessions in the economic cycle.

7.Methodological Individualism

Methodological individualism is a principle of analysis and approach in the social sciences, especially in economics, that emphasizes the importance of focusing on the individual as the basic unit of study. This approach contends that explanations and understandings of social phenomena should be derived from individual actions and decisions, rather than attributing properties or behaviors to abstract groups.

Individual Action: Methodological individualism starts from the principle that all social action is the result of individual actions. Instead of treating social groups as homogeneous entities with inherent properties, it seeks to understand social interactions and dynamics through individual actions and choices.

Individual Agency: Methodological individualism recognizes individual agency as the primary driver of social action. Each individual is seen as an active agent making decisions and taking actions based on their own goals, preferences, and circumstances.

Rejection of Group Homogeneity: It opposes the idea of treating social groups as homogeneous entities with inherent properties. Instead of making generalizations about how certain groups act or think, it seeks to understand the diversity of choices and individual actions within those groups.

Context and Personal Circumstances: Understanding individual action involves taking into account the context and personal circumstances. Each individual acts in a specific environment and responds to a variety of factors, including their past experiences, beliefs, available resources, and perceived opportunities.

Social Interactions and Dynamics: Social interactions and group dynamics emerge from individual actions. Through the interconnection of individual decisions, broader social patterns and structures form. However, these patterns should not be treated as autonomous entities but as the result of interconnected individual choices.

Reciprocal Influence: While individual action is emphasized, methodological individualism does not deny the reciprocal influence between individuals. The actions of one individual can influence the actions of others, creating broader patterns of social behavior. However, this process is still analyzed from the perspective of individual actions.

Individual Utility Maximization: In the economic realm, methodological individualism is often associated with the idea of individual utility maximization. Individuals are perceived as making rational decisions to maximize their personal well-being, although the notion of utility may vary depending on the context and discipline.

Methodological individualism highlights the importance of understanding individual actions and choices as the foundation for understanding broader social phenomena, avoiding simplistic generalizations about social groups.

Individual Rationality: It is assumed that individuals act rationally, pursuing their own goals and maximizing their personal utility. Individual decision-making and the pursuit of self-interest are considered fundamental to understanding social and economic phenomena.

Assumption of Rationality: In the context of methodological individualism, it is assumed that individuals act rationally. This implies that they make informed decisions, carefully evaluating their options and choosing the one that maximizes their personal utility, given constraints and circumstances.

Utility Maximization: Utility maximization refers to the idea that individuals seek to increase their well-being or personal satisfaction as much as possible. This may include the pursuit of happiness, satisfaction of basic needs, accumulation of wealth, among other individual goals.

Economic Perspective: In the economic realm, individual rationality is crucial for explaining the behavior of economic agents, such as consumers and producers. It is assumed that individuals make economic decisions with the goal of maximizing their utility, either in terms of personal satisfaction or financial gain.

Informed Decision-Making: Rationality implies that individuals have access to relevant information and use it in an informed manner when making decisions. This does not mean that individuals always make perfect decisions, but it is assumed that their overall behavior follows a logic of choice based on available information.

Pursuit of Self-Interest: The pursuit of self-interest implies that individuals act in their own benefit, pursuing their own goals and individual objectives. This principle aligns with the idea that individual actions are driven by personal motivations and that social cooperation can arise when individuals find working together beneficial to their individual interests.

Critique and Deviations from Rationality: Although rationality is assumed, some approaches recognize that individuals may deviate from rationality in certain contexts or circumstances. For example, behavioral economics explores how psychological and emotional factors can influence individual decisions.

Broader Application: While individual rationality is a fundamental concept in economics, it has also been applied in other disciplines, such as game theory, sociology, and political science, to understand human behavior in various social contexts.

The assumption of individual rationality is a cornerstone of methodological individualism, providing a framework for understanding and analyzing individual actions in a variety of contexts, especially in the social and economic spheres.

Critique of Collective Generalizations: Methodological individualism criticizes collective generalizations that may conceal the diversity of individual choices and actions. Instead of speaking of "groups" as if they were entities with inherent collective behaviors, it seeks to break down explanations in terms of individual actions and decisions.

Diversity of Individual Choices: Methodological individualism emphasizes the diversity of choices and individual actions within any social group. Treating a group as if all its members act in the same way can lead to oversimplifications and the loss of valuable information about individual variations.

Complexity of Individual Motivations: Each individual has their own motivations, preferences, and circumstances. Collective generalizations often oversimplify this complexity, ignoring significant variations in the reasons why people make decisions and act in certain ways.

Effect of Individual Actions on the Whole: Methodological individualism argues that individual actions and decisions form the basis of broader social phenomena. By breaking down explanations in terms of individual actions, it seeks to understand how each person's choices contribute to the dynamics of the group as a whole.

Avoiding Group Homogenization: Collective generalizations often lead to the homogenization of groups, treating all members as if they share identical characteristics. This can result in stereotypes and prejudices, as reality is often much more complex and diverse.

Individuality in Social Decisions: Even in broader social contexts, such as institutions or organizational structures, methodological individualism emphasizes that individual decisions and actions remain the driving force. Group policies and dynamics result from complex interactions among individual choices.

Critique of Holistic Explanations: Holistic explanations attributing collective properties or behaviors as if they were independent entities from individual actions are criticized. Instead of viewing a group as a homogeneous entity, there is an advocacy for understanding how individual actions contribute to group dynamics.

Importance of Individual Variability: Recognizing individual variability is essential for understanding the complexities of society. People may have different values, goals, experiences, and circumstances, significantly influencing their choices and actions.

Critique of Collective Generalizations: Criticizing collective generalizations is a central feature of methodological individualism, emphasizing the importance of analyzing and understanding the diversity of individual choices and actions to gain a more accurate view of social phenomena.

Emphasis on the Variety of Choices: It acknowledges the variety of individual choices and preferences. Although there may be general patterns and trends, methodological individualism highlights that individual actions and decisions can be highly diverse, even in similar situations.

Diversity of Preferences and Values: Methodological individualism recognizes that people have a wide variety of preferences, values, and goals. Even in seemingly similar situations, individuals may make different decisions due to differences in their experiences, cultural contexts, and personal values.

Contextualization of Decisions: Each individual makes decisions in a unique context. Personal, historical, and social circumstances influence individual choices. Methodological individualism seeks to understand how these specific contexts shape decisions, rather than applying simplistic explanations based on group categories.

Response to Human Complexity: By recognizing the variety of individual choices, methodological individualism responds to the inherent complexity of human nature. People have diverse motivations and uniquely respond to their environments, challenging simplistic generalizations about how they should behave in groups.

Resistance to Stereotypes: By highlighting the diversity of choices, methodological individualism opposes the application of stereotypes to groups of people. It avoids assuming that all individuals within a category automatically share certain traits or behaviors, instead recognizing the uniqueness of each person.

Adaptation to Changes and Variable Contexts: The variety of choices also implies that people can adapt and change over time in response to new experiences, information, or circumstances. This underscores the importance of approaching individuals as dynamic and adaptable beings.

Differentiation of Individual Outcomes: The emphasis on the variety of choices highlights that even when people face similar situations, their outcomes may be different due to individual choices. This is essential for understanding disparities in life outcomes and individual well-being.

General Trends without Homogenization: While recognizing general patterns and trends, methodological individualism avoids homogenizing individual choices. It acknowledges that even in the presence of trends, individual variability is a fundamental feature of the human condition.

The emphasis on the variety of choices in methodological individualism underscores the need to understand and respect the diversity of motivations and individual decisions, thereby enriching our understanding of the complexity of society and human interaction.

Critique of Collective Abstractions: It opposes collective abstractions that treat groups as entities with homogeneous characteristics. This includes criticisms of the idea that collective entities, such as "society" or "the market," have intentions or behaviors separate from the individual actions that compose them.

Avoiding Group Homogenization: Methodological individualism opposes the tendency to treat groups as if they were homogeneous entities. This critique emphasizes that characteristics, behaviors, and preferences can vary significantly within any social group. It cannot be assumed that all members of a group act in the same way.

Diversity of Individual Actions: Each individual within a group may have unique motivations and goals. Collective abstractions often simplify the diversity of individual actions, thereby losing the richness of human variability and differences in decision-making.

Breakdown Analysis: Methodological individualism advocates for breaking down explanations and analyses in terms of individual actions and decisions instead of attributing abstract collective characteristics to an entire group. This allows for a more precise understanding of social and economic dynamics.

Critique of Collective Entities with their Own Intentions: The idea of attributing intentions or behaviors separate from individual actions to collective entities, such as "society" or "the market," is criticized. These abstractions can lead to simplistic interpretations and misunderstandings of how these concepts actually operate.

Recognition of Individuality: Each individual has their own experiences, values, and circumstances. By rejecting collective abstractions, methodological individualism recognizes the individuality of each person and seeks to understand how these differences contribute to the complexity of social interactions.

Approach to Complex Reality: Collective abstractions can oversimplify reality, leading to a limited understanding of social phenomena. Methodological individualism addresses the complexity of reality by considering individual actions and decisions as the fundamental units of analysis.

Resistance to Stigmatization: Criticizing collective abstractions is also related to resisting the stigmatization or labeling of entire groups based on perceived characteristics. It acknowledges that generalizations often do not reflect reality and can lead to misconceptions and prejudices.

Critiquing collective abstractions is essential for a more accurate and respectful perspective on the diversity and complexity of human action in social and economic contexts.

Development of Theories at the Individual Level: Instead of building theories based on broad social categories, methodological individualism seeks to develop theories that explain social phenomena from the perspective of individual action and interaction.

Microscopic Analysis: Methodological individualism advocates for a "microscopic" approach to social analysis. Instead of focusing on broad social structures or group categories, it concentrates on understanding the actions and decisions of specific individuals as the fundamental unit of study.

Actions as Fundamental Units: Instead of assuming that social categories, such as classes or ethnic groups, have inherent properties, methodological individualism considers individual actions and decisions as the fundamental units shaping social phenomena.

Dynamics of Individual Interactions: Emphasizing individual action leads to considering how interactions between individuals contribute to the formation of social structures and patterns. The theories developed under this approach seek to explain social phenomena through the dynamics of individual actions and their interconnections.

Avoiding Hasty Generalizations: By developing theories at the individual level, hasty generalizations about how certain groups should behave are avoided. Instead of attributing characteristics to broad social categories, the goal is to understand the diversity of behaviors within those categories.

Contextualization of Individual Decisions: The importance of contextualizing individual decisions is recognized. The theories developed under methodological individualism seek to understand how personal circumstances and specific contexts influence individual choices and actions.

Adaptability to Different Contexts: By focusing on individual action, the theories developed are more adaptable to different contexts and circumstances. This allows for greater flexibility in applying theories to various situations and avoids the rigidity associated with group-level generalizations.

Focus on Individual Responsibility: By focusing on individual actions and decisions, methodological individualism also emphasizes individual responsibility. This involves recognizing that the consequences of individual actions contribute to social and economic outcomes.

Understanding Changeability: Theories developed at the individual level can capture the changeability and adaptability of individuals over time. This allows for a more dynamic understanding of social phenomena in contrast to static models that assume fixed collective behaviors.

In summary, the development of theories at the individual level is a fundamental characteristic of methodological individualism, enabling a more detailed and contextualized analysis of social and economic phenomena. This approach influences various disciplines but is particularly prominent in economics, where economists following this methodology tend to explain economic phenomena through the lens of individual decisions and actions, rather than abstract collective properties.

8.Theory of Knowledge

The Austrian School of Economics, known for its heterodox approaches and principles based on methodological individualism, also has implications in the theory of knowledge.

Emphasis on Human Action: The Austrian School, particularly through Ludwig von Mises, places a strong emphasis on human action as the foundation of economic reality. Its main work, "Human Action," argues that the economy is the result of the conscious actions of individuals.

Individual as Rational Agent: The Austrian School assumes that individuals are rational agents making conscious and goal-oriented decisions. Each individual has their own preferences, goals, and circumstances, and acts logically to achieve those goals given the constraints and opportunities they face.

Theory of Human Action: Ludwig von Mises' central work, "Human Action," develops a comprehensive theory of how individuals make economic decisions. Mises argues that human action is the necessary starting point for any economic analysis, and all other economic categories can be derived from conscious action.

Economy as a Result of Individual Decisions: According to the Austrian School, the structure and dynamics of the economy are the direct result of the individual decisions of millions of people. The interaction of these individual actions in the market forms emerging patterns and structures that shape economic reality.

Decentralized Knowledge: The Austrian School emphasizes the idea that the knowledge needed for effective economic decisions is decentralized among individuals. Each person has specific information about their own circumstances and preferences, and effectively uses this knowledge when making decisions.

Critique of Aggregated Models: In contrast to approaches using aggregated models and abstractions, the Austrian School advocates for an analysis focused on individual action. It argues that data aggregation can lose the richness and complexity of individual decisions, and models should consider the diversity of human actions.

Rejection of Centralized Planning: The idea that the economy is the result of the conscious actions of individuals also leads to a fundamental critique of centralized planning. Austrians argue that a central authority cannot efficiently know or coordinate the decentralized and specific decisions of millions of people.

The emphasis on human action is a distinctive principle of the Austrian School, influencing how they understand and analyze economic processes, highlighting the importance of individual decisions and decentralized knowledge in shaping economic reality.

Praxeology: Praxeology is the central methodology in the Austrian School and is fundamental to its theory of knowledge. It refers to the study of human action and is based on the idea that human action and deducible logic are the foundations of economic theory. Austrians argue that praxeology is an aprioristic science, deduced a priori and not dependent on empirical experience.

Definition of Praxeology: Praxeology is the science that deals with the study of human action. Ludwig von Mises, one of the leading representatives of the Austrian School, developed this concept as a fundamental methodological approach to economics.

Human Action as the Object of Study: Praxeology focuses on understanding human action as the main object of study in economics. Action, according to Austrians, implies that individuals choose means to achieve ends and make decisions with limited knowledge in uncertain environments.

Axioms as Aprioristic Foundations: In praxeology, Austrians argue that there are certain principles or axioms that are fundamental and do not require empirical verification. These axioms, such as the existence of action, time preference, and the law of marginal utility, are considered aprioristic truths, logically deduced without relying on empirical experience.

Rejection of Empiricism in Economics: Praxeology rejects the traditional empirical approach in economics, arguing that understanding economic phenomena should not depend solely on empirical observation. Austrians contend that fundamental economic principles can be understood through logical and deductive reasoning.

Deductive Method: Praxeology uses a deductive approach to develop economic theories. Starting from fundamental axioms, logical conclusions about human behavior and economic processes are derived. This method contrasts with the inductive approach, which relies on the observation of data to formulate theories.

Emphasis on Rational Action: Praxeology assumes that human action is always rational in the sense that individuals choose means they consider appropriate to achieve valued ends. This approach emphasizes the importance of understanding the logic behind individual decisions.

Critique of Mathematization: Praxeology also criticizes the tendency toward mathematization in economics. It argues that the complexity of human action and the multitude of factors involved in decisions cannot be fully captured through mathematical models.

Importance of Qualitative Interpretation: Praxeology advocates for a qualitative interpretation of economic processes. It argues that the meaning of human actions cannot be reduced simply to numbers and that deep understanding requires an appreciation of the motives and intentions behind individual decisions.

In summary, praxeology is a distinctive and central approach in the Austrian School, providing a methodological framework based on aprioristic principles and highlighting human action as the foundation of economic theory.

Tacit and Decentralized Knowledge: The Austrian School acknowledges the existence of tacit and decentralized knowledge in economic decision-making. Individuals possess specific information about local and personal circumstances that cannot be fully expressed formally. This knowledge is crucial for understanding economic behavior and is difficult to quantify.

Tacit Knowledge: Tacit knowledge refers to knowledge that is difficult to express formally and articulately. It is a type of knowledge rooted in practical experience, skill, and intuitive understanding of specific situations. In the economic context, this could include knowledge about the quality of a product, personal relationships, or local market conditions.

Decentralization of Knowledge: The Austrian School emphasizes that the knowledge needed for efficient economic decisions is dispersed among individuals. Each person has specific information about their own situation, skills, and preferences, and this knowledge is essential for informed decision-making.

Local and Circumstantial Information: Individuals, being immersed in their local circumstances, have access to information that may not be apparent to external observers or centralized authorities. This circumstantial knowledge includes details about local supply and demand, market conditions, and other factors influencing economic decisions.

Difficulty of Quantification: The tacit nature of knowledge means that it cannot always be expressed quantitatively or formally. This poses challenges for those seeking to centrally model or plan the economy, as specific situational knowledge cannot always be captured in statistics or numbers.

Decentralized and Adaptive Action: Decentralized economic decision-making allows for continuous adaptation to changing circumstances. Individuals can adjust their actions based on the information they possess, dynamically responding to events and changes in the economic environment.

Critique of Centralized Planning: The Austrian School uses the existence of tacit and decentralized knowledge as a basis to criticize the effectiveness of centralized planning. It argues that a central authority cannot access the detailed knowledge individuals have about their own circumstances and, therefore, cannot make efficient decisions.

Emphasis on Entrepreneurial Creativity: Tacit knowledge is particularly relevant in the context of entrepreneurial creativity. Entrepreneurs, by identifying opportunities based on their specific knowledge, contribute to innovation and economic dynamism.

The Austrian School recognizes and emphasizes the importance of tacit and decentralized knowledge as a critical factor in economic decision-making, highlighting the challenges of centralized planning and advocating for a more adaptive and decentralized approach to the economy.

Critique of Centralized Planning: Austrians criticize the idea that centralized planning is effective due to the dispersion of knowledge. They argue that the information necessary to efficiently coordinate the economy is scattered among individuals and cannot be effectively collected and used by a central authority.

Dispersion of Knowledge: Austrians, following the thought tradition of Friedrich Hayek and Ludwig von Mises, argue that the knowledge necessary to efficiently coordinate an economy is dispersed among millions of individuals. This knowledge includes information about individual preferences, skills, local market conditions, and dynamic changes in supply and demand.

Tacit and Specific Knowledge: The critique focuses on the fact that much of the relevant knowledge is tacit and specific to particular situations. This type of knowledge is challenging to express formally or quantify and resides in people's direct experience in their specific roles and daily interactions.

Inability to Collect All Knowledge: Austrians argue that a central authority cannot effectively collect all the dispersed information among individuals. Even if an attempt were made to gather, classify, and process all the information, the speed at which conditions and preferences change would quickly render the collected information outdated.

Dynamism of Knowledge: The economy is a dynamic system where conditions constantly change. Knowledge about these changing local and personal circumstances is essential for informed decision-making. Austrians argue that a central authority cannot adapt as quickly as individuals making decentralized decisions.

Inefficient Planning: The Austrian critique argues that, due to the impossibility of having complete access to dispersed knowledge, attempts at centralized planning are inherently inefficient. Decisions based on incomplete or outdated information can lead to inefficient resource allocations, distortions in prices, and ultimately, suboptimal economic performance.

Importance of Decentralized Action: The critique of centralized planning reinforces the Austrian emphasis on decentralized action. They argue that allowing individuals to make decisions based on their specific knowledge and in response to market signals allows for more efficient adaptation to changing economic conditions.

The Austrian critique of centralized planning focuses on the central authority's inability to access and efficiently process dispersed knowledge among individuals, leading to efficiency and adaptability issues in the economy.

Problems with Mathematical Modeling: The Austrian School criticizes the emphasis on complex mathematical modeling in economics. They argue that mathematical complexity does not guarantee greater accuracy and often overly simplifies reality, overlooking the richness of human action and specific conditions.

Excessive Simplification: Austrians argue that complex mathematical models often overly simplify economic reality. Attempting to translate the complexity of human interactions and market conditions into mathematical equations can lead to the loss of important aspects and subtleties of human behavior.

Human Action as a Complex Phenomenon: The Austrian School maintains that human action and market interactions are complex phenomena that cannot be easily reduced to mathematical formulas. The richness of individual motivations, preferences, and responses to stimuli cannot be fully captured through equations.

Limitations of Quantification: Some aspects of human behavior and market transactions are challenging to quantify. Factors such as subjective preferences, uncertainty, and entrepreneurial creativity may not easily fit into a mathematical framework, limiting the models' ability to fully represent reality.

Heterogeneity and Variability: Individuals are heterogencous in their preferences, knowledge, and circumstances. The variability and diversity of human action may not align well with models assuming homogeneous or constant behaviors.

Dynamic Changes and Nonlinearities: The economy is dynamic and subject to constant changes. Mathematical models often assume stability that may not reflect the changing nature of economic and social conditions. Additionally, nonlinearities in human behavior and market interactions can challenge the effectiveness of simplified linear models.

Critique of the Pretense of Precision: The Austrian School criticizes the belief that mathematical complexity automatically ensures greater precision in predicting economic phenomena. They argue that economic reality is inherently uncertain, and the pretense of precision through complex mathematical models can be deceptive.

Emphasis on Deep Understanding: Instead of relying exclusively on mathematization, the Austrian School advocates for a deeper and qualitative understanding of the economy. They argue that logic and understanding the motives behind human actions are essential to grasp economic reality.

The Austrian critique of complex mathematical modeling is based on the idea that mathematical complexity does not guarantee an accurate representation of economic reality and may overlook the richness and diversity of human action and specific real-world conditions.

Emphasis on Creativity and Innovation: The Austrian School recognizes creativity and innovation as fundamental aspects of human action. These elements are difficult to predict and mathematically model but play an essential role in economic dynamics.

Entrepreneurial Creativity: The Austrian School emphasizes the importance of entrepreneurial creativity in the economic process. Entrepreneurs, seeking profit opportunities, introduce new ideas, production methods, and products to the market. This creativity is driven by the pursuit of profits and the ability to perceive opportunities before others.

Innovation as a Driver of Change: Innovation, understood as the successful application of new ideas, is seen as a fundamental engine of economic change. The introduction of new technologies, products, or production processes can significantly alter the existing economic structure, creating opportunities and challenges for businesses and consumers.

Difficulty of Predicting Innovation: The unpredictable nature of innovation is highlighted by the Austrian School. They argue that true innovations are difficult to predict and mathematically model due to their unique and often disruptive nature. Entrepreneurial creativity introduces an element of uncertainty into economic planning.

Tacit Business Knowledge: The ability to identify and capitalize on market opportunities often involves tacit business knowledge. This knowledge, rooted in the experience and specific understanding of an entrepreneur, is challenging to quantify and express formally, making it difficult for mathematical models.

Adaptation to Changes: Entrepreneurial creativity enables businesses to adapt to changes in consumer preferences, market conditions, and technology. Entrepreneurs' adaptability to changing environments is a crucial component for the efficient functioning of the economy.

Critique of Static Models: The Austrian School criticizes static economic models that do not adequately account for the dynamics of creativity and innovation. Models assuming constant equilibrium may overlook the evolutionary and changing nature of the economy.

Importance for Economic Progress: Creativity and innovation are considered essential drivers of long-term economic progress. The economy's ability to continuously adapt and improve through the introduction of new ideas and technologies is a central element in the Austrian perspective.

In summary, the Austrian School emphasizes the importance of creativity and innovation as dynamic forces shaping the economy and highlights the difficulty of predicting and mathematically modeling these forces due to their unique and nonlinear nature.

Theory of the Business Cycle: The Austrian theory of the business cycle asserts that interventions in the economic system, especially in the supply of money and credit by monetary authorities, can distort the production structure and lead to economic cycles.

Interventions in Money and Credit Supply: The Austrian theory of the business cycle is based on the idea that interventions in the economic system, especially those related to the supply of money and credit, can have significant effects on the production structure.

Monetary Expansion Phase: The theory begins with a phase of monetary expansion. During this stage, monetary authorities tend to increase the money supply and artificially reduce interest rates below their market equilibrium level. This environment of low borrowing costs stimulates investment and spending.

Distortions in Production Structure: The artificially lowered interest rates lead to investment decisions that would not be sustainable under unmanipulated market conditions. Businesses, perceiving lower interest rates, may undertake investment projects that, under normal conditions, would not be profitable. This leads to distortions in the economy's production structure.

Boom Phase: During the expansion phase, the economy experiences a boom in economic activity. The increased investment and spending create a period of apparent growth, with the appearance of prosperity.

Malinvestment and Unsustainable Projects: However, investments made during this phase are often poor due to distortions in interest rates. Projects that seemed profitable at artificially low interest rates turn out to be unsustainable when interest rates return to more realistic levels.

Contraction or Recession Phase: The contraction phase, also known as a recession, follows the boom. Poor investments become evident, and companies face financial difficulties. Recession is seen as a necessary process to correct bad investments and readjust the economy's production structure.

Importance of Liquidation and Correction: The Austrian theory emphasizes the importance of allowing the liquidation and correction process to follow its course during the recession. This involves letting insolvent companies fail and reallocating resources to more sustainable and efficient activities.

Role of the Banking System: The theory also attributes a crucial role to the banking system in creating economic cycles. The artificial expansion of bank credit contributes to malinvestment and distortions in the production structure.

The Austrian theory of the business cycle argues that interventions in the supply of money and credit, especially by monetary authorities, can lead to economic cycles characterized by expansion, malinvestment, and recession, emphasizing the importance of allowing the correction process to follow its natural course.

The Austrian School of Economics has a unique perspective on knowledge theory, highlighting human action, praxeology, and decentralized knowledge as fundamental elements for understanding economic phenomena. Additionally, it criticizes centralized planning, excessive mathematical modeling, and advocates for an approach more focused on creativity and innovation.

9.Money and Credit

Money and credit are fundamental elements in the modern economy, and their interaction has profound implications for the functioning of the economic system. Below, I will explore the role of money and how credit expansion can affect the economy:

Function of Money:

Medium of Exchange: Money facilitates the exchange of goods and services, acting as a medium of exchange accepted by all parties in a transaction.

Widespread Acceptance: Money is generally accepted by society as a medium of exchange. People trust that others will accept money as payment, facilitating trade and transactions.

Divisibility: Money must be divisible into smaller units to facilitate transactions of various sizes. For example, a currency may have different denominations to represent diverse values.

Portability: Money must be easy to transport and handle. Physical forms, such as coins and bills, as well as digital forms, meet this requirement.

Durability: Money must have a sufficiently long lifespan to be practical. Coins and bills are designed to withstand normal wear and tear.

Homogeneity: Money units must be uniform and have a constant value for people to trust their use in daily transactions.

Recognisability: It should be easy to identify and authenticate money to prevent fraud. Coins and bills often have distinctive features that make counterfeiting difficult.

The medium of exchange function is one of the three main functions of money, along with a unit of account and store of value. These combined functions make money a fundamental tool in modern economies by facilitating the efficient exchange of goods and services.

Unit of Account: It serves as a standard measure for valuing goods and services, facilitating price comparison and economic value calculation.

Standard Measure of Value: Money provides a common measure for expressing and comparing the value of goods and services. This facilitates the assessment and comparison of prices for different products and services in the economy.

Facilitates Accounting: The unit of account is essential for financial record-keeping and accounting. Businesses, individuals, and governments use money as a standard unit to assess assets, liabilities, income, and expenses.

Complexity Reduction: In an economy without money, comparing and measuring the relative value of goods and services would be complicated. The unit of account in the form of money simplifies this process and allows for easy quantification of economic transactions.

Price Stability: Price stability is important to maintain the unit of account function. If there is excessive inflation, the ability of money to act as a stable measure of value is negatively affected as prices fluctuate significantly.

Facilitates Economic Planning: Both individuals and businesses can make more efficient financial projections and plans when they have a stable and reliable unit of account.

The unit of account of money is essential for the function of measuring and comparing values in an economy. By providing a common standard, money simplifies transactions and accounting, thereby facilitating the efficient operation of markets and economic decision-making.

Store of Value: Money acts as a way to store wealth over time, allowing people to save and transfer value over time.

Long-Term Wealth Storage: Money allows individuals to preserve value over time. Instead of immediately consuming income, people can save money in the form of liquid assets, such as cash, bank accounts, or investments, to use in the future.

Transfer of Value Over Time: Money facilitates the transfer of value over time. You can earn money today and use it in the future to purchase goods and services, providing flexibility in managing financial resources over different periods.

Preservation of Purchasing Power: To effectively fulfill the store of value function, money must maintain its purchasing power over time. In other words, the real value of money should not erode significantly due to inflation or other factors.

Facilitates Savings: People use money as a tool for saving and accumulating wealth. They can save money in various forms, such as savings accounts, certificates of deposit, investments, etc.

Investment Instrument: In addition to acting as a store of value, money can also be used to invest in different financial assets, such as stocks, bonds, real estate, among others. These investments can provide additional returns and contribute to wealth growth.

It is important to note that the ability of money to function as a store of value can be affected by economic factors, such as inflation. If the inflation rate is high, the purchasing power of money may decrease over time, impacting its ability as a long-term store of value.

Deferred Payment Pattern: Facilitates the exchange over time by allowing delayed payment, which is essential for long-term transactions and investment. Credit and Loans: Money enables individuals and businesses to obtain credit or loans for purchases or investments that they may not be able to afford immediately. This is crucial for long-term economic activities, such as investing in capital goods or buying a home. Financial Instruments: Promissory notes and other financial instruments can also be used to establish deferred payment agreements. For example, a company might issue a promissory note to commit to making a payment in the future. Investments and Financing: The concept of deferred payment is fundamental in the world of investments and finance, where investors can receive returns in the future for capital invested today. Money, along with financial instruments and credit agreements, facilitates exchange over time, which is essential for long-term transactions and investment.

Credit Expansion and Its Effects: Money Creation: When banks grant loans, they are effectively creating new money. This is because the borrowed money is available for spending, increasing the money supply. Fractional Reserves: In many banking systems, banks operate on the principle of fractional reserves. This means they are not required to hold in reserve the entirety of the money deposited in their accounts. Instead, they only have to maintain a fraction (reserve) of those deposits. Money creation process: When a bank receives a deposit, it must keep a portion of that deposit as a reserve and can lend the rest. When they grant a loan, they are effectively creating money, as the borrower gets additional funds that were not in circulation before. Money Multiplier: Money creation through loans can have a multiplier effect on the money supply. For instance, if a bank lends $100 to someone, and that person deposits that money in another bank, the second bank can keep a fraction as a reserve and lend the rest, leading to more money creation. This process can repeat several times, increasing the total money supply. Importance in the Economy: The ability of banks to create money through loans is essential for the functioning of the financial system and economic activity. It facilitates access to credit, encourages investment and spending, and contributes to economic growth. It's important to note that this money creation process is also subject to controls and regulations to maintain financial stability and prevent issues like uncontrolled inflation. Central banks typically oversee and regulate banking activity to ensure a proper balance in the money supply.

Credit expansion can stimulate economic growth by providing businesses and consumers with funds to invest and spend.

Business Investment: When businesses have access to credit, they can fund investment projects, purchase equipment, and expand operations. This can boost productivity and generate employment, contributing to economic growth. Consumption: Consumers can also benefit from credit expansion as it provides them with the ability to make significant purchases, such as homes or cars, even when they don't have enough cash at the moment. This can increase demand for goods and services, stimulating production and employment in various industries. Stimulating Aggregate Demand: Access to credit can increase aggregate demand in the economy, as both businesses and consumers can spend more than they could with their own resources. This increase in demand can have positive effects on production and employment. Economic Cycle: During periods of economic slowdown or recession, governments and central banks often consider stimulus policies, including measures to facilitate credit. This is done with the intention of reviving economic activity and countering the negative effects of economic decline. However, it's important to highlight that economic stimulus through credit expansion also carries risks. Excessive credit growth can lead to financial bubbles, unsustainable debt, and other long-term economic problems. Therefore, prudent management and regulation are essential to avoid negative side effects.

An increase in the money supply, especially if it surpasses the growth of real production, can lead to inflation, as there is more money chasing the same amount of goods and services.

Demand and Supply: Inflation tends to occur when the money supply increases at a faster rate than the real growth of goods and services production in an economy. If there is more money in circulation but the quantity of goods and services available remains constant or doesn't increase enough, the demand for those goods and services can surpass the supply, leading to a widespread increase in prices.

Aggregate Demand: The increase in the money supply can boost aggregate demand in the economy, as individuals and businesses have more resources to spend. If production cannot keep up with this increased demand, prices tend to rise.

Effects on Prices: Inflation can manifest as a widespread increase in the prices of goods and services. This affects the purchasing power of money, as the same amount of money can buy fewer products and services.

Inflation Expectations: Inflation expectations can also contribute to inflation. If people anticipate that prices will rise in the future, they may act in ways that reinforce that forecast, such as spending more now before prices increase further.

Inflation Control: Central banks and monetary authorities often monitor the relationship between the money supply and inflation. They use monetary policies, such as interest rates and money supply, to control inflation and maintain price stability.

It is important to note that the relationship between the money supply and inflation can be complex and influenced by various economic factors. Furthermore, not every increase in the money supply necessarily leads to inflation if the economy has sufficient productive capacity to meet additional demand.

Economic Cycles: Credit expansion is often associated with periods of economic boom but can contribute to the creation of bubbles and financial crises when not supported by solid fundamentals. During phases of economic expansion, an increase in credit expansion is commonly observed. This drives investment and spending, thereby stimulating economic growth. However, as you mention, this process can become problematic if credit expansion is not supported by solid fundamentals.

When credit expansion flows into overvalued assets or high-risk investments, it can lead to the formation of financial bubbles. Bubbles occur when asset prices, such as stocks or real estate, inflate to unsustainable levels relative to their economic fundamentals. Investors may participate in these bubbles in the hope of quick gains, which, in turn, drives prices even higher.

However, when these bubbles burst, whether due to changes in market expectations, unforeseen economic events, or adjustments in financial conditions, a financial crisis can be triggered. Asset overvaluation corrects, leading to business bankruptcies, significant losses for investors, and a widespread economic contraction.

In response to such events, monetary authorities and policymakers often intervene to manage the crisis, stabilize markets, and prevent long-term negative effects on the economy. This intervention may include measures such as adjustments to interest rates, liquidity injections, or the implementation of fiscal policies to stimulate the economy.

In summary, while credit expansion can be beneficial for economic growth during boom phases, it is essential that it is supported by solid fundamentals and that the formation of bubbles is avoided to prevent potentially harmful financial crises.

Debt and Risks: Excessive debt can become problematic if economic conditions worsen, as borrowers may struggle to meet their obligations, leading to systemic financial problems.

Borrowing and economic conditions: During periods of economic expansion, individuals, businesses, and governments commonly resort to borrowing to finance investments and expenses. However, if this borrowing is excessive and not managed properly, it can become a problem during unfavorable economic conditions.

Difficulties in meeting obligations: When economic conditions worsen, such as during recessions or financial crises, borrowers may face difficulties in meeting their payment obligations. This is especially true if the debt is tied to assets that have significantly lost value.

Systemic risks: If many entities, whether individuals, businesses, or even financial institutions, have trouble meeting their debt obligations simultaneously, it can lead to systemic risks. This means that the financial problems of a significant group of borrowers can have a negative impact on the entire financial system.

Domino effect: The inability to meet debt obligations can trigger a domino effect in the financial system. Banks, which often hold assets linked to these debts, may face substantial losses. This, in turn, can affect the availability of credit in the economy, exacerbating the recession.

Intervention and countercyclical policies: In these situations, governments and monetary authorities often implement countercyclical measures to stabilize the economy. This may include fiscal policies to stimulate spending, measures to alleviate the burden of debt, and actions aimed at strengthening the financial system.

Excessive debt can pose a significant risk, especially during periods of adverse economic conditions. Prudent debt management and appropriate policies are essential to mitigate these risks and preserve financial stability.

Regulation and Supervision: Effective regulation and supervision are essential for managing credit expansion and preventing risky financial practices that could trigger crises.

Mitigation of systemic risks: Financial regulation is designed to mitigate systemic risks, i.e., those that could affect the entire financial system. This involves setting limits and controls to prevent the excessive accumulation of risks by a financial institution or in a specific sector from causing significant harm to financial stability.

Consumer protection: Financial regulations are also aimed at protecting consumers. This includes ensuring transparency in financial transactions, preventing deceptive practices, and ensuring that financial products are suitable and safe for consumers.

Prevention of conflicts of interest: Regulation seeks to prevent conflicts of interest that may arise in the financial sector. This could include practices that prioritize short-term gains at the expense of long-term stability or favor certain interest groups to the detriment of others.

Management of credit expansion: Regulatory authorities can implement policies that guide credit expansion prudently and prevent overindebtedness. This helps maintain a balance between access to credit necessary for economic growth and the prevention of excessive financial risks.

Supervision of financial institutions: Ongoing supervision of financial institutions by regulatory entities is essential to assess financial health, risk management, and compliance with standards. This helps identify and address potential issues before they become crises.

Adaptation to changes in the economic environment: Regulations must be adaptable to address changes in the economic and financial environment. This includes the ability to adjust rules and regulations to address new emerging risks and challenges in the financial industry.

Effective regulation and supervision are critical tools to ensure the stability and integrity of the financial system, as well as to prevent risky practices that could have negative consequences for the economy as a whole.

The role of money as a medium of exchange and store of value is essential for the economy, and credit expansion can have significant impacts. It is crucial that economic and financial policies are carefully designed to balance economic stimulus with the management of risks associated with excessive borrowing. Financial stability and long-term sustainability are key considerations in managing the relationship between money and credit in an economy.

10.Theory of Marginal Utility

The Theory of Marginal Utility is a key concept in economics that refers to the idea that the value of a good or service for an individual is determined by marginal utility, i.e., the additional utility gained from consuming one additional unit of that good or service. This theory is central to consumer theory and was developed by classical and neoclassical economists.

Jeremy Bentham and utility: Although the theory of marginal utility was formalized by 19th-century economists, the idea that utility is the basis for evaluating value has roots in utilitarianism, an ethical philosophy developed by Jeremy Bentham in the 18th century. Bentham argued that actions should be evaluated based on their utility to society, and that happiness or utility was the measure of all things.

Jeremy Bentham, an 18th-century British philosopher and jurist, founded utilitarianism, an ethical theory that posits the right action is one that maximizes total happiness or utility in society. Bentham developed a quantitative approach to measuring happiness or utility, proposing a calculation called "hedonistic calculus" in which he assigned numerical values to different dimensions of utility. From his perspective, actions should be evaluated based on the amount of pleasure (positive utility) they generate and the pain (negative utility) they avoid.

This utilitarian perspective influenced the way value was thought of in economics. While Bentham did not directly formulate the theory of marginal utility, his ideas laid the groundwork for economists' later focus on individual utility and utility-based decision-making.

It was in the 19th century, with economists like William Stanley Jevons, Carl Menger, and Alfred Marshall, that the theory of marginal utility was formalized and incorporated into economic theory. These economists expanded and refined the idea, arguing that the marginal utility of a good or service is what determines its value and price in the market.

Water and Diamonds Paradox: One of the early economists to develop the theory of marginal utility was the British economist William Stanley Jevons in the 1860s. Jevons used the "Water and Diamonds Paradox" as a notable illustration to explain this theory.

Jevons observed the apparent contradiction in the relative prices of essential and non-essential goods. He noted that water, crucial for survival, had a low price, while diamonds, non-essential luxuries, had a high price. This observation contradicted expectations if value were based simply on total utility or the total quantity of a good.

Jevons proposed that the key to understanding these price patterns lay in marginal utility. He argued that diminishing marginal utility explains why the price of water is low, despite its high total utility. Since water is so abundant, the marginal utility of an additional unit is low. On the other hand, diamonds are scarce, and the marginal utility of owning one more can be high due to their relative rarity.

This observation laid the foundation for the theory of marginal utility and marked a significant shift in how economists understood the value and prices of goods and services. The central idea is that the value of a good or service is derived from the marginal utility of the last unit consumed, not from total utility. This approach significantly influenced economic thinking and became a fundamental element of consumer theory.

Carl Menger and the Austrian School: Carl Menger, another economist of the same era, also contributed to the development of the theory of marginal utility. Menger and other economists of the Austrian School argued that the value of a good is derived from marginal utility, and that this marginal utility is subjective and varies from person to person.

Carl Menger, an Austro-Hungarian economist, was a central figure in the development of the theory of marginal utility and is considered one of the founders of the Austrian School of Economics. Along with William Stanley Jevons and Léon Walras, Menger was among the first to independently formalize and present the theory of marginal utility.

One distinctive contribution of Menger and the Austrian School was the introduction of the concept of subjective marginal utility. While classical economists had considered utility as something objective and measurable, Menger argued that utility is subjective and varies according to individual preferences.

In Menger's perspective: Subjective utility: The marginal utility of a good or service is derived from an individual's subjective preferences. The satisfaction or utility a person obtains from a specific good is unique to that person and may change over time. Subjective value: The value of a good is not objectively determined by the amount of labor invested in its production (as classical economists believed) but by the subjective utility it has for an individual. Value is subjective and depends on individual valuation. Subjective value theory: Menger developed a subjective value theory that focused on the individual decisions of consumers. He argued that the exchange of goods and services in the market is based on subjective perceptions of marginal utility.

The Austrian School, led by economists like Menger, Friedrich Hayek, and Ludwig von Mises, significantly influenced economic thinking by emphasizing the importance of human action, the subjectivity of preferences, and decentralized coordination through the market. Menger's theory of subjective marginal utility was fundamental to this perspective and contributed significantly to modern economic theory.

Alfred Marshall and Neoclassical Synthesis: In the late 19th century, British economist Alfred Marshall integrated the ideas of Jevons and Menger into a broader neoclassical synthesis. Marshall developed the concept of the "demand curve," which depicts how the quantity demanded of a good varies in response to changes in price and how this variation is related to marginal utility.

Alfred Marshall, an influential British economist who lived in the late 19th and early 20th centuries, played a crucial role in synthesizing and consolidating the ideas of marginal utility theory, developed by William Stanley Jevons and Carl Menger, in what is known as the neoclassical synthesis.

Some key contributions of Alfred Marshall include:

Demand Curve: Marshall developed the notion of the demand curve, representing how the quantity demanded of a good varies in response to changes in its price. This curve reflects the law of diminishing marginal utility: as the quantity consumed of a good increases, marginal utility decreases.

Marginal Cost: Marshall introduced the concept of marginal cost, which is related to marginal utility. He argued that firms maximize their profits by equating the market price of a good with its marginal cost, an essential idea in the theory of the firm and price determination in a competitive market.

Partial Equilibrium Theory: Marshall contributed to the development of partial equilibrium theory, focusing on the analysis of individual markets and how they reach equilibrium between supply and demand.

Neoclassical Synthesis: Marshall merged the ideas of Jevons and Menger with elements of classical theory, creating the neoclassical synthesis. He integrated marginal utility theory into a broader framework that included elements of supply and demand, production costs, and value theory.

Marshall's neoclassical synthesis became the foundation of neoclassical economic theory that predominated in the first half of the 20th century. This synthesis greatly influenced the way economics is taught and practiced, laying the groundwork for modern economic analysis.

Marginal Utility Theory is a fundamental concept that has evolved over time and has been central to consumer theory in economics. It provides a basis for understanding how individuals make consumption decisions and how prices are determined in markets.

11.Invisible Hand of the Market

"The Invisible Hand" is a key concept in economic theory and was popularized by the Scottish philosopher and economist Adam Smith in his work "The Wealth of Nations," published in 1776. The idea of the Invisible Hand is used to describe the phenomenon of spontaneous coordination of individual actions in a free market.

Decentralized Decision-Making: The Invisible Hand highlights the ability of the free market to efficiently coordinate economic activities without the need for central planning. In a free market, individuals pursue their own individual interests in making consumption and production decisions, yet these individual actions contribute to the overall coordination of the economy.

Decentralization of Decisions: In a free market, individuals, companies, and producers make decisions based on their own interests and local knowledge. There is no central entity dictating what should be produced, in what quantity, and at what prices.

Price Mechanism: The Invisible Hand operates through the price mechanism. When supply and demand interact in the market, prices adjust to reflect preferences and changing conditions. These prices serve as signals to indicate to producers and consumers where resources and goods are needed.

Competition and Efficiency: Competition in a free market drives companies to improve efficiency and meet consumer demands in the best possible way. This competitive process without centralized planning contributes to efficiency in resource allocation.

Adaptability: The Invisible Hand highlights the market's adaptability. When circumstances change, prices and individual decisions adjust dynamically without the need for a central authority to orchestrate these adjustments.

Individual Incentives: The Invisible Hand acknowledges that, although individuals act in pursuit of their own interests, their actions generate results that benefit society as a whole. The pursuit of personal benefits leads to an efficient allocation of resources.

It is important to note that, while the Invisible Hand is a powerful concept for describing spontaneous coordination in a free market, it is also recognized that market failures can occur under certain circumstances, such as negative externalities, monopolies, or asymmetric information. In such cases, some advocate for limited government intervention to correct these imperfections and improve economic efficiency.

Supply and Demand: The Invisible Hand operates through the mechanism of supply and demand. When a good or service is demanded by consumers, producers have an incentive to offer more of that good to take advantage of profit opportunities. As more producers enter the market, competition tends to balance supply and demand, thus determining prices and quantities efficiently.

Demand: Demand represents the quantity of a good or service that consumers are willing and able to buy at different prices. When the demand for a good increases, consumers are indicating that they value that good more and are willing to pay more for it.

Supply: On the other hand, supply represents the quantity of a good or service that producers are willing to offer in the market at different prices. When the price of a good is high, producers have a greater incentive to offer more of that good to the market.

Market Equilibrium: Market equilibrium is reached when the quantity demanded equals the quantity supplied at a specific price. This price and quantity form the point where the supply and demand curves intersect, representing a balance between what consumers desire and what producers are willing to supply.

Price Mechanism: The price at the market equilibrium acts as a key signal. If the demand for a good increases, the price tends to rise, indicating to producers that there is an opportunity to profit by offering more of that good. Similarly, if demand decreases, the price tends to fall, signaling to producers to offer less.

Dynamic Adjustment: The Invisible Hand operates through this dynamic price adjustment process. When conditions change, whether due to changes in supply, demand, or external factors, prices and quantities adjust automatically without the need for centralized intervention.

The interaction of supply and demand facilitates the efficient allocation of resources in a free market, allowing prices to adjust to balance consumer preferences with producers' production decisions. The Invisible Hand works through this mechanism to coordinate economic activities efficiently.

Competition and Economic Efficiency: Competition in a free market drives companies to improve the quality of their products, reduce costs, and become more efficient. This competitive process benefits consumers by providing them with a variety of options at competitive prices.

Stimulus for Improvement: Competitive pressure motivates companies to enhance the quality of their products and services. In a competitive environment, companies seek to stand out and attract consumers by offering products that are superior in terms of features, performance, or price.

Cost Reduction: Competition also compels companies to be more efficient in production and cost management. Companies that can produce goods and services at lower costs have a competitive advantage, often resulting in lower prices for consumers and higher profit margins for companies.

Innovation: Competition fosters innovation. Companies are constantly looking for ways to differentiate themselves and gain market share, and a key way to achieve this is through innovation. Intense competition can stimulate the introduction of new products, processes, and technologies.

Consumer Choice: In a competitive market, consumers have more choices. This means they can choose from a variety of products and services that suit their individual needs and preferences. Competition leads to greater diversity of options for consumers.

Allocation efficiency: Market competition contributes to an efficient allocation of resources. Resources tend to flow towards companies and sectors that are more productive and efficient in satisfying consumer demands. This process contributes to maximizing overall utility and economic prosperity.

Pressure to adapt: Competition creates constant pressure to adapt to changing market conditions. Companies must be vigilant to the needs and desires of consumers, as well as the actions of their competitors, fostering agility and responsiveness.

It is important to note that while competition can generate economic efficiency, there are also arguments in favor of government intervention in certain cases to correct market failures and promote goals such as equity and stability. The relationship between competition and efficiency is a significant topic in economic theory and policy formulation.

Individual incentives: The Invisible Hand recognizes that in a free market, individuals act in pursuit of their own interests and personal benefits. However, this selfish behavior can lead to beneficial outcomes for society as a whole.

Pursuit of personal interests: In a free market, it is acknowledged that individuals, whether consumers or producers, seek to maximize their own interests and personal benefits. This involves making decisions that enhance their well-being, either through the purchase of goods and services that meet their needs or the production of goods for profit.

Competition and efficiency: Competition in a free market means that companies are competing for consumer preference. This competition motivates companies to be efficient, innovative, and to offer high-quality products to attract customers. In this process, although companies seek their own benefits, competition leads to societal benefits in the form of better products and services at competitive prices.

Spontaneous coordination: The Invisible Hand posits that through the individual pursuit of personal interests, spontaneous coordination is achieved in the market. As individuals seek to maximize their utility and profits, their actions contribute to the overall coordination of the economy without the need for a central authority to direct the process.

Price as a signal: Price in a free market acts as a crucial signal reflecting supply and demand. Changes in prices provide information to producers and consumers about the scarcity or abundance of goods and services, guiding individual decisions in resource allocation.

Innovation and adaptation: Individual incentives also foster innovation and adaptation to changing market conditions. The pursuit of profits drives companies to improve and meet the evolving needs of consumers.

It is important to note that while individual incentives play a key role in efficient market coordination, there are also situations where market failures can occur. For this reason, some advocate for limited government intervention to correct these failures and promote goals such as equity and stability. The interaction between individual incentives and the role of government is a central theme in economic theory and policy formulation.

Despite its benefits, the Invisible Hand is not without criticism. Some argue that market failures, such as negative externalities or inequities, may require government intervention. Additionally, the success of the Invisible Hand depends on the existence of real competition and access to complete information, which may not always be the case.

The Invisible Hand assumes that markets are efficient and that, through competition, a beneficial equilibrium is reached. However, there are situations where markets can fail, leading to negative externalities (unintended impacts on third parties), monopolies, asymmetric information (differences in information available to buyers and sellers), among others. These failures can result in inefficient resource allocations and justify government intervention.

Externalities: Externalities, such as pollution or unintended side effects of production or consumption, are examples of situations where the Invisible Hand may not achieve socially optimal results. In these cases, individual actions may have negative consequences for society as a whole, and government intervention may be necessary to internalize these externalities.

Monopolies and market power: The Invisible Hand presupposes perfect competition, but in reality, monopolies and market power can arise, leading to high prices and suboptimal resource allocation. In such cases, government regulation or antitrust laws may be necessary to preserve competition and efficiency.

Incomplete information: The success of the Invisible Hand depends on the existence of complete and perfect information. However, in reality, information is often asymmetric or incomplete, leading to suboptimal decisions by market participants. Government intervention, such as regulation to ensure transparency, can address these limitations.

Another critical aspect is the possibility that the Invisible Hand contributes to economic inequality. If not managed properly, markets can generate inequities in the distribution of income and wealth, which may require policy interventions to address these disparities.

While the Invisible Hand is a useful metaphor for describing efficient coordination in a free market, it is also important to recognize its limitations and the potential need for government intervention to correct market failures and promote broader social and economic objectives. The discussion of the balance between the market and government intervention remains a central theme in economic theory and policy formulation. The Invisible Hand is a powerful metaphor that highlights how the interaction of individual decisions in a free market can lead to efficient coordination and beneficial outcomes for society as a whole.

12.Entrepreneurship Theory

The Entrepreneur Theory highlights the importance of the entrepreneur in the economy, emphasizing their key role in decision-making and innovation. Unlike more traditional views that focus on coordinating factors of production (land, labor, and capital), the entrepreneur theory focuses on the entrepreneur as an active and creative agent in the economic process. Here are some key points associated with this theory:

Decision-making and risk: Entrepreneurs are seen as agents who take risks and make important decisions in creating and managing businesses. The willingness to take entrepreneurial risks, such as investing in new projects or launching innovative products, is essential for economic dynamism.

Decision-making: Entrepreneurs are constantly involved in making strategic decisions for the success and survival of their businesses. These decisions cover a variety of areas, such as determining what products or services to offer, how to produce them, at what price to sell them, how to market them, and how to finance operations. The ability to make effective decisions is crucial for the viability and prosperity of the business.

Risk assumption: Risk assumption is a distinctive feature of the entrepreneur's role. Entrepreneurs take financial risks, whether by investing their own capital or seeking financing to start or expand a business. Additionally, they face risks associated with market uncertainty, changes in consumer demand, competition, and external economic factors. The willingness to take risks allows entrepreneurs to seek opportunities and carry out innovative projects.

Risk and innovation: The relationship between risk and innovation is particularly relevant. Innovation often involves introducing something new or unknown to the market, which carries inherent risk. Entrepreneurs who can assess and manage risk effectively are better positioned to undertake innovative initiatives and seize disruptive opportunities.

Learning and adaptation: Since decision-making and risk-taking are intrinsically linked, entrepreneurs must also be able to learn from their experiences, both successes and failures. Adaptability and the ability to adjust strategies in response to changes in the business environment are essential for long-term survival.

The combination of decision-making and risk assumption distinguishes the entrepreneur's role in the Entrepreneur Theory. This perspective recognizes the importance of initiative, courage, and the ability to assess and manage risks as essential components of the entrepreneurial process.

Innovation: The entrepreneur theory emphasizes the innovative role of entrepreneurs. Entrepreneurs not only replicate what already exists but seek opportunities to introduce novelties in products, services, processes, and business models. Entrepreneurial innovation is viewed as a key driver of economic progress.

Introduction of novelties: Entrepreneurs are seen as agents introducing novelties into the economy. These novelties can be products, services, production processes, business models, or strategic approaches that differ from what already exists in the market.

Adaptation and change: The ability to innovate allows entrepreneurs to adapt to changing market conditions. Innovation not only involves creating something entirely new but also adapting and continuously improving existing products and processes to better meet market needs.

Stimulus for economic progress: The successful introduction of innovations can stimulate economic progress by improving efficiency, increasing productivity, and creating new market opportunities. Innovations such as new technologies, efficient production methods, or new products can have significant impacts on the economy.

Risk and innovation: Innovation involves risks as it entails the introduction of something new and unknown. Entrepreneurs willing to take risks may be more prone to undertake innovative initiatives, which, in turn, can yield significant rewards in terms of competitive advantages and business success.

Competition and differentiation: Innovation can be a key competitive strategy. Innovative entrepreneurs can differentiate their products or services in the market, allowing them to stand out among competitors and gain consumer preference.

Entrepreneurial life cycle: The ability to innovate can be crucial at different stages of a company's life cycle. In the initial phase, innovation may be fundamental for business creation and differentiation, while in later stages, continuous innovation may be essential to maintain relevance and competitiveness.

In summary, the Entrepreneur Theory recognizes that the innovative function of entrepreneurs plays an essential role in economic dynamism. The ability to identify opportunities, take risks, and implement changes and improvements significantly contributes to economic progress and societal development.

Discovery of opportunities: Entrepreneurs are considered discoverers of market opportunities. Through the identification of unmet needs or the creation of new and improved solutions, entrepreneurs contribute to efficiency and economic growth.

Identification of unmet needs: Entrepreneurs are constantly alert to unmet needs in the market. They observe unsatisfied consumer demands, areas where existing products or services can be improved, or even identify needs that consumers are not yet aware of.

Creativity and vision: Discovering opportunities requires creativity and vision. Entrepreneurs not only respond to current needs but are also able to visualize future opportunities before they become evident to others. This forward-looking vision can be crucial for long-term business success.

Innovation as a response to opportunities: The identification of opportunities often leads to innovation. Entrepreneurs seek unique ways to address the opportunities they have discovered, whether through the development of new products, the improvement of existing processes, or the introduction of innovative business models.

Risk and Reward: The discovery of opportunities is linked to the willingness to take risks. Entrepreneurs who identify opportunities often must be willing to risk resources, time, and effort to capitalize on those opportunities. The assumed risk can lead to significant rewards if the opportunity is successfully exploited.

Adaptation to Change: Entrepreneurs are open to change and adaptation. The discovery of opportunities often involves recognizing changes in the business environment, technology, consumer preferences, or other factors. The ability to adapt to these changes is crucial to capitalize on discovered opportunities.

Competition and Differentiation: Discovering market opportunities can also be a key competitive strategy. Entrepreneurs who are successful in this aspect can differentiate their products or services from the competition, creating a unique advantage in the market.

Opportunity discovery is an essential skill for entrepreneurs. This ability to identify and capitalize on opportunities not only drives innovation but also contributes to economic development by meeting the changing needs and desires of consumers.

Adaptability and Change: Entrepreneurial theory recognizes the entrepreneur's ability to adapt to changing market conditions. In a dynamic environment, entrepreneurs are constantly assessing opportunities and threats, adjusting their strategies accordingly.

Dynamic Environment: Economies and markets are inherently dynamic and subject to constant changes. Entrepreneurs must be able to adapt to these changing conditions, whether in terms of consumer preferences, technological advancements, changes in competition, or other variables in the business environment.

Resilience: The ability to adapt implies resilience in the face of challenges and adversities. Entrepreneurs must overcome obstacles, learn from negative experiences, and adjust their strategies to remain competitive and successful.

Innovation as a Response to Change: Adaptability often manifests through innovation. Faced with market changes, entrepreneurs can respond with new ideas, products, or business approaches that allow them to stay relevant and competitive.

Opportunity Evaluation: Adaptability is linked to the recognition of opportunities amid change. Entrepreneurs who can adapt efficiently are also more likely to identify new opportunities that arise as market conditions evolve.

Continuous Learning: Adaptability involves a continuous learning process. Entrepreneurs must be open to acquiring new knowledge, skills, and perspectives as circumstances evolve. Continuous learning contributes to the ability to make informed decisions and constant improvement.

Business Agility: Adaptability is associated with business agility, the ability to move quickly and effectively in response to changes in the environment. Agility enables entrepreneurs to capitalize on opportunities timely and mitigate risks.

Recognition of Trends: Successful entrepreneurs can recognize emerging trends before they become evident to everyone. This anticipation allows them to strategically position themselves and lead rather than simply react to change.

In summary, adaptability is essential for long-term business success. Entrepreneurs who are flexible, resilient, and capable of managing change are more likely to thrive in dynamic and competitive business environments.

Coordinating Function: In addition to decision-making and innovation, entrepreneurs also fulfill a coordinating function by gathering and organizing the resources necessary for their projects. This coordinating function contributes to efficiency and effective resource allocation.

Resource Organization: Entrepreneurs are responsible for gathering and organizing various resources needed for their business projects. These resources may include financial capital, labor, technology, raw materials, and other essentials for business operation.

Resource Optimization: The coordinating function involves optimizing available resources. Entrepreneurs must make strategic decisions on how to efficiently allocate resources to maximize production, minimize costs, and ensure the long-term viability of the business.

Planning and Organization: Coordination requires effective planning and organization. Entrepreneurs must develop robust business plans and efficient organizational structures that facilitate the successful execution of their projects.

Team Management: The coordinating function also involves team management and creating effective work environments. Entrepreneurs must lead, motivate, and supervise their staff to ensure that all team members are aligned with business objectives.

Negotiation and Collaboration: In many cases, entrepreneurs must negotiate and collaborate with various stakeholders, such as suppliers, customers, investors, and other entrepreneurs. The ability to establish collaborative relationships and negotiate beneficial agreements is crucial.

Adaptation to Demand Changes: The coordinating function also involves the ability to adapt to changes in market demand. Entrepreneurs must adjust production and supply according to fluctuations in demand to avoid surpluses or shortages of products or services.

Logistic Coordination: In industries involving the physical production and distribution of goods, logistic coordination is essential. Entrepreneurs must ensure that products move efficiently from the production phase to end customers, managing the supply chain effectively.

In summary, the coordinating function of the entrepreneur focuses on the efficient management of resources and the creation of an organizational environment that allows the successful execution of business projects. The ability to coordinate these elements is crucial for the effective operation of a business in a dynamic business environment.

Business Competition: Competition among entrepreneurs is seen as a positive factor driving continuous improvement and economic efficiency. Rivalry among entrepreneurs to offer better products, services, or prices benefits consumers and promotes market efficiency.

Continuous Improvement: Competition creates an environment in which entrepreneurs constantly seek to improve their products, services, and processes to stand out in the market. Competitive pressure stimulates innovation and efficiency as entrepreneurs look for ways to offer greater value to consumers.

Innovation: Competition drives innovation as entrepreneurs seek new and creative ways to differentiate their offerings and gain customer preference. This innovative drive can lead to technological advancements, improvements in product and service quality, and the introduction of new solutions to the market.

Economic Efficiency: Competition fosters economic efficiency as entrepreneurs seek to reduce costs and improve productivity to be more competitive. This optimization process contributes to a more efficient allocation of resources in the economy.

Benefits for Consumers: Competition benefits consumers by offering them more choices, competitive prices, and higher-quality products and services. Consumers can leverage the rivalry between companies to obtain products and services that best suit their needs at more attractive prices.

Price Reduction: Competition can lead to price reduction as companies strive to attract consumers by offering products and services at lower rates than their competitors. This can result in increased accessibility for consumers and a constant pressure to provide better value.

Differentiation: Competition can also drive product and service differentiation. Entrepreneurs aim to stand out in the market through unique features, distinctive branding, and innovative marketing strategies.

Pressure for Quality: Competition puts pressure on companies to maintain and improve the quality of their products and services. Those that do not meet quality standards may lose market share to competitors offering superior products.

Business competition is considered beneficial for the overall economy and consumers in particular. It stimulates continuous improvement, innovation, and efficiency, thereby contributing to economic development and satisfying the needs and desires of consumers.

The Entrepreneurship Theory highlights the role of the entrepreneur as a dynamic and creative actor in the economy. It recognizes the importance of decision-making, risk-taking, and the ability to innovate as essential elements for economic progress and efficiency in the economic system.

13.Critique of Socialism

Critiques of socialism often focus on various aspects, including economic efficiency, resource allocation, and private property.

Economic Inefficiency: It is argued that socialist systems, by centralizing the ownership of the means of production in the hands of the state, tend to be less efficient compared to market systems. Competition and market incentives are considered efficient drivers for improving productivity and the quality of goods and services.

The argument about economic inefficiency in socialist systems is based on the idea that state ownership of the means of production and centralized planning can lead to resource allocation problems and a lack of incentives for efficiency.

Lack of Incentives: In a socialist system where the state owns and controls the means of production, it is argued that the lack of individual private property and economic incentives can lead to a decrease in motivation and productivity. Private property, according to this argument, provides individuals with incentives to work hard and be innovative as they can directly benefit from the results of their efforts.

Centralized Information and Calculation Problems: Centralized planning in socialist systems often involves decision-making at the government level. It is argued that this centralized planning can face significant challenges in collecting and accurately evaluating the information needed for efficient economic decisions. In contrast, the market system, through price mechanisms, allows for a more effective allocation of resources based on supply and demand.

Rigidity in Adaptation: Centralized planning can become rigid and slow to adapt to changes in consumer preferences or economic conditions. Market systems, being decentralized, allow for greater flexibility and quick adjustment to changing dynamics.

Bureaucracy and Corruption: Some criticisms focus on socialism's tendency to generate extensive government bureaucracies. It is argued that bureaucracy can hinder efficient decision-making and foster corruption, negatively affecting economic efficiency.

Lack of Competition: Competition in a free market is considered a key driver for efficiency. In socialist systems where the ownership of the means of production is centralized, there may be a lack of business competition, which, according to the argument, reduces the pressure to improve quality, reduce costs, and be more innovative.

It is important to note that these criticisms generally apply to specific forms of socialism involving significant government intervention in the economy and property centralization. Additionally, there are diverse interpretations and experiences of socialism implementation, and specific criticisms may vary depending on the context and the particular application of socialist policies.

Lack of Incentives: In a socialist system where the means of production are state-owned, it is argued that the lack of individual incentives to work hard and be innovative can lead to lower productivity. Private property and the possibility of personal benefits are considered more effective motivational factors.

Collective Ownership: In socialist systems, the means of production, such as factories and land, are often collectively or state-owned rather than privately owned. It is argued that when ownership and associated benefits are not directly attributable to individuals, there may be a lack of personal incentives to work hard or be innovative.

Disconnection between Effort and Reward: The lack of individual private property can lead to a disconnection between personal effort and economic rewards. In a system where benefits are not directly related to individual performance, some argue that individuals may lack the necessary stimulus to strive beyond the minimum required.

Incentive Against Entrepreneurship: In an environment where private property and individual profit are limited, it is argued that there may be a lack of entrepreneurial initiative. Entrepreneurship often relies on the possibility of making profits and taking risks, and some argue that socialism may discourage this initiative.

Lack of Competition: In a socialist system, where competition among businesses may be limited, it is argued that the lack of incentives to stand out can result in lower product and service quality, as well as a lack of innovation.

Inefficiency in Human Resource Allocation: The lack of individual incentives can lead to inefficient human resource allocation. Not being directly related to individual performance, some argue that workers may lack motivation to seek more challenging roles or improve their skills.

It is important to emphasize that these criticisms are based on specific interpretations and historical experiences of socialism. Not all socialist models share these characteristics, and there are diverse interpretations and approaches within the broad spectrum of socialist thought. Additionally, measures and policies may be implemented to address these challenges in specific contexts.

Inefficient Resource Allocation: It is argued that the market system is more efficient in allocating resources as prices act as signals indicating scarcity and demand. In a socialist system where the state plans the economy, there may be difficulties in assessing and satisfying changing consumer preferences and needs.

The argument about inefficient resource allocation in socialist systems focuses on the market system's efficiency in optimally allocating resources through price mechanisms.

Price Mechanism: In a market system, prices act as signals conveying information about the supply and demand for goods and services. It is argued that these relative prices reflect the scarcity and perceived utility of resources, guiding producers and consumers in decision-making.

Dynamic Adjustment: Market prices are not static and can continuously adjust in response to changes in supply and demand conditions. This allows for dynamic adjustment of resource allocation based on changing consumer preferences, technology, and other factors.

Efficiency in Allocation: Economic theory maintains that, under market competition, resources tend to be allocated efficiently. Producers seek to maximize profits, and consumers seek to maximize utility, leading to resource allocation that reflects the preferences and needs of society.

Adaptability to Scarcity: In a market system, prices rise in response to the scarcity of a resource, indicating higher demand. This price increase serves as a signal for producers that there is an opportunity to gain higher profits by meeting that demand, incentivizing efficient resource allocation where it is most needed.

Incentives for Efficiency: Competition in the market creates incentives for efficiency. Companies that use their resources more efficiently can reduce costs and offer more competitive prices, giving them an advantage in the market. This competitive process is considered an effective mechanism for fostering economic efficiency.

Challenges of Centralized Planning: In contrast, it is argued that centralized planning in socialist systems may struggle to efficiently assess and respond to changing economic conditions and consumer preferences, lacking the dynamism and adaptability of the market system.

It is important to note that these arguments reflect a specific perspective on the efficiency of economic systems, and there are ongoing debates about the relative merits of market systems and socialist systems in the efficient allocation of resources. Furthermore, there are various forms of socialism, and criticisms may vary depending on the specific implementation of socialist policies.

Innovation and Creativity: Critics of socialism argue that market competition fosters innovation and creativity as companies strive to stand out and gain market share. In a socialist system, where competition may be limited, it is argued that innovation could stagnate.

The argument about innovation and creativity highlights market competition as a fundamental driver of innovation and notes that socialist systems, by limiting competition, may experience stagnation in terms of innovative development. Here are some key points related to this argument:

Competition as a stimulus for innovation: In a competitive market system, companies have incentives to innovate to stand out among the competition. The need to gain market share and attract consumers drives companies to develop new products, improve existing ones, and adopt more efficient technologies.

Pressure to improve: Competition creates constant pressure to improve the quality of products and services. Companies that do not innovate risk losing customers to competitors offering more advanced and appealing solutions.

Adaptation to changing consumer preferences: Competition also compels companies to quickly adapt to changing consumer preferences. Those that can anticipate and efficiently respond to market demands have a greater chance of success.

Innovation as a competitive strategy: In a competitive environment, the ability to innovate becomes a key strategy to differentiate and gain a competitive advantage. Companies constantly seek ways to offer something unique that sets them apart from their competitors.

Lack of competition in socialist systems: It is argued that in socialist systems, where competition may be limited due to state ownership of the means of production, the absence of a competitive market may result in a lack of incentives for innovation. Without the pressure of competition, companies may lack incentives to invest in research and development.

Market dynamics as a facilitator of creativity: Market dynamics, with consumers making decisions based on their individual preferences, is presented as a conducive environment for creativity. Companies are motivated to think creatively and respond to specific needs of consumers.

It is important to note that this argument is based on the idea that market competition is an essential driver of innovation. However, there are diverse interpretations and approaches within socialism, and some advocates argue that it is possible to foster innovation within a socialist framework through planning and strategic state investment. The debate on the relationship between economic systems and innovation continues to be a subject of discussion.

Lack of Economic Freedom: It is pointed out that socialism, involving greater state intervention in the economy, can limit individual economic freedom. The ability to make decisions about property, production, and exchange may be restricted, negatively affecting entrepreneurial initiative and freedom of choice.

The argument about the lack of economic freedom in socialism focuses on the idea that state intervention in the economy can limit individual freedom in terms of decision-making regarding property, production, and trade. Here are some key points related to this argument:

State ownership and control: In socialist systems, ownership of the means of production is often in the hands of the state or is collectively owned. This may mean that decisions about what to produce, how to produce, and to whom to sell are more centralized and can be determined by the government. It is argued that this limits individuals' freedom to own and control property privately.

Restrictions on entrepreneurial initiative: State intervention in the socialist economy sometimes involves stricter regulations and controls on entrepreneurial initiative. Limitations on the ability to start and operate businesses independently can be seen as restrictions on economic freedom.

Centralized planning: In socialist systems that employ centralized planning, the government may have a more active role in key economic decision-making. This could limit the autonomy of individual and business decisions on what to produce, in what quantity, and at what price.

Intervention in resource distribution: State intervention may involve the redistribution of resources, influencing economic freedom by determining who owns what and how goods and services are distributed. This can raise concerns about fairness and individuals' ability to make autonomous decisions about their resources.

Restrictions on trade: In some socialist systems, freedom to engage in commercial activities may be subject to government restrictions and regulations. This can limit individuals' freedom of choice in terms of where to buy, sell, or exchange goods and services.

Incentives for conformity: Centralized planning and state ownership may create incentives for conformity with government-established policies. It is argued that this can reduce freedom of choice and the diversity of business approaches, as individual decisions may align more with state policies.

Critiques often focus on specific implementations of socialism, and there are various forms of socialism with varying degrees of state intervention. Additionally, socialist proponents argue that measures can be taken to safeguard individual freedom and balance state intervention. The debate about the balance between state intervention and economic freedom remains a significant topic in economic theory and policy formulation.

History of Socialist Experiences: Many criticisms of socialism are based on historical experiences, such as those of the Soviet Union and other socialist states of the 20th century, where economic problems, lack of incentives, and lack of individual freedom are argued to have been evident.

Economic problems: One of the central arguments is that socialist systems faced significant economic problems. Centralized planning often led to inefficiencies in resource allocation, a lack of adaptability to market conditions, and difficulties in meeting changing consumer demands.

Lack of incentives: It is argued that the absence of individual incentives in socialist systems contributed to a lack of entrepreneurial initiative and less motivation for innovation and efficiency. The lack of private property and a direct connection between effort and reward were seen as discouraging factors.

Lack of individual freedom: Criticisms focus on the restriction of individual freedom in terms of choosing occupation, private property, and participation in independent economic activities. State intervention in the economy and centralized planning were perceived as limitations on individual autonomy.

Bureaucracy: The implementation of socialist models often led to the formation of extensive government bureaucracies. It is argued that these bureaucracies were inefficient in decision-making and prone to corruption, negatively affecting economic management.

Collapse of the Soviet Union: The fall of the Soviet Union in 1991 is often cited as an example of systemic problems in socialism. It is argued that the lack of economic dynamism, inefficiency, and failure to adapt to market demands contributed to the collapse of the Soviet socialist regime.

The collapse of the Soviet Union in 1991 is a significant event often cited in the context of criticisms of socialism. Here are some key points related to the collapse of the Soviet Union and its connection to perceived systemic problems of socialism:

Economic Dynamism: It is argued that the Soviet economy lacked economic dynamism compared to market economies. Centralized planning and the absence of market incentives were seen as obstacles to sustainable economic growth and innovation.

Economic Inefficiency: Centralized planning and state ownership of the means of production were perceived as causes of economic inefficiencies. The inability to adapt to changing market conditions and the centralized allocation of resources were cited as factors contributing to economic inefficiency.

Market Adaptation Failure: The Soviet economy failed to effectively adapt to the demands of the global market. The absence of market mechanisms, such as competition and supply and demand-based pricing, was considered a limitation for effective participation in the global economy.

Scarcity and Low Living Standards: Throughout the decades, the Soviet Union experienced scarcity issues, especially in consumer goods. Low living standards and lack of access to a variety of goods and services were argued to contribute to widespread discontent.

Political and Social Reforms: In addition to economic issues, the Soviet Union faced political and social challenges, including a lack of political freedoms and the repression of dissent. Dissatisfaction with the political regime also played a role in the collapse.

Political Disintegration: The Soviet Union experienced ethnic and nationalist tensions leading to political disintegration. The declared independence of several Soviet republics and the creation of independent states marked the collapse of political union.

The collapse of the Soviet Union does not necessarily condemn socialism as a whole, as there are diverse interpretations and approaches within the socialist spectrum. Some socialist proponents argue that the specific model implemented in the Soviet Union does not represent all forms of socialist thought. However, this historical event continues to be cited in debates on the viability and effectiveness of socialist systems.

Comparison with Market Economies: Criticisms are also based on comparisons with market economies that experienced more dynamic economic growth and higher quality of life during the same period. Competition and private ownership in market economies are suggested as key factors in their success.

It is crucial to note that these criticisms are based on specific experiences and particular models of socialism, and there is diversity within the socialist spectrum. Additionally, socialist advocates argue that lessons learned from these experiences can inform future models, addressing historical criticisms. The debate on socialism and its implementations remains a complex and discussed topic.

Bureaucracy Development: Some criticisms focus on socialism's tendency to generate extensive government bureaucracies, leading to inefficient decision-making and a lack of agility in economic management.

Centralization of Decision-Making: In some socialist systems, centralized planning and state ownership of the means of production can lead to increased centralization of economic decision-making. Key decisions about production, distribution, and resource allocation are made by government bodies, resulting in a larger bureaucracy.

Inefficiency and Rigidity: Critics suggest that extensive bureaucracies can be inefficient and rigid in decision-making. The need for multiple layers of approval and the complexity of bureaucratic processes can hinder quick adaptation to changes in economic conditions and market demands.

Corruption: Bureaucracy expansion can also increase the risk of corruption. The complexity of bureaucratic processes and the concentration of power in the hands of government officials can provide opportunities for corrupt practices, negatively affecting efficiency and fairness in economic management.

Lack of Incentives for Efficiency: In socialist systems where ownership is state or collective, the lack of market incentives for efficiency and profitability can lead to bureaucratic management not driven by the need to compete in an open market.

Disconnect from Market Needs: Extensive bureaucracy can result in a disconnect between decision-makers and the needs and preferences of the market. The lack of direct market feedback can contribute to decision-making that does not efficiently reflect economic demands and dynamics.

Rigidity in Resource Allocation: Extensive bureaucracy can also contribute to rigid resource allocation. Lack of flexibility to adapt to changes in supply and demand can lead to inefficiencies in resource distribution.

These criticisms do not necessarily apply to all models of socialism, as there is a variety of approaches within the socialist spectrum, and some advocates promote mechanisms to reduce bureaucracy and encourage more efficient management. However, criticism of bureaucracy in socialist systems has been a recurring concern in debates about the viability and effectiveness of these economic models.

These criticisms represent common arguments in the debate on economic systems, and there are diverse perspectives on these issues. It is also relevant to note that there are different forms of socialism, and criticisms may vary depending on the specific implementation of socialist policies. The debate between socialism and capitalism remains an important topic in economic theory and policy formulation.

14.Ethics and Capitalism

.

The ethics of capitalism involves the evaluation of ethical principles associated with private property, respect for individual rights, and market dynamics within a capitalist system. Below, some key aspects of ethics in the context of capitalism are explored:

Private property: In a capitalist system, private property is valued as a fundamental right. The ethics of private property maintains that individuals have a legitimate right to own, use, and dispose of their own goods and resources. This principle is based on the idea that private property is essential for individual freedom and autonomy.

Valuing private property as a fundamental right in the context of capitalism has deep philosophical and ethical roots. Here are some key aspects of the ethics of private property in a capitalist system:

Freedom and autonomy: The ethics of private property argues that the ability to privately own, use, and dispose of goods and resources is essential for individual freedom and autonomy. Private property allows people to make decisions about how to use their resources according to their own values, needs, and goals.

Incentives and responsibility: Private property is associated with the efficient allocation of resources and individual responsibility. When individuals own goods and resources, they have incentives to use them productively and efficiently, as they are directly linked to the outcomes of their decisions.

Protection against coercion: Private property is considered a defense against external coercion. In a system where property rights are respected, individuals are protected against unfair interference in their possessions and activities. This contributes to an environment where transactions are voluntary and based on consent.

Economic growth: The ethics of private property maintains that respecting this right drives economic growth. Private property provides incentives for investment, innovation, and wealth creation, as individuals can expect to benefit from their efforts and ventures.

Fair distribution: From an ethical perspective, private property is associated with the idea of a fair distribution of resources. It is argued that the system allows people to earn and own property based on their contributions and efforts, rather than allocating resources arbitrarily.

Personality development: Private property is considered fundamental for personality development. By having control over their possessions, individuals can express their preferences, develop their identity, and pursue life goals autonomously.

Critiques and challenges: Despite these arguments in favor, the ethics of private property has also faced criticism. Some argue that it can lead to significant inequalities and concentration of power, posing ethical challenges in terms of fairness and social justice.

The ethics of private property in capitalism advocates the idea that this right is essential for individual freedom, responsibility, economic growth, and justice in resource allocation. However, its application and ethical implications continue to be topics of debate in ethical and economic theory.

Individual rights: The ethics of capitalism advocates for the importance of individual rights, including freedom of choice, freedom of contract, and freedom of association. Capitalism proponents argue that these rights are fundamental for the development of just and prosperous societies, as they allow individuals to pursue their goals and aspirations autonomously.

Freedom of choice: The ethics of capitalism maintains that freedom of choice is essential for the development of just and prosperous societies. Individuals must have the freedom to make decisions about their own lives, including their economic choices. This involves the ability to choose occupation, consume goods and services, and make financial decisions according to their preferences and values.

Freedom of contract: The ethics of capitalism defends freedom of contract, which involves the ability of individuals to enter into voluntary agreements and mutually beneficial contracts. Advocates argue that minimal intervention in contractual agreements allows transactions to be efficient and based on consent.

Freedom of association: The ethics of capitalism values freedom of association, which involves the ability of individuals to form relationships, partnerships, and organizations according to their own choices. This freedom also extends to the formation of businesses, unions, charities, and other entities that reflect the interests and values of individuals.

Protection against coercion: Individual rights in capitalism are linked to protection against external coercion. The ethics argues that government interventions and undue restrictions should be kept to a minimum to preserve the freedom and autonomy of individuals.

Personality development: The ethics of capitalism suggests that the recognition and protection of individual rights contribute to the full development of personality. By having the freedom to make decisions and pursue personal goals, individual expression and personal growth are fostered.

Individual responsibility: The ethics of capitalism also emphasizes individual responsibility as an integral part of rights. With the freedom to make decisions, individuals assume responsibility for the consequences of those decisions, contributing to a society where people are accountable for their actions.

Critiques and challenges: Despite these arguments, the recognition and application of individual rights in capitalism have also been subject to criticism. Some argue that the system can lead to significant inequalities and that certain interventions are necessary to ensure fairness and social justice.

The ethics of capitalism advocates for the importance of individual rights as fundamental to the flourishing of just and prosperous societies. However, the implementation of these rights and how to balance them with other ethical considerations continues to be a topic of debate.

Free Market: Capitalism is commonly associated with the existence of a free market, where economic exchanges are voluntary and based on supply and demand. From an ethical perspective, the free market is considered a mechanism that enables peaceful and mutually beneficial cooperation among individuals, without the coercion of government intervention.

Voluntariness and Consent: The ethics of the free market emphasizes the importance of voluntariness and consent in economic transactions. In a free market, interactions between individuals are based on voluntary agreements, where both parties agree to participate in an exchange without external coercion.

Supply and Demand: The free market operates according to the principles of supply and demand. Prices of goods and services are determined by the interaction between available supply and market demand. From an ethical perspective, this mechanism is considered to efficiently reflect consumers' preferences and needs.

Peaceful Cooperation: The free market is seen as a mechanism that facilitates peaceful cooperation among individuals and businesses. Instead of relying on government coercion, transactions are conducted voluntarily, contributing to an environment where people can interact and collaborate in achieving their goals.

Competition: The ethics of the free market values competition as a driver of efficiency and innovation. Competition among businesses motivates continuous improvement in product quality, cost reduction, and innovation, benefiting consumers.

Access to Opportunities: From an ethical perspective, the free market is associated with the idea of providing equal access to opportunities. People have the freedom to engage in economic activities, start businesses, and compete in the market, contributing to social mobility and personal fulfillment.

Autonomy and Individual Freedom: The ethics of the free market highlights the importance of autonomy and individual freedom. Allowing people to make economic decisions according to their preferences and values respects their autonomy and encourages individual freedom.

Critiques and Challenges: While the free market has its proponents, it also faces criticisms. Some argue that it can lead to significant inequalities, labor exploitation, and unethical business practices. Regulation and government intervention are debated topics to address these concerns without completely sacrificing the benefits of the free market.

The ethics of the free market in the context of capitalism emphasizes voluntariness, peaceful cooperation, competition, and individual freedom as fundamental principles contributing to societal well-being.

However, proper implementation and regulation are also important considerations to address potential ethical challenges.

Meritocracy: The ethics of capitalism often includes the principle of meritocracy, suggesting that economic success should be related to individual effort, skill, and merit. The idea that financial and social rewards should be linked to performance and personal contribution is valued.

Relationship between Effort and Reward: Meritocracy posits that financial and social rewards should be linked to individual effort, skill, and merit. From an ethical perspective, it is argued that those who contribute more and exert more effort should receive greater benefits and recognition in society.

Encouragement of Excellence: Meritocracy is perceived as an encouragement for excellence. By linking success to ability and effort, it is expected that people will strive to improve their skills, performance, and contributions, leading to a more dynamic and efficient society.

Incentives for Innovation: In a meritocracy-based system, individuals are expected to seek innovation and improvement. The prospect of rewards provides incentives for creativity and problem-solving, leading to technological advancements and improvements in quality of life.

Justice in Resource Distribution: Meritocracy is associated with the idea of a fair distribution of resources. Those who contribute more and perform better are rewarded proportionally. From an ethical perspective, this is considered fairer than a distribution based on arbitrary factors.

Challenges and Criticisms: Despite its perceived benefits, meritocracy has also faced criticisms and challenges. Some argue that initial conditions, such as access to education and opportunities, may not be equal for everyone, undermining meritocracy in practical application. Additionally, it is highlighted that certain external factors, such as socioeconomic background, can influence success and may not always reflect individual merits.

Balance with Social Justice: Meritocracy must be balanced with considerations of social justice to address systemic inequalities and ensure equal opportunities. The ethics of capitalism must address how to reconcile meritocracy with the responsibility to create an equitable and accessible environment for all.

Meritocracy is an ethical principle within the context of capitalism that seeks to link economic success with individual effort and merit. However, its application and ethical implications require careful considerations to address challenges and ensure social justice.

Competition and Cooperation: In capitalism, competition and cooperation coexist. Competition is considered a driver of efficiency and innovation, while cooperation through voluntary exchanges is seen as an ethical way to meet people's needs and desires.

Driver of Efficiency: Competition in capitalism is perceived as a driver of efficiency. Companies compete for resources and consumer attention, motivating them to improve product quality, reduce costs, and seek innovations.

Stimulus for Improvement: Rivalry between companies creates an environment where each one seeks to outperform the other, leading to constant improvement in the offering of goods and services. From an ethical perspective, this is considered beneficial for consumers and society as a whole.

Cooperation: Voluntary Exchanges: In capitalism, cooperation manifests through voluntary exchanges. Economic transactions are based on mutual consent, where both parties involved expect to benefit from the exchange. This form of cooperation is considered ethical as it occurs voluntarily.

Meeting Needs: Cooperation through voluntary exchanges allows people to meet their needs and desires more efficiently. By facilitating the production and distribution of goods and services, individuals have the opportunity to improve their quality of life.

Ethical Balance:

Harmonization of Interests: The ethics of capitalism seeks to balance competition and cooperation. While companies compete with each other, they also cooperate through supply chains, partnerships, and trade agreements. This balance is essential to ensure that competition does not lead to harmful practices and that cooperation does not result in monopolistic agreements.

Ethical Challenges:

Negative Externalities: Although competition and cooperation are fundamental, they can also pose ethical challenges. Negative externalities, such as labor exploitation or environmental impact, may arise when competitive incentives are not properly balanced with broader ethical considerations.

In capitalism, competition and cooperation coexist and are considered essential ethical elements. Competition drives efficiency and innovation, while cooperation through voluntary exchanges facilitates the ethical satisfaction of needs and desires. The challenge lies in balancing these elements to ensure that the system operates fairly and benefits society as a whole.

Social Responsibility: The ethics of capitalism also addresses social responsibility, emphasizing that companies and individuals have a responsibility to act ethically and contribute to the well-being of society. This includes considering environmental impacts, fair labor practices, and participation in philanthropic initiatives.

Fair Labor Practices:

Respect for Labor Rights: Companies in an ethical capitalist system must respect labor rights, provide safe and fair working conditions, and offer wages that enable a dignified quality of life. Social responsibility involves treating employees with equity and dignity.

Environmental Impact:

Sustainability: The ethics of capitalism promotes sustainability and responsible management of natural resources. Companies must consider and mitigate their environmental impact, adopting practices that minimize ecological footprints and contribute to environmental preservation.

Transparency and Business Ethics:

Ethical Business Practices: Ethical companies in a capitalist system must operate with transparency and honesty. Social responsibility involves avoiding deceptive or exploitative business practices, ensuring integrity in all transactions.

Participation in Philanthropic Initiatives:

Community Contributions: Social responsibility includes participating in philanthropic initiatives and supporting social causes. Ethical companies and individuals are committed to giving back to the community, whether through charitable donations, educational programs, or efforts to address social issues.

Ethics in the Supply Chain:

Ensuring Ethical Practices: Ethical companies consider ethics throughout their supply chain. This involves ensuring that suppliers also adhere to ethical standards in terms of labor practices, environmental impact, and fair trade standards.

Commitment to Diversity and Inclusion:

Promotion of Equality: Social responsibility also addresses diversity and inclusion in the workplace. Ethical companies commit to promoting inclusive work environments that value gender, ethnic, sexual orientation, and other forms of diversity.

Challenges and Constant Evolution:

Adaptation to Changing Expectations: Social responsibility in capitalism involves constant adaptation to changing societal expectations. Ethical companies must be willing to evolve their practices to address new social and environmental concerns.

Social responsibility in the context of ethical capitalism acknowledges that companies and individuals have an obligation to act ethically and contribute to the well-being of society in various aspects. This goes beyond the pursuit of financial benefits and focuses on creating a positive long-term impact on the community and the environment.

Critiques and Challenges: Despite its ethical principles, capitalism has also faced criticism. Some argue that it can lead to significant inequalities, labor exploitation, and unethical business practices. These challenges have sparked debates on how to balance the ethics of capitalism with the need to address social and economic issues.

Economic Inequality:

Critique: One of the main criticisms of capitalism is economic inequality. It is argued that the system can generate significant gaps between the rich and the poor, creating an unequal distribution of wealth and limiting access to opportunities for certain groups.

Labor Exploitation:

Critique: Another common criticism focuses on labor exploitation, especially in precarious working conditions or low wages. It is argued that, in some cases, companies seek to maximize their profits at the expense of workers, leading to unjust conditions.

Unethical Business Practices:

Critique: Unethical business practices, such as unfair competition, unrestricted exploitation of natural resources, and a lack of environmental responsibility in some business sectors, are also criticized.

Lack of Regulation and Control:

Critique: Some argue that the lack of adequate regulation can lead to unethical behavior by companies. The absence of a strong regulatory framework may allow practices that harm workers, consumers, and the environment.

Short-Term Focus:

Critique: The constant pursuit of short-term profits is sometimes criticized for leading to business decisions that do not consider long-term consequences, such as the depletion of natural resources or a lack of investment in sustainable practices.

Negative Externalities:

Critique: Negative externalities, such as pollution and unintended side effects of production, are also subject to criticism. Some argue that companies often do not fully bear the costs of these externalities, leading to harmful impacts on society.

Lack of Equal Access to Opportunities:

Critique: Criticism regarding the lack of equal access to opportunities points out that initial conditions, such as access to education and resources, may not be equal for everyone, undermining meritocracy in practice.

Impact on Social Well-being:

Critique: Some argue that the market-centered focus of capitalism can jeopardize aspects of social well-being, such as health, education, and housing, when primarily considered as commodities.

These critiques are not inherent to capitalism itself but rather to its implementation and how its ethical aspects are managed. Many advocates of capitalism argue that effective regulation, corporate social responsibility, and a balance between competition and cooperation can address these criticisms and strengthen the system.

The ethics of capitalism are based on the defense of private property, individual rights, competition, and voluntary cooperation as fundamental principles for social and economic organization. However, these principles also face critiques and challenges, highlighting the importance of addressing ethical issues within a capitalist framework.

15.Analysis of the Labor Market

Human Action and the Labor Market:

Austrian theory is based on the principle of human action, which asserts that economic decisions result from individual choices based on the information available at a given moment.

In the labor market, human action implies that both employers and workers make rational decisions based on their preferences and expectations.

Principle of Human Action:

Austrian theory, developed by economists such as Carl Menger, Ludwig von Mises, and Friedrich Hayek, is grounded in the principle of human action. This principle holds that economic and social decisions result from the individual choices of actors in the economy.

Methodological Individualism:

Austrian theory advocates for methodological individualism, meaning it focuses on the individual as the basic unit of analysis in economics. In the context of the labor market, each worker and employer makes decisions based on their own circumstances, preferences, and knowledge.

Rational Decision-Making in the Labor Market:

In the labor market, human action implies that both employers and workers make rational and autonomous decisions. Workers evaluate job opportunities based on their preferences, skills, and needs, while employers assess the potential contribution of workers to the production process.

Subjective Valuation of Work:

Subjective valuation is a key concept in Austrian theory. In the labor market, individuals assign subjective value to their time and effort. The decision to accept a job and the accepted wage level reflect the worker's subjective valuation of the perceived benefit from that transaction.

Adaptability and Change:

Austrian theory highlights the adaptability of individuals in response to changes in labor market conditions. Human action drives workers to adjust their skills and preferences according to the evolution of labor supply and demand.

Entrepreneurship in Labor Choice:

The principle of human action also addresses the role of entrepreneurship in labor choice. Individuals act as entrepreneurs of themselves by seeking job opportunities that maximize their utility and personal satisfaction.

Limitations of Information:

Austrian theory acknowledges the limitations of information individuals face when making decisions in the labor market. Human action takes place with the information available at a given moment, and errors and adjustments are part of the market process.

The Austrian theory emphasizes the importance of human action in the labor market, where individual decisions influence wage formation, resource allocation, and the overall dynamics of employment. Subjective valuation and adaptability are key elements shaping the interaction between workers and employers in this theoretical approach.

Wage Formation:

According to Austrian theory, wages result from the subjective valuation individuals assign to their time and effort. Workers assess the offered wage in comparison to the subjective value of their time and skills, while employers value the worker's contribution to the production process.

Wages are formed through a voluntary negotiation process in which employers and employees seek an agreement that maximizes their individual utility.

Subjective Valuation of Work:

In Austrian theory, it is emphasized that the value of a job is not inherent to the work itself but is subjective and varies from person to person. Each individual, both the worker and the employer, values work differently based on their needs, preferences, and circumstances.

Evaluation by Workers:

Workers evaluate the offered wage based on their subjective valuation of time and skills. They consider factors such as working conditions, development opportunities, and the perceived value of the wage in relation to their personal needs and goals.

Voluntary Negotiation:

Austrian theory highlights that wage formation is the result of voluntary negotiation between workers and employers. Both parties seek an agreement that maximizes their individual utility, and the transaction takes place if both parties are willing to accept the terms.

Evaluation by Employers:

Employers, in turn, assess the worker's contribution to the production process. They evaluate efficiency, skills, and the perceived productivity of the worker. The decision to hire a worker and the level of wage offered reflect the subjective valuation of the worker's contribution to the company's success.

Competition and Flexibility in the Labor Market:

Austrian theory recognizes the importance of competition and flexibility in the labor market. Competition between companies and workers contributes to efficiency in wage formation, as companies seek to retain talent by offering competitive wages, and workers seek the best opportunities.

Changes in Subjective Valuation:

Wage formation can change over time as labor market conditions and individual preferences change. Subjective valuation can adjust in response to changes in the supply and demand for skills, technological advances, and other factors.

Government Intervention and Distortions:

Austrian theory warns of potential distortions in wage formation when there is government intervention, such as the imposition of minimum wages or labor regulations affecting free negotiation between workers and employers.

Austrian theory highlights that wage formation is a dynamic and decentralized process, influenced by the subjective valuation of individuals in the labor market. Voluntary negotiation and competition are essential elements contributing to the efficiency and adaptability of this process.

Supply and Demand for Labor:

Austrian theory considers labor supply as the offering of a service by workers. The quantity of labor offered depends on the subjective valuation of workers regarding wages and working conditions.

On the other hand, labor demand is derived from the subjective valuation of employers regarding the worker's contribution to the production process. The quantity demanded depends on the company's needs and the perceived productivity of the worker.

Labor Supply as a Service Offering:

Austrian theory regards labor supply as the offering of a service by workers. In this approach, work is seen as a service that individuals are willing to provide in the labor market.

Subjective Valuation of Wages:

The quantity of labor offered is based on the subjective valuation of workers regarding wages and working conditions. Each worker evaluates the value of their time and effort based on their own preferences, needs, and individual circumstances.

Voluntary Negotiation:

Austrian theory emphasizes that labor supply occurs through voluntary negotiation between workers and employers. The amount of labor offered depends on the willingness of the worker to accept working conditions, including the proposed salary.

Flexibility and Adaptability:

Flexibility and adaptability are key elements in Austrian theory. Labor supply can be adjusted as the worker's circumstances change, such as changes in preferences, acquired skills, or shifts in labor market conditions.

Competition among Workers:

Competition among workers is also considered in labor supply. Workers compete to secure employment, which can influence the amount of labor they are willing to offer and the conditions they are willing to accept.

Changes in Skill Demand:

Labor supply can be affected by changes in skill demand in the market. Workers may adjust their labor supply in response to industry needs or the introduction of new technologies.

Government Intervention and Distortions:

Austrian theory warns about distortions that may arise when there is government intervention in the labor market, such as regulations affecting the flexibility of labor supply or imposing restrictions on salary negotiation.

Austrian theory views labor supply as a service, where the quantity offered is determined by workers' subjective valuation of salary and working conditions. Voluntary negotiation, competition, and adaptability are essential elements in this process.

Labor Market Dynamics:

Austrian theory highlights the dynamic nature of the labor market, where conditions and preferences are constantly changing. Fluctuations in labor supply and demand, as well as changes in required skills, can influence wage formation.

The flexibility of the labor market allows individuals to adapt to changes in skill demand, facilitating the efficient allocation of human resources.

Constant Changes in Conditions and Preferences:

Austrian theory acknowledges that economic conditions and individual preferences are constantly changing. Factors such as technology, consumer demand, and other economic events influence labor market conditions.

Fluctuations in Labor Supply and Demand:

Labor market dynamics involve fluctuations in labor supply and demand. These changes can result from external factors, such as shifts in the global economy, technological advances, or changes in government regulation.

Individual Adaptability:

Austrian theory emphasizes the adaptability of individuals in the labor market. Workers can adjust their skills and preferences in response to changes in market demand. Training and acquiring new skills are examples of this adaptability.

Impact on Wage Formation:

The dynamics of the labor market directly impact wage formation. Fluctuations in labor supply and demand can influence wages as employers seek to attract or retain talent in a changing labor environment.

New Skills and Technologies:

Changes in required skills and the introduction of new technologies are integral to labor market dynamics. Workers may need to adapt and acquire new skills to remain competitive and relevant in the market.

Competition and Adjustment:

Competition between workers and companies is a key component of labor market dynamics. Competition can drive workers to improve their skills and companies to offer competitive salaries to attract the best talent.

Response to Economic Changes:

Austrian theory recognizes that the labor market responds to broader economic changes, such as recessions, economic expansions, and shifts in growth rates. These events can have a significant impact on labor supply and demand.

Employment Flexibility:

Labor market dynamics also address employment flexibility. Employment models, such as freelancing and temporary hiring, are examples of how individuals can adapt to changing labor market conditions.

Austrian theory highlights the dynamic nature of the labor market, where economic conditions, individual preferences, and changes in labor supply and demand constantly interact. Individual adaptability and competition are fundamental aspects of this approach.

Government Intervention and Distortions:

Austrian theory warns about distortions that may arise when there is government intervention in the labor market, such as labor laws, minimum wages, or regulations affecting employment flexibility.

Such interventions can create imbalances by imposing artificial restrictions on wage formation and limiting individuals' ability to make decisions based on their preferences and skills.

Labor Laws:

Austrian theory points out that labor laws, regulating working conditions, hours, and other employment aspects, can introduce rigidities into the labor market. These rigidities can limit flexibility for both employers and workers.

Minimum Wages:

The imposition of minimum wages is viewed cautiously from the Austrian perspective. It is argued that setting a minimum wage above the level determined by market forces can result in unemployment, especially for workers with limited skills and experience.

Regulations Affecting Employment Flexibility:

Any regulation affecting employment flexibility, such as restrictions on temporary contracts or independent work practices, is considered a potential source of distortions. Austrian theory advocates for the ability of individuals and companies to adapt to changing labor market conditions.

Impact on Competition:

Government intervention can influence competition in the labor market. Regulations that impose additional costs on businesses or establish barriers to entry for new participants can reduce competition, potentially negatively affecting market efficiency.

Perverse Incentives and Unintended Effects:

Austrian theory highlights the possibility that government interventions may create perverse incentives and unintended effects. For example, policies aiming to protect certain groups of workers may have unintended consequences, such as indirect discrimination or a reduction in job opportunities.

Bureaucracy and Administrative Costs:

The implementation and enforcement of labor regulations can generate significant bureaucracy and administrative costs for both businesses and the government. These additional costs can impact the efficiency and adaptability of the labor market.

Restrictions on Wage Negotiation:

Austrian theory warns that certain restrictions on wage negotiation, such as limiting the ability of companies and workers to freely agree on conditions, can distort wage formation and discourage market adaptability.

Austrian theory maintains that government intervention in the labor market can introduce distortions affecting market flexibility, competition, and efficiency. The central concern is to preserve the ability for adaptation and voluntary negotiation among the parties involved in the labor process.

Role of Entrepreneurship and Innovation:

Austrian theory emphasizes the role of entrepreneurship and innovation in the labor market. The introduction of new technologies and innovative forms of organization can affect the demand for certain skills and change the overall structure of employment.

Entrepreneurial Role:

Austrian theory views entrepreneurship as a dynamic force driving change in the economy and, consequently, in the labor market. Entrepreneurs are seen as individuals who identify market opportunities, take risks, and undertake new business initiatives.

Innovation and Technological Change:

The introduction of new technologies and innovative forms of organization is a key element in Austrian theory. Technological innovation can affect the demand for certain skills, generate new job opportunities, and change the overall structure of the labor market.

Impact on Skill Demand:

Innovation can have a significant impact on the demand for labor skills. The adoption of advanced technologies can increase the demand for specialized skills, while certain tasks may be automated, altering the skills required in some occupations.

Dynamics of Entrepreneurial Creativity:

Austrian theory highlights entrepreneurial creativity as a driver of change. Creative entrepreneurs can develop new products, services, and business models that create employment and contribute to the adaptability of the labor market.

Adaptation to Economic Changes:

The ability of entrepreneurs to adapt to economic changes and embrace innovation is essential in Austrian theory. This adaptability contributes to the labor market's ability to adjust to new conditions and opportunities.

Decentralization of Innovation:

Austrian theory advocates for the decentralization of innovation. Instead of being driven by large centralized companies, innovation can arise from agile entrepreneurs and small businesses responding to market needs.

Risk and Reward of Entrepreneurship:

The assumption of risks by entrepreneurs is a central aspect. Austrian theory recognizes that the entrepreneurial process involves risks but also emphasizes the importance of potential rewards for those who succeed in creating economic value.

Changes in Business Structure:

Innovation and entrepreneurship can lead to changes in the business structure. New companies may emerge and grow, while others may decline. These changes affect the dynamics of employment and the distribution of skills in the labor market.

Austrian theory highlights the crucial role of entrepreneurship and innovation in the dynamics of the labor market.

16.Production Theory

Production theory according to the Austrian School differs from more conventional approaches by focusing on the temporal structure of production and the importance of time and uncertainty.

Temporal Structure of Production:

The Austrian School introduces the concept of the temporal structure of production, which refers to the variety of productive processes spanning different time periods. These processes vary in duration, from short-term production activities to long-term projects.

Variety of Productive Processes:

The temporal structure of production refers to the diversity of productive processes in the economy. These processes cover different time periods, with some completing in the short term, while others are long-term projects.

Duration of Processes:

Productive processes can have various durations, ranging from activities that yield quick results in the short term to projects requiring significant time investment before producing results. The variability in the duration of these processes is essential for understanding the temporal structure of production.

Short Term vs. Long Term:

The temporal structure of production distinguishes between short-term activities and long-term projects. In the short term, actions with immediate effects are taken, while in the long term, more extensive projects requiring considerable time and resources are undertaken.

Interconnection of Processes:

Processes in the temporal structure of production are interconnected. The completion of a short-term process may depend on the outcomes of longer-term processes. This interconnection reflects the complexity of production and how different elements relate to each other.

Importance of Time:

The temporal structure of production highlights the importance of time in economic decision-making. Economic agents must consider not only the quantity of goods produced but also when they are produced and how they are distributed over time.

Temporal Preferences:

Individuals' temporal preferences, i.e., how they value present consumption compared to the future, influence the temporal structure of production. Decisions about the duration of productive processes are affected by consumers' and producers' temporal preferences.

Risk and Uncertainty:

The temporal structure of production also incorporates the notions of risk and uncertainty. Decisions about long-term projects are influenced by the perception of future risks and uncertainty in the economic environment.

Dynamic Adaptability:

The temporal structure of production is not static; it is dynamic and can adapt to changes in preferences, technology, and market conditions. Dynamic adaptability is a fundamental feature that allows the economy to adjust to new circumstances.

The Austrian School's temporal structure of production provides a detailed perspective on how production is organized in the economy, considering the diversity of processes, their duration, interconnection, and the crucial influence of time and temporal preferences.

Importance of Time:

Austrian theory emphasizes the importance of time in production. Resources and effort are allocated to different stages of production, and the choice to allocate resources in the short or long term is influenced by temporal preferences and the expectations of economic agents.

Allocation of Resources to Different Stages:

Austrian theory argues that resources and effort are allocated to different stages of production. This allocation refers not only to the quantity of resources used but also to when they are employed in the production process.

Choice between Short and Long Term:

The choice to allocate resources in the short or long term is a crucial component of economic decision-making. Economic agents must decide whether to allocate resources to activities that yield quick results in the short term or to more extensive projects that will require time before producing results.

Influence of Temporal Preferences:

Temporal preferences of individuals, i.e., how they value present consumption compared to the future, have a significant impact on the temporal allocation of resources. Decisions about the duration of productive projects are influenced by these preferences.

Expectations of Economic Agents:

The importance of time is also tied to the expectations of economic agents about the future. Resource allocation decisions are made based on perceptions and predictions about future market conditions, demand for goods and services, and other relevant factors.

Risk and Uncertainty:

Temporal decision-making in production is also influenced by risk and uncertainty. The assessment of potential risks and uncertainty about future events affects the duration of production commitments.

Adaptation to Changes in Time:

The Austrian economy recognizes that time is a dynamic factor, and resource allocation must adapt to changes in preferences, emerging technologies, and market conditions. Temporal flexibility allows continuous adjustments in production.

Coordination of Temporal Structure:

Efficient coordination of the temporal structure of production is essential for the harmonious functioning of the economic system. Proper allocation of resources to different stages helps prevent poor investments and facilitates adaptation to changing conditions.

The importance of time in production according to Austrian theory highlights how economic decisions are intrinsically linked to temporal considerations. The allocation of resources in the short or long term, influenced by temporal preferences, expectations, and adaptability, plays a fundamental role in the dynamics of the economy.

Effect of Temporal Preference:

Temporal preference, reflecting how individuals value present consumption compared to the future, affects production decisions. The temporal structure of production adapts according to temporal preferences and the perception of risk and uncertainty in the future.

The effect of temporal preference is a central aspect of Austrian theory and plays a crucial role in economic decision-making and the configuration of the temporal structure of production.

Definition of Temporal Preference:

Temporal preference refers to the subjective valuation individuals assign to present consumption compared to future consumption. It is the expression of how individuals evaluate the satisfaction they derive from consuming goods and services in the present in relation to deferring consumption to the future.

Influence on Production Decisions:

Temporal preference directly influences production decisions. Companies and entrepreneurs must make decisions about resource allocation and timing based on how consumers value present consumption versus the future.

Temporal Structure Adaptation:

The production's temporal structure, covering different periods of time and production processes, adapts to the temporal preferences of consumers. If preferences shift towards a higher valuation of future consumption, the structure can be adjusted to reflect this changing demand.

Impact on Project Duration:

Temporal preferences affect the duration of projects and production processes. If temporal preferences indicate a higher valuation of present consumption, short-term projects are likely preferred. Conversely, if there is a higher valuation of future consumption, longer-term investments may arise.

Risk and Uncertainty Perception:

The perception of risk and uncertainty about future events is also linked to temporal preferences. Individuals may be willing to take on more risks or prefer secure investments depending on how they value present and future consumption in relation to uncertainty.

Changes in Temporal Preferences:

Austrian theory acknowledges that temporal preferences can change over time and in response to various factors, such as economic conditions, external events, or changes in individual preferences. These changes impact the dynamics of the temporal production structure.

Market Adaptability:

Market adaptability is essential to respond to fluctuations in temporal preferences. Prices and market signals reflect changing preferences, and entrepreneurs respond by adjusting production to meet consumer demand.

The effect of temporal preference highlights how economic decisions, including those related to production, are strongly influenced by the subjective valuation of time and consumption. Market adaptability and temporal production structure are key aspects in understanding this phenomenon from the Austrian perspective.

Risk and Uncertainty:

Austrian theory recognizes the presence of risk and uncertainty in production decisions. Economic agents must make decisions under conditions of uncertainty, as the future is inherently uncertain. This influences investment choices and the duration of production processes.

Considering risk and uncertainty is an essential element in Austrian theory, affecting production decisions and the dynamics of the temporal structure.

Inherent Presence of Risk and Uncertainty:

Austrian theory starts from the recognition that the future is inherently uncertain and that there is an element of risk in all economic decisions.

Economic agents must make decisions in an environment where they cannot fully foresee all future events.

Influence on Investment Decisions:

The presence of risk and uncertainty directly influences investment decisions. Entrepreneurs must assess not only opportunities but also associated risks. Uncertainty about future demand, costs, and other factors affects the choice of investment projects.

Duration of Production Processes:

Uncertainty about future events can impact the duration of production processes. Economic agents may opt for short-term projects if uncertainty is high and prefer not to commit to long-term projects in an unpredictable environment.

Adaptability and Flexibility:

Adaptability and flexibility are key elements in responding to uncertainty. Entrepreneurs must be able to adjust their strategies and decisions as new information is revealed and market conditions change.

Importance of Risk Perception:

Risk perception is subjective and may vary among different economic agents. Austrian theory recognizes that how individuals perceive and assess risk affects their economic and investment decisions.

Role of Competition:

Market competition also influences how risk and uncertainty are managed. Companies compete not only in offering goods and services but also in efficiently managing risks and adapting to unexpected changes.

Austrian theory emphasizes the role of entrepreneurship in managing risk and uncertainty. Entrepreneurs not only take risks but are constantly seeking and discovering opportunities in a dynamic and uncertain environment.

Risk vs. Uncertainty:

The distinction between risk and uncertainty is important in Austrian theory. While risk involves events whose probability can be estimated, uncertainty refers to situations where probabilities are unknown or impossible to calculate.

Austrian theory recognizes the reality of risk and uncertainty in economic decision-making. How economic agents face and manage this risk impacts the temporal production structure and the market's adaptability to changing conditions.

Capital and Productive Structure:

The concept of capital in Austrian theory is closely related to the productive structure. Capital is not homogeneous but varies in its specificity for certain production processes. The production structure consists of a series of interconnected capital goods in different stages.

Non-Homogeneity of Capital:

In contrast to the classical conception of capital as a homogeneous factor, Austrian theory emphasizes the non-homogeneity of capital. Capital goods are not interchangeable uniformly but vary in their specificity and application for certain production processes.

Interconnected Production Structure:

The production structure consists of a series of interconnected capital goods in different stages. Each stage represents a phase in the production process, from raw material extraction to the final product's manufacture. These stages are linked by production relationships.

Specific Capital Goods:

Capital goods are specific to certain production processes and are not easily transferable to other production lines. The specificity of capital implies that its value is linked to its application in particular contexts, influencing investment decisions and the configuration of the production structure.

Duration of Production Processes:

The duration of production processes is related to the production structure. Long-term investment projects requiring specific capital goods are linked to more advanced stages of the production structure, while short-term projects may be associated with initial stages.

Importance of Time in Production:

Austrian theory emphasizes the importance of time in production, and the production structure reflects how capital goods are distributed over time. The temporal allocation of resources is essential to efficiently coordinate production across various stages.

Production and Consumption Cycle:

The production structure is also related to the production and consumption cycle. Proper coordination between production stages and time is essential to avoid poor investments and ensure that goods are available when consumers demand them.

Impact of Changes in Temporal Preferences:

Changes in temporal preferences, reflecting how present and future consumption is valued, can affect the production structure. If there is a shift in preference towards future consumption, there may be increased demand for capital goods associated with long-term projects.

Entrepreneurship and Opportunity Discovery:

Entrepreneurs play a crucial role in shaping the production structure by identifying investment opportunities and adjusting resource allocation in response to changes in market conditions and consumer preferences.

In summary, the concept of capital in Austrian theory, along with the production structure, offers a dynamic perspective on how production processes are organized over time and how they respond to changes in the economy and individual preferences.

Dynamic Adjustment:

Austrian theory addresses the economy as a dynamic system that is constantly adjusting to changes in temporal preferences, supply and demand, and market conditions. Adjustments in the production structure are integral to this process.

Dynamic Vision of the Economy:

Austrian theory views the economy as a dynamic system in constant flux. This approach diverges from static views and recognizes that preferences, market conditions, and other economic factors are continually evolving.

"Adjustments to Changes in Time Preferences:

Since time preference is a key factor in Austrian theory, dynamic adjustments occur in response to changes in how present and future consumption are valued. These changes influence the production structure and resource allocation over time.

Flexibility of the Productive Structure:

The productive structure, composed of interconnected capital goods at different stages, exhibits flexibility to adapt to changing conditions. Entrepreneurs can readjust resource allocation and the duration of production processes to meet market demands.

Entrepreneurship and Opportunity Discovery:

Dynamic adjustment involves entrepreneurs' ability to identify opportunities in a changing environment. Discovering investment opportunities and strategic adaptation are essential for entrepreneurial success in a dynamic system.

Coordination between Supply and Demand:

The dynamics of adjustment manifest in the coordination between supply and demand. Prices and market signals play a crucial role in this coordination, guiding producers on resource allocation and consumers on spending distribution.

Production and Consumption Cycle:

Dynamic adjustment is related to the production and consumption cycle. Proper coordination of production stages over time prevents poor investments and ensures goods are available when consumers demand them.

Competition and Natural Market Selection:

Market competition acts as a mechanism of natural selection, where more efficient and adaptable firms have a greater chance of survival and thriving. This contributes to the dynamic adjustment of the economic system.

Response to Changes in Supply and Demand:

Dynamic adjustments also occur in response to changes in supply and demand. Variations in consumer demand and market conditions lead to adjustments in the production and supply of goods and services.

In summary, dynamic adjustment is a central principle in Austrian theory that highlights the economic system's ability to adapt and evolve in response to changes in market conditions and individual preferences. The flexibility of the productive structure and entrepreneurial initiative are key aspects of this dynamic process.

Poor Investments and Economic Cycles:

The Austrian School argues that poor investments can occur when there are distortions in market signals, such as those generated by expansive monetary policies. These poor investments can lead to economic cycles with phases of boom and crisis.

Distortions in Market Signals:

Austrian theory argues that poor investments can occur when there are distortions in market signals. These distortions can result from external interventions, such as expansive monetary policies implemented by authorities.

Expansive Monetary Policies:

The expansion of money supply by monetary authorities can artificially lower interest rates. When interest rates do not adequately reflect market time preferences, incentives for investments that would otherwise not be profitable may arise.

Economic Boom:

The economic boom phase is characterized by an increase in investment and economic activity. Companies and individuals may be more willing to borrow due to low interest rates, leading to credit expansion and increased investments.

Poor Resource Allocation:

Poor investments result from the misallocation of resources to projects that, under normal conditions, would not be economically viable. This may include investments in specific sectors benefiting from artificially low interest rates.

Economic Cycle:

The Austrian economic cycle involves a sequence of boom and crisis phases. During the boom phase, poor investments proliferate. However, the unsustainability of these investments becomes apparent when market conditions change or when interest rates begin to adjust.

Crisis Phase:

The crisis phase is an inevitable correction after the boom. Poor investments are revealed, and companies relying on easy financing may face difficulties. This can lead to economic contraction, bankruptcies, and unemployment.

Market Adjustment:

The crisis phase is part of the market adjustment process. During this period, resources are reallocated more efficiently, and excesses accumulated during the boom are eliminated. It is a period of economic restructuring.

Role of Government Intervention:

Austrian theory argues that government intervention, especially in financial and monetary markets, can be a significant source of distortions leading to poor investments and economic cycles.

Importance of Financial Prudence:

From the Austrian perspective, financial prudence and caution in entrepreneurial decision-making are essential to avoid the pitfalls of the economic cycle and associated poor investments.

Austrian theory highlights how poor investments, driven by distortions in market signals, can trigger economic cycles with boom and crisis phases. Market adjustment and the correction of misallocations are integral parts of this approach.

Economic and Socialist Calculation:

Ludwig von Mises, a prominent economist of the Austrian School, also emphasized the importance of economic calculation in a market economy. He argued that socialism, by eliminating private ownership of the means of production, lacks an efficient mechanism for allocating resources and coordinating the production structure.

Importance of Economic Calculation:

Ludwig von Mises emphasized the importance of economic calculation in making efficient decisions in a market economy. This calculation involves evaluating costs and benefits, allocating resources, and making business decisions based on profitability.

Private Property and Means of Production:

In a market economy, private ownership of the means of production is essential. Entrepreneurs and private owners can perform economic calculations to determine the efficiency and profitability of various business activities.

The Challenge of Socialism:

Mises posed the challenge that socialism faces in eliminating private ownership of the means of production. He argued that, without private property, there are no markets for factors of production, and thus no market prices reflecting relative scarcity and consumer preferences.

Absence of Market Prices:

In a socialist economy where the means of production are owned by the state, Mises argued that genuine market prices for factors of production do not exist. The lack of prices makes it impossible to efficiently calculate economic decisions and determine the most efficient allocation of resources.

Economic Discoordination:

Without a market price system, Mises argued that economic coordination becomes extremely difficult. Information about relative scarcity and consumer preferences, transmitted through prices, is lost, leading to discoordination in production and resource allocation.

Efficiency and Social Welfare:

Mises argued that economic calculation based on private property and market prices is essential for achieving efficiency and social welfare. The absence of these elements in socialism can result in misallocations of resources, scarcity, and a lack of incentives for innovation and continuous improvement.

Contribution to Central Planning:

Mises also pointed out that central planning in a socialist system cannot efficiently substitute decentralized decision-making based on economic calculation by entrepreneurs and consumers in a free market.

Ludwig von Mises's perspective on economic calculation highlights how private property and market prices are essential for economic efficiency and how their absence in socialism can lead to significant challenges in resource allocation and economic coordination.

Austrian Production Theory:

The Austrian theory of production focuses on the temporal structure of production, the importance of time, risk, capital specificity, and dynamic market adjustment. These elements provide a unique perspective on how production processes form and adjust in the economy.

17.Critique of Centralized Planning

Critique of centralized planning and arguments in favor of decentralization and autonomy are fundamental in the context of various economic theories and political philosophies.

Inefficiency in Resource Allocation: One of the primary arguments against centralized planning is the inefficiency in resource allocation. Without the information provided by market prices and competition, the central authority may struggle to allocate resources efficiently to areas of greatest need.

Absence of Price Signals: In a centralized system, the absence of a free market impedes the formation of prices through the interaction of supply and demand. Prices are vital signals indicating the relative scarcity of resources and consumer preferences. Without these prices, the central authority lacks information to make informed decisions about resource allocation.

Difficulty in Valuing Preferences: Centralized planning often faces difficulties in accurately valuing consumer preferences. The diversity of individual preferences and needs is challenging to capture without an efficient mechanism like the market, where transactions directly reflect consumer choices.

Lack of Incentives for Efficiency: Without market competition, producers may lack incentives to improve efficiency and reduce costs. In a centralized environment, where production is not subject to competitive pressure, there may be less stimulus to innovate and find more efficient ways of using resources.

Disconnection from Local Reality: The central authority may struggle to understand local needs and conditions. Lack of decentralization can lead to decisions that do not align properly with the specific realities of particular communities or regions.

Risk of Overproduction or Scarcity: Without market feedback, centralized planning can lead to overproduction of some goods and scarcity of others. Difficulty in foreseeing and adjusting to changing market needs can result in imbalances in supply and demand.

Disincentive for Innovation: Market competition fosters innovation by rewarding those who introduce improvements. In a centralized economy, where there is no direct competition, there may be less incentive for innovation and technological development.

Slow Response Time: Centralized decision-making can be slower and less agile than decisions made locally by actors responding directly to changing conditions. This can lead to inefficient responses to unforeseen events or sudden changes in demand.

The inefficiency in resource allocation in a centrally planned system highlights inherent limitations when market signals and competition are disregarded. These challenges are fundamental in debates about the effectiveness of economic and political systems.

Lack of Incentives and Motivation: Decentralization and autonomy are considered more effective in providing incentives and motivation. In centralized systems, where decisions come from a central authority, individuals and companies may lack the necessary stimulus to innovate and improve efficiency.

The lack of incentives and motivation in centralized systems is a key argument in favor of decentralization and autonomy.

Disconnection from Individual Interests: In a centralized system, decisions may deviate from individual interests and needs. Lack of participation in decision-making can decrease people's and companies' motivation to strive and contribute significantly.

Lack of Differentiated Rewards: Without market mechanisms that differentially reward effort and innovation, individuals may perceive a lack of incentives to excel in their efforts. Equality of rewards, regardless of performance, can discourage the pursuit of excellence.

Stagnation in Efficiency: Competition and the pursuit of efficiency are fundamental drivers in a decentralized environment. Decentralization provides companies and individuals with incentives to continuously improve, as those offering higher quality products or services at lower costs are more likely to succeed.

Limited Innovation and Creativity: Autonomy and decentralization encourage innovation and creativity by allowing individuals and companies to experiment and test new ideas. In a centralized system, where decisions are centralized, there may be less room for experimentation and creativity.

Workplace Demotivation: Lack of participation in decision-making and the perception that individual efforts do not translate into direct benefits can result in workplace demotivation. Autonomy, in contrast, allows workers to see a more direct connection between their efforts and the outcomes achieved.

Resistance to Bureaucracy: Centralized systems often involve more bureaucracy and slower decision-making processes. This bureaucratic environment can demotivate individuals and limit their ability to make quick and efficient decisions.

Entrepreneurship and Business Initiative: Decentralization fosters entrepreneurship and business initiative by allowing individuals to take risks and pursue opportunities. A centralized system may inhibit these qualities by imposing restrictions and limitations on individual initiative.

The lack of incentives and motivation in centralized systems underscores the importance of decentralization and autonomy in stimulating innovation, efficiency, and active participation of individuals and companies in decision-making. These elements are crucial for the dynamic development of an economy and society.

Decentralized Knowledge:

The critique of centralized planning underscores the idea that knowledge about local conditions, preferences, and needs is inherently decentralized. Central planners may lack the detailed information needed to make effective decisions at the local level.

The emphasis on decentralized knowledge is a central argument against centralized planning.

Specific Local Information:

The knowledge necessary for effective decision-making is often specific to local conditions. This includes factors such as local supply and demand, cultural characteristics, and consumer preferences in particular areas. Local individuals and businesses have more direct and detailed knowledge of these circumstances.

Adaptability to Changing Conditions:

Economic and social conditions can change rapidly. Local actors are better positioned to adapt to these changes due to their immediate understanding of the environment. In a centralized system, decision-making may be slow and less responsive to local variations.

Tacit and Experiential Knowledge:

There is a type of "tacit" and experience-based knowledge that is difficult to formalize and communicate effectively. This knowledge often resides in the direct experience of local individuals and businesses and is valuable for effective decision-making. Centralized planning may overlook this form of knowledge.

Instant Market Feedback:

In a decentralized system, the market provides instant feedback through transactions and prices. This feedback is essential for adjusting decisions and allocating resources efficiently. Centralized planning lacks this direct and agile mechanism.

Variety of Consumer Preferences:

Consumer preferences can vary significantly from one region to another. Central planners may struggle to understand and anticipate this diversity of preferences. Decentralization allows for more effective adaptation to variations in demand.

Local Innovation:

Innovation often arises from local communities in response to specific challenges and opportunities. A decentralized system fosters local innovation by allowing solutions to develop from the closest level to particular circumstances.

Active Community Participation:

Decentralization facilitates active community participation in decision-making that directly affects their lives. This strengthens the connection between decisions made and perceived consequences, leading to greater engagement and responsibility.

Decentralized knowledge highlights the importance of leveraging specific local information for more informed and efficient economic decisions. Centralized planning, unable to capture this knowledge effectively, may encounter significant challenges in resource allocation and adapting to changing market conditions.

Adaptability and Flexibility:

Decentralization allows for greater adaptability and flexibility as conditions change. Local actors can respond more quickly to market fluctuations and changing demands compared to a centralized entity that may have more rigid and bureaucratic procedures.

Adaptability and flexibility are key aspects supporting the critique of centralized planning in favor of decentralization. Here are some points related to this argument:

Quick Response to Local Changes:

In a decentralized environment, local actors have the ability to quickly adapt to changes in market conditions, consumer demands, or local economic situations. Decisions can be made swiftly and directly, without depending on a distant central authority.

Innovation and Experimentation:

Decentralization encourages innovation and experimentation at the local level. Companies and individuals have the freedom to try out new ideas and approaches without waiting for central approval. This can lead to more creative and efficient solutions, especially in contexts requiring constant adaptation.

Diversity of Approaches:

Since different communities and regions may have diverse needs and contexts, decentralization allows for the implementation of specific approaches tailored to those particular conditions. This contrasts with the uniformity that may arise from centralized decisions that do not take local variations into account.

Decentralization of Decision-Making:

Decentralization involves delegating decision-making to the local level. This means decisions can be made closer to the people and businesses affected, increasing the likelihood that solutions are relevant and effective for local circumstances.

Greater Business Agility:

Local businesses can adjust their strategies and operations more quickly and efficiently in a decentralized environment. They can respond immediately to changes in market demand, local economic conditions, and other variables affecting their operations.

Less Bureaucratic Rigidity:

Bureaucratic processes are often less rigid in a decentralized environment. Local authorities can adapt and adjust procedures more easily to meet changing needs without going through extensive layers of bureaucratic hierarchy.

Local Empowerment:

Decentralization empowers local communities and businesses by giving them more control over their own decisions. This not only drives adaptability but also strengthens the sense of local responsibility and participation.

The inherent adaptability and flexibility of decentralization make it a more dynamic and responsive option to changes, allowing for quick and personalized responses to local needs and conditions. This stands in contrast to the potential rigidity of centralized planning, emphasizing the importance of decentralization in economic and social environments.

Innovation and Creativity:

Decentralization fosters innovation and creativity by allowing multiple entities to try different approaches and experiment with diverse solutions. Decentralized competition can drive continuous improvement and the pursuit of more effective solutions.

The relationship between decentralization, innovation, and creativity is a fundamental point in the critique of centralized planning.

Variety of Approaches:

In a decentralized environment, various entities have the freedom to try different approaches to address problems or meet needs. This variety of perspectives and strategies can lead to innovative solutions that might not have been considered in a more centralized system.

Competition among Entities:

Decentralization encourages competition among various entities, whether businesses, organizations, or communities. Competition acts as a stimulus for innovation, as each entity seeks to stand out and offer more effective solutions or improved products and services to gain a competitive advantage.

Learning Through Experimentation:

Decentralization allows for experimentation at the local level. Entities can try out new ideas, adjust strategies, and learn directly from experience. This process of learning through experimentation is essential for the continuous generation of innovative ideas.

Market Feedback: In a decentralized system, market feedback plays a crucial role in guiding innovation. Market responses to new ideas or products provide valuable information about their viability and acceptance. This feedback contributes to continuous improvement and adaptation to changing needs.

Empowerment of Local Creativity: Decentralization empowers local communities and businesses to be creative and seek solutions tailored to their own realities. Local creativity can be more effective in addressing specific challenges facing a community compared to general solutions from a central authority.

Diversity of Innovation: Decentralization fosters diversity in innovation. Different entities can excel in specific areas or find unique approaches to solving problems. This diversity in innovation contributes to a broader landscape of possible solutions.

Agility to Adopt New Ideas: Decentralized entities can adopt new ideas more quickly and efficiently. They are not constrained by bureaucratic processes and extensive hierarchies that can hinder the adoption of innovations in a more centralized environment.

Decentralization creates a conducive environment for innovation and creativity by allowing diverse entities to explore ideas and strategies autonomously. This adaptability and experimentation contribute to a dynamic process of continuous improvement.

Citizen Participation: Local or individual autonomy also promotes citizen participation. When decisions are made centrally, there can be a sense of alienation and lack of control among citizens.

Citizen Empowerment and Local Control: Decentralization gives communities and individuals greater control over decisions affecting their lives. This autonomy promotes a sense of empowerment and responsibility while reducing the perception of alienation often associated with distant centralized decisions.

Active Participation: When decisions are made locally, there is a higher likelihood of citizens actively participating in the decision-making process. Active participation involves contributing ideas, opinions, and efforts to decisions that directly affect the community.

Connection to Local Issues: Decentralization facilitates a direct connection between citizens and local issues. With greater control over decisions, citizens can more effectively address the specific challenges their community faces, as they have a deeper understanding of their needs and circumstances.

Sense of Belonging: Citizen participation strengthens the sense of belonging to a community. When citizens have the ability to contribute to local decisions, the sense of identity and connection to the place they live is reinforced.

Transparency and Accountability: Decentralization promotes transparency and accountability at the local level. Citizens have more direct access to information about decisions made and how they impact the community. This contributes to a more transparent process and greater accountability for decision-makers.

Variety in Participation: Different communities can adopt unique approaches to citizen participation, adapting to their own preferences and needs. Decentralization allows for a variety of participatory models that may be more effective and meaningful for each community.

Strengthening Civil Society: Citizen participation strengthens civil society by fostering organization and collaboration among citizens. Communities can come together to address common problems and work toward shared goals.

Citizen participation is an essential component of decentralization, empowering citizens to be active participants in decision-making that affects their lives and communities. This contributes to more inclusive, transparent, and locally tailored governance.

Risk of Bureaucracy and Corruption: Centralized systems are often associated with increased bureaucracy and the risk of corruption. Decentralization can help reduce these problems by placing more decisions in the hands of local actors and limiting the concentration of power.

Decentralization as an Anti-corruption Measure: Decentralization is considered an anti-corruption measure as it distributes power and responsibilities among local entities. By limiting the concentration of authority in the hands of a central entity, the opportunity for large-scale corruption is reduced.

Greater Transparency and Accountability: Decentralized decision-making favors transparency and accountability at the local level. Decision-making processes are more accessible to citizens, making it easier to detect and report corrupt practices. Additionally, direct local accountability may deter officials from engaging in corruption.

Less Bureaucracy: Centralized systems tend to generate extensive bureaucratic structures to manage and coordinate a wide range of activities. Decentralization, by shifting decisions and responsibilities to the local level, can reduce the need for excessive bureaucracy, thereby decreasing opportunities for corrupt practices.

Active Civil Society Participation: Active participation of civil society, facilitated by decentralization, can act as a counterbalance to corruption. When citizens are directly involved in local decision-making, they are more likely to monitor and question officials' actions, contributing to a more transparent environment.

Adaptability and Efficiency: Decentralization can also make administration more efficient and adaptable. Local entities often have a deeper understanding of specific needs and conditions, reducing the need for bureaucratic layers to interpret and implement decisions from above.

Less Concentration of Resources: In centralized systems, the concentration of resources and authority in the hands of a few can create opportunities for corruption. Decentralization disperses both authority and resources, decreasing the likelihood of corruption having a systemic impact.

In summary, decentralization is presented as a strategy to mitigate the risk of bureaucracy and corruption by promoting transparency, accountability, and active citizen participation at the local level. This contributes to more efficient, adaptable, and ethical governance.

Respect for Diversity: Decentralization and autonomy respect the diversity of cultural, social, and economic contexts. They allow for the adaptation of policies and approaches according to the specific characteristics of each region or community.

Adaptation to Local Contexts: Decentralization allows for more effective adaptation of policies and approaches to local contexts. Different regions or communities may have unique needs, challenges, and priorities, and decentralization facilitates the customization of strategies to address these differences.

Valuing Cultural Identities: By decentralizing decision-making, diversity of cultural identities is recognized and valued. Policies and programs can be designed to respect and reflect local cultural identities, promoting greater social cohesion.

Active Community Participation: Local autonomy encourages active community participation in decision-making. This means that people who know their communities best can contribute significantly to the formulation and implementation of policies that respect diversity.

Flexibility in Implementation: Decentralization allows for greater flexibility in the implementation of programs and policies. Local authorities can adjust strategies based on the specific characteristics of their communities, recognizing that there is no one-size-fits-all approach.

Local Problem Solving: Local autonomy empowers communities to effectively address specific problems they face. This may include issues related to culture, the environment, the economy, and other aspects that are distinctive to each region.

Promotion of Tolerance: Decentralization contributes to the promotion of tolerance by recognizing and respecting differences. Allowing different communities to choose their own policies fosters an environment in which diverse perspectives can coexist and enrich each other.

Strengthening Local Identities: Through decentralization, local identities and self-determination are strengthened. Communities have the ability to define and protect their own identities, preserving their unique traditions and values.

Decentralization and autonomy are essential for respecting diversity, allowing policies and decisions to adapt to the richness of cultural, social, and economic contexts present in different regions and communities. This contributes to more inclusive governance that respects differences.

The critique of centralized planning is based on the idea that decentralization and autonomy are more effective in harnessing decentralized knowledge, fostering innovation, adapting to changing conditions, and promoting citizen participation. These arguments are central to debates on efficiency and equity in the organization of economic and political systems.

18.Theory of Time Preference

The theory of time preference is fundamental in economics and highlights how people value goods and services in relation to time.

Definition of Time Preference: Time preference refers to the idea that people tend to value present goods and services more than future ones. In other words, there is a bias toward immediate gratification compared to waiting for benefits in the future.

Discounting Future Value: The theory implies that the value of a good or service decreases as it is projected into the future. This phenomenon is known as time discounting. The discount rate represents how quickly people discount the value of future benefits.

Discounting future value is a fundamental feature of time preference. This idea suggests that, in general, people tend to assign less value to future benefits compared to present ones. The discount rate is a measure of the speed at which this discount occurs and may vary depending on individual circumstances and market interest rates. The discount rate is crucial in contexts such as the evaluation of long-term investment projects, where the present value of future cash flows is considered.

Influence on Economic Decisions: Time preference influences a variety of economic decisions. For example, it affects saving and investment decisions, the evaluation of long-term investment projects, and consumption decisions. It can also have implications in areas such as financial planning and business decision-making.

Saving and Investment: Time preference affects saving decisions by influencing the choice between consuming now or postponing consumption for the future. Additionally, it influences investment decisions as people assess the profitability of investing money today for future benefits.

Evaluation of Long-Term Investment Projects: In the evaluation of long-term projects, where the flow of benefits over time is considered, time preference is essential. Discount rates are used to calculate the present value of future cash flows, affecting the feasibility of these projects.

Consumption Decisions: Time preference influences consumption decisions by determining whether people are willing to delay satisfaction to acquire goods or services later or if they prefer to enjoy them immediately.

Financial Planning: In personal financial planning, time preference plays a crucial role in determining how people allocate their income among current consumption, savings, and investments to meet their short and long-term goals.

Business Decision-Making: Companies also consider time preference when making investment and financing decisions. Long-term strategic planning and project evaluation require taking into account how time is valued in decision-making.

Time preference is a key consideration in economics and decision-making, and its understanding is essential to grasp how individuals and businesses allocate resources over time.

Considerations in Decision-Making: In decision-making, individuals balance their time preferences with other factors, such as uncertainty about the future, investment opportunities, and long-term goals. These factors can modulate how time preference is applied in specific situations.

Uncertainty about the Future: Uncertainty about future events can influence how people apply their time preference. Risk aversion and perceptions of economic stability can affect the willingness to delay gratification

Investment Opportunities: Investment opportunities can alter decisions based on time preference. If there are investment opportunities offering significant returns in the future, people may be more willing to postpone consumption.

Long-Term Goals: Long-term goals, such as buying a house, children's education, or retirement, can influence how people apply their time preference. Setting clear long-term goals can affect saving and investment decisions.

Cultural and Social Context: Cultural and social factors also play a role. In some cultures, there may be a greater preference for saving and long-term planning, while in others, the emphasis may be more on immediate consumption.

Income Level: An individual's income level can influence their ability to satisfy their time preferences. Those with higher incomes may have more flexibility to balance present and future consumption.

The complex interaction of these factors means that the practical application of time preference can vary considerably between individuals and situations. Economic decisions often result from weighing multiple considerations rather than relying solely on time preference.

Relationship with Interest Rate: The interest rate plays a crucial role in time preference. A higher interest rate can incentivize saving by offering more attractive returns for postponing consumption. On the other hand, lower interest rates may favor immediate consumption.

Savings Incentive: A higher interest rate can incentivize saving, as it offers the possibility of significant returns in the future. People may be more willing to postpone present consumption if rewarded with attractive interest rates.

Cost of Borrowing: On the flip side, a higher interest rate can also make borrowing more expensive. This can influence financing decisions for present consumption. Lower interest rates may make borrowing more attractive.

Evaluation of Investment Projects: In the business realm, the interest rate is crucial when evaluating long-term investment projects. Projects promising returns higher than the interest rate may be more attractive, while higher interest rates can make some projects less viable.

Impact on Investment Decisions: The interest rate also affects investment decisions in financial markets. Investors constantly evaluate interest rates in comparison to available investment opportunities.

Future Expectations: Expectations about how interest rates will change in the future also influence time preference. Individuals and businesses may adjust their decisions based on projections about interest rates.

The interest rate acts as a key mechanism that modulates time preference by influencing consumption, saving, and investment decisions.

Implications in Behavioral Economics: Time preference is also a relevant topic in behavioral economics, which explores how psychological factors influence economic decisions. Lack of self-control and a tendency toward instant gratification are aspects related to time preference.

Self-Control and Instant Gratification: Behavioral economics acknowledges that people often face challenges in self-control, meaning they may have a preference for instant gratification rather than waiting for larger rewards in the future. This phenomenon can influence decisions related to consumption, saving, and investment.

Hyperbolic Discounting: A related concept is hyperbolic discounting, which suggests that people tend to value short-term benefits more than long-term benefits, even if the difference in magnitude is small. This can explain behaviors such as procrastination in financial decision-making.

Temporal Dissonance: Temporal dissonance is the discrepancy between an individual's current preferences and future preferences. Behavioral economics studies explore how interventions and strategies can help better align time preferences with long-term goals.

Interventions to Improve Decision-Making: Interventions have been proposed to enhance decision-making in situations where temporal preference may lead to suboptimal outcomes. These interventions may include reminders, long-term incentives, and choice design strategies that encourage decisions more aligned with long-term goals.

Applications in Public Policies: Understanding temporal preference is crucial for designing effective public policies. For instance, in the realm of pensions and retirement savings, understanding how individuals value the future can inform the implementation of policies that encourage long-term savings.

Overall, the intersection of temporal preference and behavioral economics offers valuable insights for understanding and addressing challenges associated with decision-making in economic and financial contexts.

Challenges in Long-Term Planning: Temporal preference poses challenges for long-term planning, as individuals may struggle to commit to actions that yield benefits in the future due to a preference for immediate rewards.

Difficulties in Retirement and Savings: In the financial domain, temporal preference may translate into difficulties committing to long-term savings, especially for retirement. Individuals may underestimate the importance of early saving due to a preference for immediate consumption.

Investment Decisions: Long-term investment, which often involves tolerance for volatility and waiting for returns over time, can be challenging for those with a strong preference for quick results. This can impact decision-making in the investment market.

Health and Well-being: In the health domain, individuals may find it challenging to commit to habits and behaviors that yield long-term benefits, such as a healthy diet and regular exercise. Instant gratification may override the adoption of health-beneficial behaviors.

Public Policies and Education: Public policies and educational programs may face challenges in motivating people to commit to actions that yield future benefits. Strategies addressing temporal preference, such as persuasive messages and choice design approaches, may be necessary.

Effective Communication: Effective communication about long-term benefits and the importance of future planning is essential. Clear messages highlighting long-term rewards, perhaps using approaches that also present short-term benefits, can help overcome temporal preference.

Nudging Approaches: Aligned with behavioral economics, nudging approaches have been proposed to leverage human psychology to influence decisions. These approaches can be used to assist individuals in making decisions that better align with their long-term goals.

In summary, temporal preference presents significant challenges for long-term planning in various areas, and addressing these challenges requires approaches that consider psychology and human behavior. The theory of temporal preference is essential for understanding how individuals value and make decisions based on time, with important implications in various aspects of economic decision-making.

19.Institutions and Economic Development

The Austrian School of Economics emphasizes the fundamental importance of institutions in economic development.

Institutional Framework: The Austrian School asserts that the institutional framework within which economic agents operate is crucial in determining economic development. Institutions, understood as the rules of the game in a society, influence individual and collective decision-making.

Definition of Institutions: From the Austrian perspective, institutions are the rules of the game that structure economic and social interactions in a society. They include norms, laws, regulations, and cultural practices that define how people conduct transactions and make decisions.

Impact on Individual Decisions: These institutions have a direct impact on individual decisions. Institutional rules and structures influence how people assess risks, make investment decisions, undertake projects, and engage in economic exchanges.

Private Property and Contracts: The protection of private property and the ability to make and enforce contracts are crucial institutions. Private property provides incentives for care and investment in resources, while contracts are agreements that enable cooperation and exchange.

Social Coordination: Ludwig von Mises, a prominent Austrian economist, argued that property rights are essential for social coordination. Private property allows individuals to allocate resources efficiently and respond to market signals.

Entrepreneurship Development: Institutions supporting entrepreneurial freedom and the ability to take risks are fundamental for economic development. Entrepreneurship is seen as a key driver of innovation and the introduction of new goods and services.

Competition and Discovery: Competition in a solid institutional framework allows the discovery of market opportunities and continuous adjustment to changing consumer preferences. Adaptability is essential for sustainable economic development.

Critiques of State Intervention: From the Austrian perspective, excessive state intervention in the economy can distort market signals and create artificial barriers, negatively affecting economic development. Government policies can harmfully alter the institutional game.

Crises and Institutional Adjustment: According to the Austrian School, economic crises are often linked to institutional mismatches. Changes in policies and regulations can influence the direction of economic development, either facilitating or hindering entrepreneurial activity and investment.

The Austrian School emphasizes that economic development is intrinsically linked to the institutional framework, and the quality of institutions can determine the efficiency, innovation, and adaptability of an economy.

Private Property and Contracts: The protection of private property and the ability to make and enforce contracts are fundamental institutions for the efficient functioning of an economy. Security in property and reliable contract enforcement are pillars that foster investment, innovation, and cooperation.

Protection of Private Property: Private property, from the Austrian perspective, is fundamental to economic development. It provides individuals with a clear incentive to care for and improve their resources. When people have secure property rights, they are more inclined to invest time and resources in the maintenance and improvement of their properties.

Incentives for Investment: Property security creates an environment conducive to investment. When individuals are certain they will reap the rewards of their efforts, they are more willing to undertake long-term projects. This fosters capital accumulation and contributes to sustainable economic growth.

Contract Enforcement: The ability to make and enforce contracts is another key institution. Contracts are voluntary agreements that facilitate cooperation and exchange in society. When parties trust that contracts will be executed fairly and efficiently, they are more willing to engage in commercial transactions and long-term collaborations.

Social Cooperation: Ludwig von Mises, in his work "Human Action," highlighted that private property and contracts are essential for social cooperation. In a society where these principles are respected, individuals can coordinate their actions more efficiently, responding to market signals and satisfying the needs and desires of others.

Conflict Prevention: The clear definition of property rights and reliable contract enforcement also help prevent conflicts. When property rights are respected, disputes over resource possession are less likely, contributing to social and economic stability.

Innovation and Entrepreneurship: Property security and the ability to enter into contracts are fundamental to fostering innovation and entrepreneurship. Entrepreneurs are more willing to take risks when they are confident they will enjoy the benefits of their successes.

Critiques of Governmental Intervention: The Austrian School often criticizes excessive government intervention in the economy, as it can undermine the protection of private property and contract enforcement. Excessive regulations and interventionist policies can distort these fundamental institutions.

In summary, private property and contracts, as fundamental institutions, provide the necessary framework for coordinated human action, long-term investment, and economic development from the Austrian perspective.

Property Rights and Social Coordination: Ludwig von Mises, a prominent representative of the Austrian School, emphasized that property rights are essential for social coordination. Private property allows individuals to allocate resources efficiently and respond to market signals.

Property Rights and Social Coordination according to Ludwig von Mises: Ludwig von Mises, an influential Austrian economist, developed the idea that property rights are fundamental to social coordination and the efficient functioning of the economy. Here are some key points highlighting his perspective:

Coordination through Market Signals: Mises argued that private property enables social coordination by facilitating the transmission of information through market signals. In a system based on private property, prices act as indicators of scarcity and demand, providing valuable information on how to allocate resources efficiently.

Human Action and Private Property: In his work "Human Action," Mises contended that private property is a natural outcome of human action. As individuals seek to satisfy their needs and goals, property relationships emerge to facilitate cooperation and coordination in society.

Conflict Prevention and Efficient Resource Use:

Mises also emphasized that property rights help prevent conflicts over resource use. When property rights are clearly defined, individuals have incentives to use resources efficiently and avoid unnecessary conflicts.

Entrepreneurship and Economic Calculation:

Private property is essential for economic calculation and entrepreneurship. Mises argued that without the existence of markets and private property, centralized planning cannot efficiently carry out economic calculation, as it lacks the prices and dispersed information necessary for informed decision-making.

Challenges of Government Intervention:

Mises also criticized excessive government intervention, considering it undermines property rights and distorts market signals. Interference with private property, according to Mises, leads to misallocations of resources and economic imbalances.

In summary, Ludwig von Mises advocated for the importance of property rights in social coordination and the efficient functioning of the economy. Private property, from his perspective, not only allows for efficient resource allocation but also serves as the foundation for entrepreneurship, economic calculation, and conflict prevention in society.

Entrepreneurship and Development:

The Austrian perspective highlights the role of entrepreneurship in the economic development process. Institutions supporting entrepreneurial freedom and risk-taking are vital for introducing new ideas, products, and services to the market.

Innovation and Change:

From the Austrian perspective, entrepreneurship is closely linked to the introduction of innovations and economic change. Entrepreneurs are agents of change seeking to identify undiscovered opportunities and create value through new ideas, products, or services.

Opportunity Discovery:

Entrepreneurs, according to Austrian theory, are actors who discover profit opportunities in the market. These opportunities may arise from changes in consumer demand, technological advances, or simply the entrepreneur's ability to see connections and possibilities that others may overlook.

Competition and Coordination:

Competition among entrepreneurs is seen as a mechanism driving continuous improvement and economic efficiency. While competing to satisfy consumer needs and desires, entrepreneurs contribute to the effective coordination of resources in the economy.

Risk and Return:

Entrepreneurship involves taking risks. Entrepreneurs are willing to invest time, effort, and financial resources in projects that may succeed or fail. The potential reward for taking this risk is economic profit and the development of new opportunities.

Entrepreneurial Freedom:

Institutions supporting entrepreneurial freedom are essential for the flourishing of entrepreneurship. The ability of individuals to initiate and manage businesses, as well as to compete in the market, contributes to a dynamic environment where innovative ideas can thrive.

Economic Cycles:

Austrian theory also highlights how entrepreneurs can play a role in economic cycles. During boom phases, entrepreneurial activity often intensifies, but overinvestment and poor business decisions can contribute to contraction phases.

In summary, the Austrian perspective views entrepreneurship as a key driver of economic development. Entrepreneurs, by discovering opportunities and taking risks, bring about changes, promote competition, and contribute to the efficient coordination of resources in the economy. Entrepreneurial freedom and the ability to innovate are considered crucial institutions for this process.

Competition and Discovery:

Competition in a solid institutional environment allows for the discovery of market opportunities and continuous adjustment to changing consumer preferences. Adaptability is key to sustainable economic development.

Competition as a Dynamic Process:

From the Austrian perspective, competition is not seen solely as a static state but as a dynamic process. Competition is a mechanism through which economic actors seek to improve and differentiate themselves to attract consumers.

Competition and Adaptation:

In a competitive environment, companies constantly seek to adapt to changing market conditions. This adaptation process is essential for the discovery of new opportunities and efficiency in resource allocation.

Opportunity Discovery:

Effective competition drives companies to be attentive to market opportunities The introduction of new products, services, or innovative approaches arises as a response to market signals and competition among companies to satisfy consumer needs.

Decentralized Information:

Competition decentralizes information about consumer preferences. Companies compete to understand and respond to these preferences, contributing to the continuous discovery of untapped opportunities.

Effects on Production Structure:

Competition can have significant effects on the production structure of an economy. More efficient companies capable of meeting market demands tend to thrive, while less adaptable ones may face difficulties.

Institutions Facilitating Competition:

Robust institutions, such as protection of private property, contract enforcement, and a clear legal framework, are crucial for effective competition. These elements provide the necessary environment for companies to compete fairly and for the discovery process to be efficient.

Adaptability and Economic Development:

Competition-driven adaptability contributes to sustainable economic development. Companies that can quickly adjust to market changes are more likely to thrive, and this overall dynamism benefits the economy.

In summary, the Austrian perspective argues that competition, when rooted in robust institutions, is not only an efficiency driver but also a facilitator of continuous opportunity discovery. This dynamic process of competition and adaptation is fundamental for long-term economic development.

Critiques of State Intervention:

The Austrian School tends to be critical of excessive state intervention in the economy. It argues that government institutions can distort market signals and create artificial barriers to entry and exit, negatively affecting economic development.

Distortion of Market Signals:

State intervention, through regulations and economic policies, can distort market signals that normally guide economic actors' decisions. This can lead to inefficient business decisions and inadequate resource allocation.

Artificial Barriers to Entry and Exit:

Government interventions sometimes create artificial barriers to market entry and exit. This can result in the persistence of inefficient companies and hinder the ability of new businesses to enter and compete, impeding innovation and improving economic efficiency.

Lack of Local Knowledge:

Centralized decision-making often lacks detailed knowledge of local conditions and the specific preferences of individuals and companies. The Austrian School argues that this decentralized knowledge is crucial for economic efficiency and that government interventions may ignore it.

Perverse Incentives:

State intervention can create perverse incentives by discouraging competition and innovation. Economic actors may rely on political favors instead of improving their efficiency and meeting market needs.

Central Planning and Economic Calculation:

The Austrian School, following Ludwig von Mises' reasoning, highlights the practical impossibility of efficient central planning due to the lack of an effective economic calculation mechanism without free market prices.

Rigidities and Lack of Adaptability:

State intervention sometimes introduces rigidities into the economy, making it difficult for companies to quickly adapt to changes in market conditions. Lack of adaptability can negatively affect sustainable economic development.

The Austrian School's critique of state intervention focuses on its negative impact on market signals, competition, innovation, and the economy's adaptability. These arguments reinforce the importance the Austrian School places on market forces and individual freedom in pursuing economic development.

Crisis and Institutional Adjustment:

The Austrian School also examines how economic crises are often related to institutional imbalances. Changes in policies and regulations can influence the direction of economic development, either facilitating or hindering entrepreneurial activity and investment.

Discoordination and Economic Cycles:

According to the Austrian School, economic crises are often the result of discoordination in the production structure caused by market interventions, such as excessive credit expansion or manipulation of interest rates. These imbalances can lead to economic cycles with boom and bust phases.

Monetary and Credit Policies:

Government intervention in financial markets, especially through monetary and credit policies, is viewed critically. Excessive money creation and manipulation of interest rates can distort investment decisions and contribute to misallocations of resources, contributing to economic crises.

Institutional Adjustment in Crisis:

During crises, the Austrian School suggests that institutional adjustment may be necessary to correct imbalances. This involves reconsidering and, in some cases, reversing policies that contributed to the crisis, restoring conditions favorable to effective market coordination.

Liquidation Process:

The Austrian School advocates for a natural liquidation process during crises. This involves allowing inefficient companies to fail and reallocating resources to more productive activities. This perspective contrasts with approaches that seek to sustain nonviable companies through government interventions.

Structural Imbalances and Rationalization:

Crises often reveal structural imbalances in the economy. The Austrian School suggests that, instead of trying to artificially maintain the existing structure, it is beneficial to allow the natural rationalization of production and investment to align with market realities.

Lessons Learned:

From the Austrian perspective, crises offer important lessons about the need to avoid interventions that distort market signals and the importance of institutions that foster entrepreneurial freedom, competition, and economic adaptability.

The Austrian School examines economic crises as the result of institutional interventions that create imbalances in the production structure and advocates for institutional adjustments and liquidation processes to restore conditions conducive to efficient market coordination.

20.Game Theory and Markets

Game theory is a mathematical field that models strategic interactions among different "players" or rational agents in specific situations. Applying game theory to market situations provides an analytical tool to understand how participants' strategic decisions impact market outcomes and dynamics. Here are some key aspects of how game theory is applied to market situations:

Strategic Games in Markets: Markets can be understood as strategic game environments where participants, such as producers and consumers, make decisions to maximize their own interests. Competition, pricing, and other strategic decisions are central elements of these games.

Rationality of Participants: Game theory in markets assumes that participants are rational and seek to maximize their own interests. This implies that strategic decisions are made based on a careful evaluation of available options and possible responses from other participants.

Competition and Business Strategies: In a competitive market, companies must carefully consider their strategies to stand out. This includes decisions about pricing, advertising, product quality, and other factors that can affect their market position.

Collusion and Cooperation: Strategic games can also model situations where companies may cooperate (collude) to maximize joint benefits. However, competition and the possibility of companies pursuing their own interests often prevail.

Information and Asymmetries: Information asymmetry among participants is a key element. Some participants may have access to information that others do not, affecting their strategies and decisions.

Market Entry and Exit: The decision to enter or exit the market can be modeled as a strategic game. Companies carefully consider entry barriers, existing competition, and market opportunities when making participation decisions.

Pricing is a crucial component of strategic games in markets. Companies must consider how their pricing decisions will affect their market share and how competitors might respond.

Network Effects and Marketing Strategies: In markets where network effects are relevant (e.g., technology and social networks), marketing strategies and standard adoption can be modeled as strategic games. Companies seek to gain consumer preference to strengthen their market position.

Regulation and Policy: Government intervention and regulatory policies can also be considered as elements in strategic games in markets. Companies must anticipate and respond to changes in regulations to adapt to new playing conditions.

The application of game theory to markets allows for the analysis of participants' strategies and decisions, modeling the complexities of competition, cooperation, and decision-making in an economic environment.

Strategies and Outcomes: Game theory analyzes the strategies participants can follow and how these strategies affect game outcomes. In the context of markets, this involves examining how pricing decisions, advertising, market entry, and other strategic actions impact competition and profits.

Nash Equilibrium: Game theory seeks to identify Nash equilibrium, where each participant makes the best possible decision given the set of decisions made by other participants. In the context of markets, this could be an equilibrium where no individual company can unilaterally improve its position.

Zero-Sum Games vs. Cooperative Games: In some cases, market competition can be modeled as zero-sum games, where one participant's gains equal another's losses. However, situations can also be modeled where participants can cooperate for mutual benefits, known as cooperative games.

Strategic Competition: Market strategies go beyond pricing. They include decisions about advertising, product differentiation, market expansion, mergers, and acquisitions, among others. Analyzing how these strategies affect game outcomes is essential to understanding market dynamics.

Reputation and Long-Term Strategies: Building reputation is a long-term strategy that can have significant impacts on market behavior.

Companies may pursue strategies that not only maximize short-term profits but also build a strong reputation for sustainable gains.

Sequential Games: In some markets, decisions are not made simultaneously but sequentially. Analyzing sequential games involves considering how actions taken at one moment affect decisions and strategies in future moments.

Market Entry and Exit: Entry and exit strategies are also fundamental. Companies must carefully evaluate when and how to enter or exit a market to maximize their benefits.

Strategy Changes: Game theory allows for the analysis of how changes in participants' strategies affect market outcomes over time. This is crucial for understanding competition dynamics as they evolve.

Learning and Adaptation: Market participants can learn from past interactions and adapt their strategies accordingly. Game theory addresses how learning and adaptation influence market dynamics.

The analysis of strategies and outcomes in game theory provides a powerful tool for understanding and predicting the behavior of market participants, as well as evaluating how strategic decisions affect economic outcomes.

Competition and Collusion: Game theory can model competition between companies and also the possibility of collusion, where companies cooperate to set prices and market shares for their own benefit. The application of non-cooperative and cooperative games can shed light on competition dynamics in the market.

Competition (Non-Cooperative Games): In competitive situations, companies make decisions independently, without coordinating with others. Modeling this competition as a non-cooperative game involves analyzing strategies such as pricing, advertising, product development, and market expansion.

Prisoner's Dilemma in Collusion: Game theory can also be applied to the prisoner's dilemma when it comes to collusive agreements. Companies face the temptation to break collusion for individual gains, but if all make this decision, the result is worse for everyone. This prisoner's dilemma can explain why maintaining collusive agreements in the long term can be challenging.

Collusion Equilibrium: Modeling collusion involves seeking equilibriums where companies cooperate to maximize their joint benefits. In these cooperative games, companies can set prices jointly, divide the market, or coordinate strategies to avoid destructive competition.

Collusion Traps: Game theory can also help understand collusion traps, where companies may be tempted to break collusive agreements for a competitive advantage. Analyzing the strategies and consequences of these traps is crucial for understanding the stability of cartels and other collusive agreements.

Sequential Games in Collusion: In some cases, collusion can be a sequential game where companies make decisions sequentially. A leader may set the tone for cooperation, and other companies may follow or deviate. This type of modeling can help understand how collusion unfolds over time.

Regulation and Oversight: Game theory also applies to the analysis of regulatory and oversight strategies to prevent collusion. Authorities can design incentives and sanctions to discourage collusion and encourage competition.

Anti-Collusion Strategies: Companies can develop anti-collusion strategies to protect themselves against anticompetitive practices. These strategies may include adopting transparent practices, constant innovation, and seeking efficiencies to remain competitive without resorting to collusive agreements.

In summary, game theory provides a powerful analytical framework for understanding the dynamics of competition and collusion in markets, as well as for designing effective business and regulatory strategies.

Nash Equilibrium:

The concept of Nash equilibrium is fundamental in game theory and refers to a situation where no player can unilaterally improve their position. In the context of markets, this can represent an equilibrium of prices and strategies where no individual firm has incentives to change its strategic focus.

Strategic Stability: In Nash equilibrium, no firm has incentives to change its strategy given the current strategies of others. This state is associated with a certain strategic stability, as firms have no reasons to deviate from their current course.

Application to Pricing: In the context of price competition, Nash equilibrium may reflect a situation where no firm can unilaterally change its price to gain higher profits, given the current prices of competitors.

Cartels and Collusion: In the case of collusive agreements or cartels, Nash equilibrium in this context implies that no firm has incentives to defect from the agreement, as doing so could result in a loss of profits. However, these equilibriums can be fragile due to the prisoner's dilemma and collusion traps.

Equilibrium in Non-Cooperative Strategies: Nash equilibrium particularly applies to non-cooperative strategies, where each firm maximizes its own interests without direct coordination with others. In this context, Nash equilibrium can represent a form of self-regulation in the market.

Dynamics of Change in Equilibrium: Although Nash equilibrium implies that no firm has incentives to change its strategy given the strategies of others, market dynamics can change over time, and new strategies may emerge in response to changes in market conditions.

Monopolistic Competition: In situations of monopolistic competition, where several firms offer similar but not identical products, Nash equilibrium may reflect the situation where each firm chooses its production level and price to maximize profits, given the prices of others.

Regulation and Antitrust Policy: The analysis of Nash equilibrium can also be applied to the design of antitrust policies and regulations to promote competition and prevent firms from reaching equilibriums that may be harmful to consumers.

In conclusion, Nash equilibrium is a valuable tool for understanding and analyzing strategies and outcomes in strategic situations, providing important insights into how firms interact in markets.

Information Asymmetry: Game theory also addresses information asymmetry, where some participants have more information than others. In markets, this can refer to situations where sellers know more about the quality of a product than buyers. Modeling these asymmetries can help understand how markets develop in the presence of unequal information.

Adverse Selection: In the presence of information asymmetry, the problem of adverse selection can arise. This occurs when one party has private information about certain relevant aspects (e.g., the quality of a product) and uses this information for their own benefit at the expense of the other party.

Principal-Agent Problem: Information asymmetry also relates to the principal-agent problem, where one party (the principal) delegates decision-making to another party (the agent) who has private information. Here, the principal may have difficulty ensuring that the agent acts in their best interest due to unequal information.

Effects on Competition and Prices: Information asymmetry can affect competition and prices. For example, if buyers do not have complete information about the quality of products, sellers may have incentives to offer lower-quality products at higher prices.

Guarantees and Signaling: Companies can use guarantees and signaling strategies to overcome information asymmetry problems. For example, a company with a high-quality product may offer strong guarantees as a way to signal its quality to consumers.

Credibility of Information: The credibility of information is crucial in situations of asymmetry. Parties may have incentives to convey misleading information. Building reputation over time can be a strategy to establish the credibility of provided information.

Regulation and Transparency: Regulation and promoting transparency in markets are common approaches to addressing information asymmetry problems. By ensuring that relevant information is available to all parties, market efficiency and fairness can be improved.

Signaling Theory and Credible Costs: Signaling theory explores how parties can send credible signals about their private information. In some cases, incurring significant costs can be a credible signal of the quality or intentions of a party.

Negotiation Strategies: Information asymmetry also plays a role in negotiation strategies. Parties may try to obtain additional information through negotiation tactics, and the ability to do so can affect the outcome of transactions.

In summary, information asymmetry is an important phenomenon in game theory and economics, and understanding it is essential for addressing challenges in markets and designing effective policies.

Evolutionary Games: Some advanced applications of game theory in economics explore the concept of evolutionary games. This involves successful strategies tending to replicate and spread in a population of economic agents, leading to the evolution of strategic patterns over time.

Reproduction and Selection of Strategies: In evolutionary games, strategies can be seen as "genes" that reproduce and transmit from one generation to another. More successful strategies have a higher probability of being selected and transmitted, similar to the process of natural selection in biological evolution.

Adaptation and Change Over Time: Unlike static games, evolutionary games consider change over time. Successful strategies proliferate but can also change in response to new conditions and challenges in the economic environment.

Diversity of Strategies: Throughout iterations, evolutionary games can lead to the diversification of strategies. This reflects how different approaches can be effective in different contexts, and diversity can be an adaptive response to variability in the environment.

Stability of Strategies: In some cases, certain strategies can stabilize and persist over time if they are successful in continuous adaptation. However, stability does not imply rigidity; strategies can still change in response to new challenges.

Applications in Business Competition: In the business realm, evolutionary games are applied to model competition among firms and how business strategies evolve in response to market conditions, technology, and consumer behavior.

Learning and Imitation: Learning and imitation are key components in evolutionary games. Economic agents can learn from experience and adjust their strategies accordingly. Successful imitation can also lead to the spread of effective strategies.

Applications in Innovation Theory: Evolutionary games also apply to innovation theory, where the evolutionary process models how innovations compete and spread in a population, influencing the direction of technological progress.

Implications for Public Policies: Understanding how strategies evolve in economic environments can have implications for the design of public policies. For example, policies that promote competition and innovation can influence the evolutionary dynamics of the market.

Evolutionary games offer a framework for analyzing the dynamics of competition and adaptation in the economy over time, incorporating concepts from biological evolution into the study of economic strategies.

Mechanism Design and Auctions: Game theory is used to design efficient exchange mechanisms, such as auctions. Analyzing participants' incentives and designing rules that encourage desirable outcomes is a key aspect of applying game theory in market situations.

Mechanism Design: Game theory addresses how to design mechanisms that achieve efficient and desirable outcomes. This is crucial in situations where participants have private information, and outcomes depend on individual actions.

Incentives and Desirable Outcomes: Mechanism design involves understanding participants' incentives and how these affect game outcomes. Game structures are sought that motivate participants to reveal accurate information and take actions leading to socially efficient results.

Auctions and Competition: In the specific case of auctions, game theory analyzes how to design auctions that promote competition and efficiently allocate goods. Different types of auctions, such as English auctions, Dutch auctions, and first-price auctions, have distinct strategic properties.

Information Revelation: Game theory addresses information revelation problems in auctions. Questions like what information participants should reveal, how competition affects information revelation, and how auction design can influence revealed information are critical aspects.

Learning and Iterative Strategies: Repeated interactions, as in recurrent auctions, allow participants to learn and adjust their strategies over time. Game theory analyzes how strategies evolve in dynamic environments.

Bayesian Equilibrium: Bayesian equilibrium is an important concept in mechanism design. It refers to strategies and outcomes that are consistent with rational expectations and beliefs about participants' private information.

Ascending vs. Descending Auctions: Game theory can help compare the strategic properties of ascending and descending auctions. Ascending auctions, where prices increase, may have different strategic effects compared to descending auctions, where prices decrease.

Practical Applications: Conclusions from game theory in mechanism and auction design apply to real-world contexts, such as spectrum allocation in telecommunications auctions, carbon emissions auctions, and government tendering.

Game theory is a valuable tool for designing mechanisms that promote efficiency and competition in exchange situations, especially in the context of auctions and resource allocation.

Game theory provides a valuable analytical framework for understanding strategic decision-making in market situations, from competition among firms to price formation and the design of efficient exchange mechanisms.

21.Globalization and Free Trade

A positive attitude towards globalization and free trade is based on the idea that these phenomena are key drivers of economic growth and have significant benefits.

Economic Growth: Globalization and free trade enable access to broader markets, which can stimulate economic growth. Opening up to international competition can foster efficiency, innovation, and productivity.

Access to Broader Markets: Globalization facilitates access to larger and more diverse markets. Companies can expand their reach beyond national borders, increasing their customer base and, consequently, their growth opportunities.

Stimulation of Competition: Opening up to international competition encourages companies to become more efficient and innovate to remain competitive. This process of competition favors continuous improvement and economic growth.

Technology Diffusion: Globalization allows the transfer of technology between countries. Companies can adopt and adapt advanced technologies in use elsewhere in the world, contributing to economic growth.

Utilization of Global Resources: Countries can leverage natural and human resources available in other regions, promoting economic development by allowing a more efficient allocation of resources.

Stimulation of Foreign Investment: Opening up to foreign direct investment is common in a globalized environment. This investment can generate employment, knowledge transfer, and contribute to infrastructure development, thus driving economic growth.

Global Value Chains: Participation in global value chains, where different production stages occur in different countries, can enhance efficiency and create opportunities for economic growth.

Expansion of Export Sectors: Globalization allows countries to specialize in sectors where they have comparative advantages and export those products worldwide. This can lead to a significant increase in income and employment.

Income Generation: Opening up to international markets can generate additional income for companies and the government through exports. These revenues can be reinvested in the economy, stimulating growth.

In summary, access to broader markets, competition, technology transfer, and efficient global resource allocation are key factors contributing to the economic growth associated with globalization and free trade.

Increased Efficiency: Specialization and trade based on comparative advantages allow countries to focus on producing goods and services in which they are most efficient. This leads to a more efficient global resource allocation.

Specialization: Globalization promotes countries' specialization in producing goods and services in which they have comparative advantages. Each country focuses on what it can produce most efficiently in relative terms, leading to a more efficient global resource allocation.

Productive Efficiency: By allowing each country to specialize in the production of goods and services in which it is most efficient, global productive efficiency is maximized. This means achieving more production with fewer resources, freeing up resources for other uses.

Cost Reduction: Specialization and international trade can lead to a reduction in production costs. Countries can import goods and services that they can produce more efficiently elsewhere, resulting in more affordable end products for consumers.

Global Production Growth: By facilitating specialization and exchange, globalization contributes to the growth of global production. Countries can benefit from the diversity of resources and skills available in different parts of the world.

Innovation and Continuous Improvement: Global competition fosters innovation and continuous improvement. Companies seek ways to improve the quality of their products and reduce costs to stay competitive in a global market.

Access to Foreign Goods and Services: Consumers benefit from accessing a wide variety of goods and services from different parts of the world. This improves their well-being by providing more diverse and often more affordable options.

Optimization of Natural Resources: Globalization allows the optimization of natural resources worldwide. Countries can leverage their specific natural resources for production in which they are most efficient, rather than trying to produce everything locally.

The increased efficiency derived from specialization and exchange based on comparative advantages is a key component of the economic benefits associated with globalization and free trade.

Access to Resources and Technology: Globalization facilitates access to resources and technology from around the world. Companies can leverage knowledge, skills, and technologies from different regions, promoting innovation and continuous improvement.

Technology Transfer: Globalization facilitates the transfer of technology between countries. Companies from different parts of the world can collaborate and share knowledge, contributing to the spread of technological advances.

Innovation: Global competition drives innovation by constantly encouraging companies to improve. The adoption of new technologies and business practices accelerates when companies can access the latest innovation from anywhere.

International Collaboration: Companies can form international alliances and collaborate on research and development projects. This not only facilitates access to financial resources but also to specialized knowledge and technical expertise.

Utilization of Specific Resources: Globalization allows countries to leverage specific resources that may not be available locally. For example, some countries may have advantages in the production of certain minerals or renewable energies, and globalization facilitates collaboration to use these resources efficiently.

Development of Skills and Talent: Companies can recruit talent from around the world, tapping into specific skills and diverse experiences. This benefits not only companies but also contributes to the development of skills and talent globally.

Global Supply Chains: Globalization has led to global supply chains, where product components can come from different parts of the world. This improves efficiency by allowing production in places that can do so more cost-effectively.

Infrastructure Development: Foreign direct investment and international cooperation can drive infrastructure development in different regions. This not only facilitates trade but also improves conditions for innovation and production.

Access to Capital Markets: Globalization provides companies with access to international capital markets, facilitating financing for investment and expansion projects.

Collectively, access to resources and technology through globalization significantly contributes to economic progress and development globally.

Cost Reduction for Consumers: International competition often leads to cost reduction for consumers. The availability of products and services from different parts of the world can result in greater variety and lower prices.

Variety of Products: Globalization allows consumers to access a wide variety of products and services from different parts of the world. International competition drives innovation and product diversification, offering consumers more choices to meet their needs and preferences.

Lower Prices: Global competition among companies often results in lower prices for consumers. The ability of companies to produce on a larger scale and benefit from operational efficiencies can translate into more affordable products in local markets.

Access to Foreign Goods: Consumers can access goods and services that are not available locally or are more expensive to produce domestically. This expands purchasing options and allows consumers to enjoy products that would otherwise be inaccessible.

Production Efficiency: Globalization facilitates efficient production by allowing companies to leverage comparative advantages from different regions. Companies can produce components or goods in locations where it is more cost-effective, contributing to global efficiency.

Price Innovation: International competition not only affects current prices but also drives innovation in pricing strategies. Companies seek creative ways to offer products at competitive prices, such as special offers, discounts, and bundles, benefiting consumers.

Development of New Markets: Globalization can open new markets for companies and entrepreneurs. By reaching consumers in different parts of the world, companies can leverage economies of scale while providing products at more affordable prices.

Access to More Affordable Technologies: Globalization makes technologies more accessible to consumers. Competition among technology companies from different regions can lead to the availability of more advanced devices and services at more affordable prices.

Improvement of Quality: International competition focuses not only on prices but also on the quality of products and services. Companies strive to enhance quality to stand out in a global market, directly benefiting consumers.

Globalization and free trade have the potential to significantly improve consumers' quality of life by offering a greater variety of products at lower prices.

Job Generation: Opening up to international markets can contribute to job creation, especially in sectors benefiting from external demand. Exports can become a significant source of employment opportunities.

Expansion of Export Sectors: Participation in international trade provides companies with the opportunity to expand into sectors in demand in international markets. This can result in increased production and, consequently, job creation in those sectors.

Global Supply Chain: Many companies are part of global supply chains, involving collaboration among businesses from different regions to produce goods and services. This interconnectedness can generate employment throughout the chain, from manufacturing to distribution and sales.

Multinational Companies: Multinational companies, by expanding across borders, contribute to job creation both in their home countries and in the countries where they operate. Establishing subsidiaries or branches in different regions can create local job opportunities.

Stimulation of Innovation: Global competition can stimulate innovation and the development of new technologies. Companies seeking international competitiveness often invest in improving efficiency and adopting advanced technologies, which can boost job creation in innovative sectors.

High-Value Added Sectors: Participation in international markets can drive specialization in high-value-added sectors, such as technology, research and development, and professional services. These sectors tend to create highly skilled and well-paying jobs.

Tourism and Services: Opening up to international markets extends beyond tangible goods; it also includes services such as tourism. Countries attracting foreign tourists can experience growth in the tourism sector, generating employment in hotels, restaurants, transportation, and related activities.

Development of Small and Medium Enterprises (SMEs): Globalization can offer opportunities for small and medium-sized enterprises (SMEs) to participate in international trade. Access to broader markets can allow these businesses to expand their operations, leading to local job creation.

Development of Workforce Skills: Participation in a global environment may require specialized skills and specific knowledge. This can incentivize training and the development of workforce skills, benefiting workers by making them more employable in the global economy.

Job generation is another positive aspect associated with globalization and free trade, as opening up to international markets can drive demand for labor in various economic sectors.

Development of Global Value Chains: Globalization has facilitated the development of global value chains, where different stages of the production process take place in different countries. This allows for greater efficiency and specialization.

Efficient Specialization: The formation of global value chains allows different countries to specialize in specific stages of production where they have comparative advantages. This leads to a more efficient allocation of resources and the production of goods and services at a lower cost.

Interconnection of Businesses: Global value chains involve close interconnection between businesses located in different parts of the world. This facilitates collaboration and cooperation among companies contributing to different components or manufacturing processes.

Cost Reduction: By distributing different production phases in locations with lower costs, companies can achieve significant savings. This may include manufacturing in a country with lower labor costs, assembling in another with lower logistical costs, etc.

Access to Specific Resources: Global value chains enable companies to access specific resources and specialized skills that may not be available or may be costly in their primary locations. This drives efficiency and quality in production.

Flexibility and Adaptability: Companies participating in global value chains are more flexible and can quickly adapt to changes in demand or market conditions. They can adjust production and distribution as needed by leveraging different locations and suppliers.

Innovation and Technology Transfer: Collaboration in global value chains fosters innovation and the transfer of technology. Companies can benefit from the specialized knowledge of partners in different regions, driving the development of more advanced products and processes.

Economic Growth: The development of global value chains can contribute to global economic growth by improving efficiency and productivity in the production of goods and services. This, in turn, can have positive impacts on employment and income.

Improvement of Competitiveness: Companies participating in global value chains can enhance their competitiveness by focusing on activities in which they are stronger and more efficient. This can lead to increased participation in international markets and a larger market share.

Risk Diversification: The geographical diversification of production and supply activities reduces the risks associated with specific events in a region. For example, climatic events, natural disasters, or disruptions in the supply chain may have less impact when operations are distributed globally.

The development of global value chains is a key aspect of globalization that has transformed how businesses operate and collaborate worldwide, providing significant benefits in terms of efficiency, innovation, and economic growth.

Promotion of Peace and Cooperation: The economic interdependence resulting from globalization and free trade can promote peace and cooperation among nations. Economic collaboration often reduces incentives for conflicts and tensions.

Economic Interdependence: Globalization and free trade create a network of economic interdependence among different nations. When countries depend on each other for their trade relationships, there is a stronger incentive to resolve disputes peacefully and avoid conflicts that could harm both parties.

Diplomatic Collaboration: Economic interconnectedness through trade can facilitate diplomatic collaboration. Nations with strong trade ties have more motivation to resolve differences through dialogue and negotiation rather than resorting to hostile actions that could negatively impact their economies.

Forum for Dialogue: Trade agreements and international trade-related organizations provide platforms for dialogue and cooperation. Trade challenges are often addressed through negotiations rather than military conflicts, promoting a more peaceful environment.

Regional Integration: Regional integration agreements, such as customs unions and free trade areas, can strengthen economic and political ties between countries. Regional integration can contribute to stability and peace by fostering greater understanding and cooperation among members.

Incentives for Stability: Political stability and security are crucial for economic development and trade. Countries wanting to maintain strong trade relations have incentives to keep a stable political environment and avoid conflicts that could disrupt their economic activities.

Economic Diplomacy: Economic diplomacy becomes a fundamental tool in a globalized environment. Political leaders recognize the importance of maintaining positive relations to ensure economic cooperation and avoid measures that could negatively affect the involved economies.

Building Personal Connections: Economic interaction can lead to the creation of personal and business connections among individuals from different countries. These connections can foster mutual understanding and empathy, contributing to the building of more peaceful relations between nations.

Disincentive for Armed Conflicts: Economic interdependence can act as a significant disincentive for armed conflicts. Countries engaged in extensive economic exchanges have more to lose in terms of income loss and economic development in case of a military conflict.

Globalization and free trade not only promote peace by reducing incentives for conflicts but also establish the foundations for broader cooperation between nations in various aspects.

Poverty Reduction: Opening up to international markets can contribute to poverty reduction by stimulating economic growth and generating economic opportunities for populations in different parts of the world.

Inclusive Economic Growth: Globalization and free trade can drive economic growth, and when this growth is inclusive, meaning it benefits a wide range of sectors and populations, it has the potential to reduce poverty. Access to international markets can create opportunities for businesses and workers, especially in developing countries.

Job Generation: Opening up to international markets can result in increased demand for goods and services, which, in turn, can lead to the expansion of production and job creation. Industries finding new markets may need to hire more workers, providing job opportunities for those seeking employment.

Empowerment of Local Communities: Participation in international trade can empower local communities by offering the possibility to sell products and services in global markets. This is especially relevant for rural communities or minority groups that may find new economic opportunities through exports.

Access to Resources and Technology: Globalization facilitates access to resources and technology from around the world. This can be beneficial for entrepreneurs and small businesses that, by integrating into global value chains, can access advanced knowledge and technologies that may have been out of reach previously.

Development of Key Sectors: Opening up to international markets can drive the development of key sectors of the economy, such as agriculture, manufacturing, and services. This not only diversifies the economy but also creates opportunities for different skills and talents.

Inclusion in Global Value Chains: Participating in global value chains allows countries to specialize in areas where they have comparative advantages, which can increase efficiency and productivity. This benefits not only companies but also generates employment and development in specific sectors.

Improvement of Working Conditions: As companies strive to compete internationally, they may be motivated to improve working conditions and offer competitive wages to attract and retain talent. This can have a positive impact on the standard of living for workers and contribute to poverty reduction.

Transfer of Skills: Interaction with companies and individuals from different parts of the world can facilitate the transfer of skills and knowledge. This can be especially beneficial for those in developing countries, where adopting advanced business practices and technologies can improve productivity and quality of life.

Opening up to international markets can play a significant role in poverty reduction by generating economic opportunities, promoting the development of key sectors, and improving living conditions for communities worldwide.

Transfer of Knowledge and Cultures: Global economic interaction facilitates the transfer of knowledge and cultures. The connection between people and businesses from different regions promotes diversity and the exchange of ideas.

Cultural Exchange: Globalization and free trade foster cultural exchange by facilitating connections between people from different parts of the world. Exposure to diverse cultures through international trade, travel, and online interactions contributes to broader understanding and appreciation of cultural diversity.

Transfer of Technology: Global economic interaction involves not only the transfer of goods and services but also the transfer of technology. Companies operating internationally can share technical knowledge and scientific advancements, contributing to technological progress in different parts of the world.

Scientific Collaboration: Globalization facilitates international scientific collaboration. Researchers from different countries can work together on scientific and medical projects, sharing their knowledge and resources to address global challenges such as diseases, climate change, and emerging technologies.

Access to Educational Resources: Global connectivity allows broader access to educational resources. Students and professionals can benefit from the availability of online courses, virtual lectures, and educational materials from various international sources, enriching their knowledge and skills.

Development of Best Practices: Interaction between businesses from different regions can lead to the development and adoption of best business practices. Observing and incorporating successful approaches from other business cultures can improve efficiency and quality in various industries.

Promotion of Innovation: Exposure to different perspectives and approaches can foster innovation. International collaboration in research and development, as well as global competition, motivates companies to innovate to stay competitive, with potential global benefits.

Cultural Enrichment: Global economic interaction enriches culture by introducing new forms of art, music, cuisine, and lifestyles. Cultural exchanges through international trade contribute to cultural diversity and mutual understanding among communities worldwide.

Promotion of Multilingualism: Globalization promotes multilingualism as people and businesses interact in different languages. This can lead to greater recognition and appreciation of linguistic diversity, as well as the development of language skills in the population.

In summary, the transfer of knowledge and cultures through globalization and free trade not only enriches individuals' lives on an individual level but also contributes to global progress by facilitating the exchange of ideas, technologies, and innovative practices.

Sustainability and Sustainable Development: International cooperation in trade can facilitate more sustainable approaches to economic development by sharing best practices and environmentally friendly technologies.

Trade in Sustainable Goods: International cooperation in trade can facilitate the exchange of sustainably produced goods. Countries can specialize in the production of goods that meet environmental and social standards, promoting sustainable practices globally.

Transfer of Green Technologies: Opening up to international cooperation allows the transfer of green technologies and sustainable practices between countries. Adopting cleaner and more efficient technologies can contribute to reducing environmental impact and promoting sustainable development.

International Standards and Regulations: Collaboration in international trade can lead to the creation and adoption of international standards and regulations that promote sustainability. These standards can address environmental issues, labor rights, and ethical practices, creating a global framework for sustainable development.

Investment in Renewable Energies: Globalization can facilitate investment in international renewable energy projects. Cooperation in the trade of sustainable technologies and energy resources can help address challenges related to climate change and transition to cleaner energy sources.

Development of Sustainable Supply Chains: Cooperation in trade can also drive the development of sustainable supply chains. Adopting practices such as ethical production, efficient resource use, and waste reduction can promote more sustainable business models throughout global value chains.

Economic Incentives for Sustainability: International trade can create economic incentives for sustainability. Consumers and businesses may prefer sustainable products and services, motivating companies to adopt more environmentally friendly practices to maintain and increase their market share.

Access to Markets for Sustainable Products: Trade agreements can open markets for sustainable products by removing trade barriers and facilitating the entry of goods produced sustainably. This can benefit producers committed to environmentally friendly practices.

Financing for Sustainable Projects: Globalization allows access to international financing for sustainable projects. Foreign direct investment and cooperation in trade can provide financial resources for initiatives promoting sustainable development in different regions of the world.

International cooperation in trade can play a crucial role in promoting sustainable business and economic practices, contributing to environmental preservation and global sustainable development.

The positive attitude towards globalization and free trade is based on the belief that these processes significantly contribute to economic development, efficiency, innovation, and peaceful cooperation between nations.

22. Capital Theory

Capital Structure:

Capital theory examines how productive resources are combined in different capital structures to carry out production processes. Capital structure includes physical, financial, and human assets used in production.

Physical Assets:

This encompasses facilities, machinery, technologies, and other tangible goods used in production. The efficiency and adequacy of these assets directly impact a company's ability to generate goods and services.

Financial Assets:

These include monetary resources, investments, and capital that a company owns. Financial management plays a crucial role in capital structure as it affects the ability to finance operations, investments, and growth.

Human Assets:

Refers to the workforce and their level of skills, knowledge, and experience. The quality and training of employees are key factors in efficiency and innovation in production.

The optimal combination of these assets, considering the duration of production processes and long-term planning, is essential to maximize efficiency and profitability. Additionally, capital theory addresses the renewal and obsolescence of these assets over time, recognizing the importance of adapting to technological and economic changes.

Factors of Production:

Analyzes the interaction between factors of production, such as land, labor, and capital. The efficient combination of these factors affects the productivity and profitability of companies.

Land:

This factor includes not only the land itself but also the natural resources found in it, such as minerals, water, and other renewable or non-renewable resources.

Labor:

Refers to human effort dedicated to production, including the skills, knowledge, and physical efforts of workers.

Capital:

Represents produced goods used as inputs in the production of other goods and services. It can include both physical goods (machinery, tools) and financial goods (money, investments).

Efficiency in the combination of these factors is crucial for optimizing production. Capital theory examines how capital investment can increase productivity and how the proper combination of land, labor, and capital contributes to economic success. It also considers how changes in the availability and quality of these factors can affect capital structure and production overall.

Duration and Long-Term Production:

Capital theory emphasizes the importance of considering the duration of long-term production processes. Projects spanning longer periods require different planning and resource allocation.

Strategic Planning:

In long-term projects, strategic planning is essential. This involves anticipating resource needs over time and allocating them efficiently to ensure project continuity and success.

Capital Investment:

The duration of production processes affects the decision to invest in capital. Long-term projects often require significant investments in machinery, technology, and other assets that contribute to efficiency and productivity over time.

Time and Profitability Factors:

Capital theory considers how time influences the profitability of investment. Returns on certain projects may accumulate over time, and the choice between short and long-term projects is based on evaluating these returns over time.

Economic Cycles:

The duration of production processes is also related to economic cycles. In periods of economic expansion, there may be more long-term investments, while in recessions, companies may adjust their strategies to adapt to changing economic conditions.

Capital theory provides a comprehensive perspective on how the duration of production processes affects business decision-making and economic efficiency over time.

Decreasing Marginal Returns:

Examines the principle of decreasing marginal returns, which suggests that, at some point, increasing investment in a production factor may lead to diminishing increases in production.

Definition:

The principle of decreasing marginal returns states that, holding at least one factor of production constant, the additional increase in another factor will lead to diminishing marginal increases in production over time.

Example:

For example, consider a factory that produces automobiles. As we increase the number of workers (a production factor) in relation to the fixed amount of machinery and factory space (constant production factors), at some additional point, each new worker may contribute less to the overall increase in production.

Application to Business Decisions:

Companies must consider decreasing marginal returns when making decisions on resource allocation. As investment in a specific production factor increases, it is important to assess whether the additional costs generated by that investment lead to proportional increases in production.

Production Optimum:

Production optimum is reached when the additional cost of using an additional production factor is equal to the additional benefit obtained. When marginal returns begin to decrease, the company may have reached its optimal production level.

Importance in Planning:

Understanding decreasing marginal returns is essential for long-term strategic planning. It helps companies allocate resources efficiently and avoid excessive investments that may not translate into significant increases in production.

The principle of decreasing marginal returns underscores the importance of critically evaluating how changes in the investment of production factors affect efficiency and profitability in production.

Capital-Intensive vs. Labor-Intensive:

Addresses the choice between a capital-intensive and a labor-intensive production structure. This choice may depend on factors such as relative costs and resource availability.

Definition:

A capital-intensive production structure involves a higher investment in machinery, technology, and other capital assets, while a labor-intensive structure involves a greater reliance on human labor in the production process.

Influencing Factors:

Relative Costs: The relationship between capital costs and labor costs is a critical factor. If labor is relatively inexpensive compared to capital, it might be more profitable to adopt a labor-intensive structure, and vice versa.

Available Technology: The availability and efficiency of technology are also determinants. If automated technologies are more advanced and affordable, it could encourage the adoption of a capital-intensive structure.

Division of Labor: The complexity and specialization required in the production process can influence the choice. Some industries may benefit more from the skill and adaptability of human labor.

Scalability: The ability to quickly adjust production in response to changes in demand can affect the choice between capital-intensive and labor-intensive. Technologies may be more scalable in certain contexts.

Specific Industries:

Some industries naturally tend toward a specific structure. For example, automobile manufacturing may be capital-intensive due to automation, while the garment industry may rely more on labor.

Economic Considerations:

Economic conditions, such as interest rates, fiscal policies, and labor market conditions, can also influence the decision. Changes in these factors can make one structure more attractive than the other at a given time.

Flexibility and Adaptability:

Flexibility to adapt to changes in demand or market conditions can be a key factor. Some production structures are more adaptable to variations in demand or technological changes.

Ultimately, the choice between capital-intensive and labor-intensive is unique to each company and may change over time in response to changes in the business and economic environment.

Capital Theory explores the relationship between capital investment and long-term economic growth. The accumulation of capital can be a significant driver of sustainable economic development.

Capital Accumulation:

Capital investment involves the acquisition and expansion of productive assets, such as machinery, technology, buildings, and other resources that enhance the productive capacity of an economy.

Increased Productivity:

Capital accumulation can increase labor productivity and improve efficiency in production. The introduction of more advanced technologies and improved production methods can lead to an increase in production per worker.

Effects on Employment:

While capital investment is often associated with automation and the substitution of labor in some tasks, it can also generate employment in sectors related to production, maintenance, and the development of new technologies.

Infrastructure Improvement:

Capital investment can also include improvements in infrastructure, such as roads, railways, and telecommunications. This enhanced infrastructure can facilitate the transport of goods and services, fostering trade and economic efficiency.

Sustainable Growth:

Capital accumulation can contribute to sustainable long-term economic growth. Continuous improvement in technology and productive capacity can boost the global competitiveness of an economy.

Innovation and Technological Development:

Investment in research and development (R&D) is a crucial form of capital investment. The resulting innovation and technological development can open new business opportunities, create emerging industries, and transform the economic structure.

Challenges and Considerations:

Despite the benefits, it is important to address challenges related to the distribution of the benefits of capital investment, workforce adaptation to technological changes, and environmental sustainability.

Macroeconomic Context:

The macroeconomic environment, including fiscal, monetary, and trade policies, can influence the effectiveness of capital investment in driving economic growth. A strong economic framework can facilitate the flow of investment and its positive impact.

In summary, capital investment plays a crucial role in economic growth by boosting productivity and innovation. However, effective management of this investment and consideration of its social and environmental implications are essential for equitable and sustainable economic development.

Obsolescence and Capital Renewal:

Considers the phenomenon of obsolescence and the need for capital renewal. Technological advances and changes in consumer preferences can make certain capital assets obsolete.

Technological Obsolescence:

Obsolescence can occur when technological advances make existing equipment and assets less efficient or surpassed by new technologies. Companies may face pressure to update their capital to remain competitive.

Changes in Consumer Preferences:

Consumer preferences can also influence obsolescence. For example, changes in market demand can cause certain products or services to lose relevance, leading to the obsolescence of associated assets.

Product Life Cycle:

Products and services have life cycles, and obsolescence can occur at the end of these cycles. Capital renewal involves the introduction of new products or the update of existing ones to maintain relevance in the market.

Renewal and Modernization:

Capital renewal involves the adoption of new technologies, equipment modernization, and process improvement to adapt to changes in the business environment. This may be essential for operational efficiency and long-term sustainability.

Investments in Research and Development (R&D):

Companies often make significant investments in R&D to develop new technologies and products. R&D is a form of capital renewal as it drives innovation and enables companies to stay at the forefront of their industries.

Capital renewal can pose financial challenges as it involves costs associated with acquiring new assets and training personnel to use new technologies. Companies must balance these costs with long-term benefits.

Sustainability and Energy Efficiency:

In capital renewal, considerations of sustainability and energy efficiency are increasingly important. Adopting more energy-efficient and environmentally friendly technologies can be an integral part of renewal.

Strategic Planning:

Capital renewal requires careful strategic planning. Companies must assess when and how to upgrade their assets to maximize efficiency and profitability.

In conclusion, obsolescence and capital renewal are natural processes in the business environment. Understanding and managing these processes effectively is essential for companies to adapt to changes in technology and market preferences, ensuring their long-term relevance and success.

Investment Cycles:

Examine how economic cycles can influence investment decisions. During expansion periods, companies may increase capital investment, while during recessions, they may reduce or delay investments.

Phases of the Economic Cycle:

Economic cycles typically consist of expansion and recession phases. During expansion, the economy grows, while during recession, there is contraction. These phases affect market conditions and business expectations.

Influence on Investment Decisions:

During expansion periods, companies are often more inclined to make capital investments. Optimism about economic growth and market demand can lead to bolder decisions regarding capacity expansion.

Risks and Cautious Decisions:

In contrast, during recessions, companies tend to be more cautious in their investment decisions. Economic uncertainty, declining demand, and risk aversion can result in reductions or delays in investment projects.

Product Life Cycle and Economic Cycle:

The product life cycle can also influence investment decisions. During the introduction and growth phases of a product, investments may increase. However, in maturity, investments may decrease, especially if demand stabilizes.

Availability of Financing:

The availability of financing is also a significant factor. During economic expansions, companies are more likely to find financing for investment projects. In recessions, credit conditions may become more restrictive.

Adaptation to Market Conditions:

Companies often adjust their investment decisions based on market conditions. Flexibility to adapt to economic changes can determine a company's resilience during different cycle phases.

Impact on Employability and Productivity:

Investment cycles also have implications for employability and productivity. During expansions, jobs can be created, and productive efficiency can increase. In recessions, reduced investments can negatively affect employment and productivity.

Monetary and Fiscal Policy:

Monetary and fiscal policies play a role in investment cycles. Measures such as low-interest rates and fiscal stimuli can encourage investment during recessions, while contractionary policies can influence investment during expansions to prevent overheating.

Investment cycles are intrinsic to economic dynamics and reflect how companies respond to changes in economic conditions. Understanding these cycles is crucial for business leaders, policymakers, and economic analysts to make informed decisions and prepare for market fluctuations.

Effects of Monetary Policy:

Capital theory also considers how monetary policies, such as interest rates, can affect investment decisions and capital structure in an economy.

Interest Rates and Cost of Capital:

Interest rates are a key component of monetary policy. Changes in interest rates directly affect the cost of capital for companies. Lower rates can make investment more attractive by reducing financing costs.

Investment and Corporate Financing:

Reduced interest rates tend to stimulate corporate investment. Companies may find it more affordable to finance investment projects, which can drive expansion of production capacity and economic growth.

Investment Cycle and Monetary Cycle:

Monetary policy can also influence investment cycles. During periods of low-interest rates, companies may be more inclined to make investments. Conversely, rate increases may discourage investment.

Access to Credit:

Changes in monetary policy affect access to credit. With low-interest rates, companies can more easily access loans, which can boost investment. Higher rates may restrict credit access and discourage investment.

Inflation and Expectations:

Monetary policy also aims to manage inflation. Stable inflation expectations can provide a more predictable environment for investment decisions. Uncertainty about inflation can impact long-term decisions.

Impact on Financial Assets:

Central bank actions, such as asset purchases (quantitative easing) or changes in benchmark interest rates, can also affect financial asset prices. This can influence corporate investment decisions and capital structure.

Balance between Consumption and Investment:

Monetary policies can influence the balance between consumption and investment. Low-interest rates may encourage both consumption and investment, while higher rates may shift preference toward saving.

Coordination with Fiscal Policies:

Monetary policy often coordinates with fiscal policies to achieve economic objectives. The combination of monetary and fiscal measures can affect aggregate demand and economic activity.

In summary, monetary policy is a key component influencing investment decisions and capital structure in an economy. Effective management of monetary policy aims to balance economic stimulation with price stability and financial sustainability.

Human and Technological Capital:

It is not limited to physical capital; it also includes human capital (workforce skills and knowledge) and technological capital. Improvement in these forms of capital can have a significant impact on production.

Human Capital:

Human capital refers to the skills, knowledge, and capabilities of the workforce. Investment in education, training, and professional development contributes to the growth of human capital. A worker with enhanced skills can be more productive and adaptable to changes in the economy.

Productivity and Competitiveness:

Human capital is directly linked to labor productivity and economic competitiveness. Countries and companies that invest in developing the skills of their workforce may experience improvements in efficiency and innovation capacity.

Innovation and Creativity:

Investment in human capital fosters innovation and creativity. Workers with advanced skills are better positioned to contribute to innovative processes and adopt new technologies. The ability to adapt to constantly changing work environments is strengthened by a strong human capital.

Adaptability and Continuous Learning:

Well-developed human capital facilitates adaptability and continuous learning. Workers can more easily adjust to changes in market demands and acquire new competencies as technologies and industries evolve.

Technological Capital:

Technological capital encompasses tools, machinery, software, and technical knowledge used in production processes. Investment in technology can increase efficiency, improve quality, and enable the production of more advanced goods and services.

Automation and Efficiency:

The adoption of advanced technologies, such as automation, can increase efficiency in production. Substituting repetitive tasks with automated technologies frees up time and human resources for more complex and creative tasks.

International Competitiveness:

Human and technological capital contributes to international competitiveness. Companies and countries with highly skilled workers and cutting-edge technologies can excel in global markets, participating in international value chains and generating comparative advantages.

Sustainable Development:

Improvements in human and technological capital can contribute to sustainable development. The adoption of cleaner technologies and training in sustainable practices can align economic growth with environmental and social considerations.

Overall, human and technological capital play a crucial role in determining the productivity, innovation, and adaptability of an economy, influencing its long-term development.

23.Defense of Individual Rights

Defense of individual rights is a fundamental principle in many societies that seek to preserve the freedom and well-being of their citizens.

Human Dignity: Respecting individual rights is a recognition of the inherent dignity of every human being. Each individual has fundamental rights that must be protected regardless of their origin, gender, race, religion, or other characteristics.

The idea that every human being possesses intrinsic dignity deserving of recognition and respect aligns with many international human rights documents. They establish that all humans are born free and equal in dignity and rights. Respecting diversity and promoting inclusion are essential elements to ensure that individual rights are applied equitably to all people.

Furthermore, by recognizing the inherent dignity of each individual, an ethical framework is established that advocates for treating all people with respect and consideration. This contributes not only to the protection of individual rights but also to the construction of communities and societies that value diversity and foster peaceful coexistence.

Individual rights protect personal freedom, ensuring that individuals have autonomy to make decisions about their own lives, as long as they do not unjustly interfere with the rights of others.

Autonomy and Self-Determination: Personal freedom entails the capacity of individuals to make autonomous decisions about their own lives, covering choices related to profession, education, religion, personal expression, and other significant aspects.

Individual Development: Personal freedom is essential for individual development, allowing people to pursue their interests, goals, and aspirations, contributing to a more complete sense of self-realization.

Pluralism and Diversity: Personal freedom fosters an environment where the diversity of opinions, beliefs, and lifestyles is respected. In societies that value personal freedom, it is recognized that plurality is an enriching and beneficial aspect.

Personal Responsibility: Personal freedom comes with individual responsibility. While individuals have the freedom to make choices, they must also take responsibility for the consequences of those decisions, as long as they do not violate the rights of others.

Ethical Limitations: While personal freedom is advocated, there are often ethical limits to prevent the exercise of that freedom from causing unjustified harm to others. These limits aim to balance individual freedom with the protection of rights and the overall security of society.

Empowerment and Social Participation: Personal freedom empowers individuals and encourages active participation in society. When individuals feel free to express their ideas and contribute to the community, democracy and civic life are strengthened.

Personal freedom, supported by the protection of individual rights, is an essential pillar for the functioning of just and free societies. This principle recognizes autonomy and diversity, promoting a balance between individual freedom and social responsibility.

Equality Before the Law: The protection of individual rights contributes to the idea of equality before the law. All individuals must be treated with justice and equity, without unjustified discrimination.

Fair and Equitable Treatment: Equality before the law ensures that all individuals are treated fairly and equitably. This implies that, in similar situations, people should receive comparable treatment, regardless of their personal characteristics.

Non-Discrimination: The protection of individual rights opposes unjustified discrimination. All citizens should enjoy equal opportunities and be protected against any form of discrimination based on characteristics such as gender, race, religion, sexual orientation, among others.

Equal Access to Justice: Equality before the law also implies equal access to justice. Everyone should have the opportunity to assert their rights in courts, regardless of their social, economic, or any other circumstances.

Universal Rights and Responsibilities: Equality before the law establishes that individual rights and responsibilities are universal.

There are no special privileges for certain groups or individuals; everyone is subject to the same laws and norms.

Prevention of Power Abuse: Ensuring equality before the law serves as a safeguard against potential abuses of power. When laws are applied fairly and impartially, the chances of discrimination are reduced, and protection against arbitrariness is provided.

Social Cohesion: Equality before the law contributes to social cohesion. When individuals feel they are treated justly, trust in institutions is strengthened, fostering a sense of belonging to society.

Diversity and Pluralism: Equality before the law recognizes and respects diversity and pluralism in society. It ensures that all voices carry equal weight and that differences do not translate into unjust inequalities.

Equality before the law, supported by the protection of individual rights, is essential for the establishment of just and equitable societies. This principle promotes the idea that the law should be applied impartially, ensuring that all citizens enjoy equal rights and protections.

Rule of Law: The defense of individual rights is essential for a strong rule of law. This implies that laws are applied fairly and consistently, providing a legal framework that protects individual rights.

Limitation of Governmental Power: The rule of law implies that government power is subject to laws and regulations. This acts as a mechanism of limitation to prevent the abuse of power and ensure that governmental actions align with legal principles.

Protection of Fundamental Rights: In a rule of law, laws are established to protect the fundamental rights of individuals. These laws serve as a framework guaranteeing freedom, equality, and other individual rights, providing a solid foundation for social coexistence.

Justice and Impartiality: The fair and consistent application of laws is a central principle of the rule of law. This implies that all individuals, regardless of their status or position, are equal before the law and must be treated impartially by the judicial system.

Legal Certainty: The existence of a rule of law provides legal certainty to citizens. Knowing that laws are predictable and applied consistently allows people to plan their lives and activities with confidence.

Conflict Resolution: A solid legal system in a rule of law facilitates the peaceful resolution of conflicts. Courts and legal mechanisms provide avenues to resolve disputes fairly, avoiding the need for violence or self-help.

Trust in Institutions: The existence of a rule of law contributes to trust in governmental institutions. When people perceive that laws are applied fairly, trust in the system and in the government's ability to protect their rights is strengthened.

Prevention of Arbitrary Actions: A rule of law prevents arbitrariness by establishing clear rules and procedures. This avoids impulsive decisions or decisions based on personal preferences, ensuring that all actions are supported by legal principles.

The defense of individual rights is intrinsically linked to the existence of a strong rule of law. This principle ensures that laws are fair, consistently applied, and protect the fundamental rights of citizens, thereby contributing to the construction of just and equitable societies.

Citizen Participation: Respect for individual rights encourages active citizen participation in decision-making and political life. Societies that value and protect individual rights often have more engaged and empowered citizens.

Individual Empowerment: When individual rights are respected, citizens are empowered to actively participate in society. The recognition of autonomy and personal freedom motivates people to express their opinions and contribute to the decision-making process.

Freedom of Expression: Freedom of expression, a fundamental right, is crucial for citizen participation. When individuals feel free to express their ideas and opinions without fear of reprisals, an environment conducive to the exchange of ideas and constructive debate is created.

Involvement in Politics: Respect for individual rights fosters involvement in political life. Citizens who trust that their rights will be respected are more inclined to participate in electoral processes, vote, and contribute to policy formulation.

Access to Information: Citizen participation benefits from access to information. When individual rights are respected, transparency is promoted, ensuring that relevant information is available to citizens, enabling them to make informed decisions.

Civic Tech and Digital Participation: In the digital age, respect for individual rights is reflected in the protection of online privacy. This is crucial to encourage citizen participation on digital platforms and the use of Civic Tech tools to engage in public affairs.

Activism and Rights Advocacy: Empowered citizens through the respect for their individual rights are more likely to engage in activism and rights advocacy activities. They become agents of change working to improve society and protect the rights of all.

Strengthening Civil Society: Respect for individual rights contributes to the strengthening of civil society. Non-governmental organizations, community groups, and other actors in civil society play a vital role in promoting citizen participation and rights advocacy.

In conclusion, respect for individual rights and citizen participation are intrinsically linked. Societies that value and protect individual rights tend to have more engaged, active, and empowered citizens, enriching democratic life and contributing to the development of just and equitable communities.

Innovation and Creativity: Individual freedom provides the necessary space for innovation and creativity. When people have the freedom to express their ideas and pursue their goals, progress and development are fostered.

Autonomy in Decision-Making: Individual freedom allows people to make autonomous decisions about their lives, including their careers and creative projects. This level of autonomy is crucial for fostering innovation, as individuals can follow their own ideas and visions.

Diversity of Thought: Individual freedom promotes diversity of thought and perspectives. When people are free to express their ideas without fear of reprisals, an environment is created where different approaches and innovations can emerge and contribute to progress.

Risk and Experimentation: Innovation often involves risk and experimentation. Individual freedom provides a space where people can take risks and try out new ideas without the constant fear of sanctions or restrictions, fostering creativity and exploration.

Entrepreneurship and Economic Development: Individual freedom is a key driver of entrepreneurship. When people have the freedom to start businesses, create and develop new technologies, economic opportunities are generated, and economic development is propelled.

Academic Freedom: Individual freedom in academic and research environments is essential for generating innovative knowledge. Freedom to explore new ideas and approaches without undue restrictions contributes to scientific and technological advancement.

Creative and Artistic Culture: Individual freedom fosters a vibrant creative and artistic culture. Artists, writers, and creatives, in general, need the freedom to express their visions authentically, enriching society with new forms of cultural expression.

Adaptation and Change: Innovation often involves the ability to adapt and change. Individual freedom allows individuals and societies in general to adapt to new circumstances, embrace change, and seek creative solutions to emerging challenges.

Individual freedom provides the fertile ground necessary for innovation and creativity. When people have the freedom to express their ideas, pursue their goals, and take risks, an environment conducive to progress and development is created in various areas of social and economic life.

Protection against Abuse of Power: Ensuring individual rights acts as a mechanism of protection against potential abuses of power, whether by the government or other citizens. Individual rights establish clear limits on what is acceptable in society.

Restrictions on Governmental Power: Individual rights set limits on the power of the government. By recognizing and protecting the fundamental rights of citizens, excessive government control over people's lives is avoided, establishing a balance that safeguards individual freedoms.

Guarantee of Fair Procedures: Individual rights include the guarantee of fair procedures in the legal system. This ensures that people have rights such as due process, the right to a fair trial, and the presumption of innocence, protecting against possible abuses of the judicial system.

Protection of Privacy: Respect for privacy as an individual right is essential to protect people against the abuse of power, whether by the government or other citizens. Privacy acts as a shield against undue intrusions into personal life.

Limits on the Use of Force: Individual rights establish clear limits on the use of force, both by the government and citizens. This contributes to preventing abuses, ensuring that law enforcement and public safety are within ethical and legal parameters.

Prohibition of Torture and Cruel Treatment: Individual rights prohibit torture and cruel and inhuman treatment. This ensures that people are not subjected to physical or psychological abuse by any entity, whether governmental or otherwise.

Access to Justice: Individual rights ensure access to justice for all. This access is crucial for people to defend themselves against possible abuses and violations of their rights.

Protection against Discrimination and Persecution: Individual rights protect against unjustified discrimination and persecution. This contributes to preventing abuses based on characteristics such as gender, race, religion, or sexual orientation.

Citizen Control over the Government: The protection of individual rights fosters citizen control over the government. Citizens have the right and ability to demand accountability from authorities, serving as a preventive mechanism against abuse of power.

Ensuring individual rights acts as an essential barrier against the abuse of power, whether by the government or other citizens. These rights establish clear limits and ethical principles that protect individuals and contribute to the construction of just and equitable societies.

The defense of individual rights is essential for preserving freedom and building just and equitable societies. When these rights are respected and protected, an environment conducive to human flourishing and social progress is created.

24.Theory of Taxation and Public Spending

Distortions in Resource Allocation: A fundamental critique is that state intervention through taxes and spending can distort the efficient allocation of resources in the economy. High taxes, in particular, can discourage production and labor, and government spending can be inefficiently directed, affecting market efficiency.

Negative Incentives for Production and Labor: High tax rates can create negative incentives for production and labor. Individuals and businesses may be disincentivized to work more or invest in productive activities if a significant portion of their income goes toward taxes.

Reduction of Entrepreneurial Initiative: High tax rates can discourage entrepreneurial initiative. Faced with significant tax rates, entrepreneurs may be less inclined to take risks and undertake new projects, potentially impacting innovation and job creation.

Less Investment in Productive Capital: High taxes on earnings and investment can deter businesses and individuals from investing in productive capital. This could negatively affect long-term economic growth and companies' ability to enhance efficiency and productivity.

Informal Labor and Tax Evasion: In response to high tax rates, some individuals and businesses may opt for the informal economy or find ways to evade taxes. This could have negative consequences for tax collection and equity in the tax system.

Workforce Displacement: High tax rates can result in a reduction in the labor supply. People may choose to work fewer hours or retire early if a significant portion of their income goes toward taxes, which could have implications for the workforce and production.

Impact on Labor Mobility: High income taxes can affect labor mobility. Workers may be less likely to change jobs or seek more challenging job opportunities if they fear losing a significant portion of their income due to tax rates.

Incentive for Innovation and Education: High tax rates can also discourage investment in education and the pursuit of innovation. Individuals may be less inclined to invest in their professional development and acquire new skills if they perceive that a substantial part of their income will be taxed.

Effects on Business Competitiveness: Globally, high tax rates can impact business competitiveness. Companies may choose to locate in countries with lower tax rates, which could have consequences for employment and investment in the country.

The effectiveness of fiscal policies and the relationship between tax rates and economic behavior are complex and contextual issues. While some argue that reducing tax rates can stimulate investment and economic growth, others contend that moderate tax rates are necessary to fund essential public services and reduce inequalities. Designing a fair and efficient tax system involves carefully considering these factors.

Private Sector Displacement: Critics suggest that excessive public spending can displace the private sector. When the government invests in areas where there is already private activity, it can create unfair competition and displace private companies, resulting in a less efficient allocation of resources.

Inefficiency and Unequal Competition: Government intervention through public spending in areas with existing private activity can generate unequal competition. Private companies, operating under competitive pressures and seeking efficiency, may face challenges when competing with government entities not subject to the same market forces and often having different bureaucratic structures.

Difficulties for Innovation: The displacement of the private sector by the government could have implications for innovation. Private companies are often driven by incentives to innovate and improve efficiency to compete in the market. When the government engages in sectors where there is already private activity, there may be less pressure for innovation and continuous improvement.

Risk of State Monopoly: In extreme cases, excessive government intervention could lead to the creation of state monopolies in certain sectors. This could have negative consequences for competition and economic efficiency, as monopolies often lack incentives to improve quality or reduce costs.

Lack of Incentives for Efficiency: Government entities may lack the same incentives as private companies to operate efficiently. The lack of direct competition and funding through tax revenue rather than generated profits may result in less pressure to optimize costs and improve service quality.

Impact on Private Investment: Fear of displacement by the government can affect the willingness of private companies to invest in certain sectors. If companies anticipate unequal competition or government interference, they may be hesitant to make significant investments, which could have implications for economic growth.

Disincentive for Entrepreneurship: Significant government presence in specific areas can disincentivize entrepreneurship. Entrepreneurs may be less likely to enter sectors where they perceive government intervention as an obstacle, limiting diversity and competition in the economy.

Imbalances in Supply and Demand: Government intervention without careful consideration of market dynamics can result in imbalances between supply and demand. Resources could be inefficiently allocated, as investment decisions are based on political considerations rather than market signals.

In summary, the critique of private sector displacement highlights concerns that excessive government intervention can distort the efficient functioning of the market and negatively impact competition and innovation in the economy. The discussion about the appropriate amount of government intervention remains a central issue in economic theory and policy formulation.

Growth of Public Debt: State intervention through public spending often involves taking on debt to finance programs and projects. The constant accumulation of public debt can raise concerns about long-term fiscal sustainability and its effects on the economy.

Long-term Fiscal Sustainability: Frequent use of debt to finance public spending raises concerns about long-term fiscal sustainability. If public debt grows constantly without a clear strategy for its management and reduction, there could be risks to financial stability and the government's ability to meet its obligations.

Interest Burden: Servicing the debt involves paying interest, which can become a significant burden on the government budget. As debt grows, the percentage of the budget allocated to interest payments may increase, limiting the availability of funds for other essential programs and services.

Possible Tax Increases: To address the debt burden, governments may be tempted to increase taxes. This can have negative implications for economic activity and private investment, as higher tax rates can discourage production and investment.

Uncertainty for Investors and Financial Markets: Constant growth in public debt can create uncertainty among investors and in financial markets. The lack of a clear plan to address the debt can affect confidence in the government's ability to handle its fiscal affairs, potentially leading to higher interest rates and stricter credit conditions.

Risks of Financial Crisis: An unsustainable level of public debt increases the risks of a financial crisis. If investors perceive the debt as too high and unmanageable, they may withdraw their support, triggering a financial crisis with negative consequences for the overall economy.

Impact on Credit Rating: Sustained increase in public debt can affect a country's credit rating. A lower credit rating can result in higher borrowing costs, further worsening the financial burden associated with the debt.

Constraints on Budget Flexibility: Accumulating debt limits the government's budget flexibility. When a significant portion of the budget is allocated to debt servicing, there is less room to respond to changes in economic conditions or to fund new initiatives without resorting to further debt.

Impact on Future Generations: The accumulation of debt can transfer the fiscal burden to future generations. Governments that accumulate debt must consider how the debt burden will be distributed among generations and how it will affect the ability of future generations to fund essential public services.

In summary, the critique of public debt growth highlights the risks associated with unsustainable fiscal management. Attention to long-term sustainability and the implementation of policies that responsibly address the debt burden are crucial for economic and financial stability.

Bureaucratic Inefficiencies: Inefficient management and bureaucracy associated with some government programs are grounds for criticism. It is argued that state intervention can lead to inefficiencies and resource wastage due to a lack of incentives for efficiency present in the private sector.

Lack of Market Incentives: Critics argue that, unlike the private sector where companies face market pressure to be efficient, government agencies sometimes lack market incentives to operate efficiently. Competition and the possibility of losing customers, which often drive efficiency in the private sector, may not be present in the government sphere.

Complex Bureaucratic Procedures: Government bureaucracy often involves complex procedures and a significant amount of red tape. This can result in delays, redundancies, and additional costs for citizens and businesses interacting with the government, perceived as inefficient.

Politically Driven Decisions: In some cases, decisions related to government programs may be influenced by political considerations rather than strictly efficiency and effectiveness criteria. This could lead to the implementation of programs not backed by sound analysis or not the most efficient option.

Lack of Competition and Choice: The lack of competition in certain government services can lead to less pressure to improve efficiency. The absence of market choices and the need to use specific government services can limit citizens' ability to choose more efficient providers.

Inefficiency in Resource Allocation: State intervention can result in inefficiencies in resource allocation. Resources may be distributed suboptimally due to decision-making processes not aligned with principles of economic efficiency.

Resistance to Change: Government bureaucracy is sometimes resistant to change. Established procedures and organizational structures can be challenging to modify, even when there are clear opportunities to improve efficiency. Resistance to change can hinder reform efforts.

Excessive Staffing and Administrative Costs: In some cases, excess staff and associated administrative costs in government programs are criticized. The lack of incentives to reduce costs and optimize efficiency can lead to unnecessary bureaucracy expansion.

Complexity in Performance Evaluation: Performance evaluation in the public sector can be more complex than in the private sector. The lack of clear indicators and the difficulty in measuring the success of government programs can make it challenging to identify and correct inefficiencies.

It is important to note that these criticisms do not negate the importance of state intervention in certain cases but emphasize the need to address inefficiencies and improve management to ensure effective and efficient use of public resources. The implementation of effective management practices, transparency, and accountability are key elements in addressing these concerns.

Negative Effects on Investment and Economic Growth: State intervention can have negative effects on investment and economic growth. Uncertainty about fiscal policies and the possibility of higher taxes can discourage investors and impact long-term economic expansion. Concerns about the negative effects on investment and economic growth due to state intervention stem from the idea that certain government policies may generate uncertainty and discourage investors and businesses.

Uncertainty about Fiscal Policies: State intervention through frequent changes in fiscal policies can create uncertainty for investors and businesses. Lack of predictability in decisions related to taxes and spending can make long-term planning and investment decision-making difficult.

Possibility of Higher Taxes: The perception that state intervention could lead to higher taxes in the future may discourage investment. Investors and businesses may be cautious about committing capital if they anticipate more burdensome tax obligations on the horizon.

Impact on Business Confidence: State intervention perceived as adverse to business can affect business confidence. Companies may be reluctant to invest and expand if they fear that present or future government policies may be detrimental to their operations and profitability.

Disincentive for Innovation and Expansion: Uncertainty about government policies can disincentivize innovation and business expansion. Companies might be more cautious about embarking on research and development projects or pursuing new opportunities in an uncertain environment.

Capital Flight: Investors and businesses may seek jurisdictions with more predictable and favorable policies for their investments. This could result in capital and talent flight to places offering a more stable and conducive investment environment.

Effects on Competitiveness: State intervention negatively impacting investment and growth can have effects on national and international economic competitiveness. Countries with more attractive investment policies may outperform those with less effective government interventions.

Delays in Investment Decisions: Political and fiscal uncertainty can lead to delays in investment decisions. Companies may postpone projects and expansions until the direction of government policies is clarified, potentially affecting short and long-term economic momentum.

Impact on Employment and Incomes: Reduced investment and economic growth can have direct effects on employment and incomes. Less investment and business expansion can limit job opportunities and affect the standard of living of the population.

The relationship between state intervention, investment, and economic growth is complex and subject to various factors. While some argue that certain levels of intervention are necessary to correct market failures and promote equity, others contend that excess intervention can have negative consequences for economic activity and investment. In practice, finding an appropriate balance between intervention and a free market is a key challenge for policymakers.

Inequity in the Distribution of Tax Burdens: Some criticisms focus on the inequity in the distribution of tax burdens. It is argued that certain groups may be disproportionately affected by certain taxes, potentially increasing economic disparities.

Regressive Taxes: Some taxes are considered regressive, meaning they disproportionately affect lower-income taxpayers compared to those with higher incomes. Indirect taxes, such as consumption taxes, are often cited as examples of regressive taxes, as all consumers, regardless of their income, pay the same rate on goods and services.

Exemptions and Deductions Favoring High Incomes: The presence of tax exemptions and deductions that primarily benefit higher-income taxpayers can contribute to inequity. If certain groups have more access to these exemptions, the tax system may indirectly favor those with higher incomes, thus increasing economic disparities.

Proportional Tax Burden: Proportional tax burden implies that all taxpayers pay the same proportion of their income in taxes. Some critics argue that this structure can result in an uneven burden, as a smaller proportion of the incomes of low-income households may be allocated to basic needs and essential expenses.

Impact on Economic Mobility: A tax system that disproportionately affects low-income groups can have implications for economic mobility. If taxes hinder the accumulation of wealth and improvement of the financial situation for those with low incomes, it could contribute to the perpetuation of economic inequality over time.

Inequality in Access to Tax Benefits: Inequality in access to tax benefits can also be a cause for concern. If certain groups have more ability to take advantage of tax benefits, such as tax credits or specific deductions, the distribution of tax burdens can become even more unequal.

Pressure on Disposable Incomes: When taxes on essential goods and services represent a significant portion of the incomes of low-income households, this can create additional pressure on their disposable incomes. This affects more strongly those who allocate a larger proportion of their incomes to basic needs.

Contribution to Overall Inequality: Inequity in the distribution of tax burdens can contribute to overall economic inequality in society. If the tax system does not effectively address income and wealth disparities, it may amplify existing gaps between different social strata.

Equity in the distribution of tax burdens is a significant topic in fiscal policy design. Policymakers seek tax structures that are fair and mitigate, rather than exacerbate, economic disparities. Ongoing review and adaptation of tax systems are essential to address these concerns and promote an equitable distribution of the tax burden.

These criticisms represent specific perspectives, and the assessment of state intervention in the economy is a complex issue subject to various approaches and economic theories. Many advocates of state intervention argue that it is necessary to correct market failures, reduce inequality, and provide public goods and services.

25.Financial and Banking Crises

The Austrian perspective on financial and banking crises is derived from the Austrian School of Economics, which includes thinkers such as Ludwig von Mises and Friedrich Hayek. From this standpoint, financial crises are seen as the outcome of distortions in the production structure caused by interventions in the financial system and excessive credit expansion.

Economic Cycle and Credit Expansion: The Austrian perspective emphasizes the central role of credit expansion in the economic cycle. It argues that when central banks increase the money and credit supply, a false sense of economic prosperity is generated. This results in artificially low interest rates, stimulating investment and spending.

Credit Expansion and False Sense of Prosperity: The Austrian perspective contends that when central banks expand the money and credit supply, it creates a false sense of economic prosperity. The abundance of credit leads to artificially low interest rates, facilitating access to credit for consumers and businesses.

Low Interest Rates and Investment Stimulus: With lower interest rates, investment becomes more attractive. Companies find it more profitable to fund investment projects, and consumers are motivated to take loans for durable goods such as homes and cars.

Distortions in the Production Structure: Credit expansion causes distortions in the economy's production structure. The low interest rate does not accurately reflect the real availability of resources and consumers' time preferences. This leads to an inefficient allocation of resources to unsustainable areas in the long term.

Investment in Unprofitable Projects: Companies may invest in projects that, under more realistic interest rate conditions, would not be economically viable. Credit expansion can result in excessive investments in specific sectors, creating asset bubbles.

Economic Boom: The initial period of credit expansion and increased investment is known as the "boom." During this time, the economy appears to be thriving, with apparent growth and increased economic activity.

Rise in Consumption and Indebtedness: Low interest rates also encourage an increase in consumption, as consumers are more likely to borrow to finance purchases. This contributes to the sense of prosperity during the boom phase.

Inevitability of Correction: The Austrian perspective argues that the credit expansion phase is unsustainable in the long run, and a correction is inevitable. At some point, interest rates must adjust to economic reality, revealing the unsustainability of investments made during the boom.

Bust or Recession Phase: The correction phase is known as the "bust" or recession. During this time, unsustainable investments are liquidated, unprofitable projects are abandoned, and the economy experiences a contraction.

Importance of Market Cleansing: The Austrian perspective highlights the importance of allowing the market to undergo necessary cleansing during the recession phase. This involves the liquidation of overvalued assets, the reallocation of resources to more sustainable uses, and the restoration of coordination between savings and investment.

Austrian Perspective Summary: According to the Austrian perspective, credit expansion driven by expansive monetary policies leads to distortions in the production structure and an economic cycle that goes through boom and bust phases. The natural market correction during the recession is considered essential to restore long-term economic health.

Malinvestment and Distortions in the Production Structure: Credit expansion at artificially low interest rates leads to poor investments and distortions in the production structure. Resources are directed toward areas that are not sustainable in the long term, creating bubbles in specific sectors of the economy.

Credit Expansion and Low Interest Rates: Credit expansion, driven by expansive monetary policies, results in artificially low interest rates. This makes borrowing more attractive for businesses and consumers, as the cost of borrowing is lower.

Investment Stimulus: Lower interest rates stimulate investment in capital projects. Companies, seeing the low cost of credit, may embark on expansion projects, new developments, and acquisitions.

Mismatch Between Supply and Demand: Low interest rates do not accurately reflect the real supply and demand for savings in the economy. This leads to a mismatch between the supply of capital goods (investments) and the actual market demand.

Investments in Unsustainable Areas: Credit expansion may lead companies to invest in areas that, under more realistic market conditions, would not be economically sustainable. Resources are allocated to projects that may not have a sustainable long-term demand.

Creation of Bubbles in Specific Sectors: Easy credit availability can lead to the creation of bubbles in specific sectors of the economy. For example, during a real estate boom, credit expansion may result in overinvestment in the construction sector and the overvaluation of real estate assets.

False Sense of Prosperity: During the credit expansion phase, the economy experiences a false sense of prosperity. Apparent growth and economic benefits are driven by credit expansion rather than solid economic fundamentals.

Need for Correction: The Austrian perspective argues that this phase of malinvestment and distortions in the production structure is unsustainable in the long term and requires correction. This correction manifests during the recession phase of the economic cycle.

Liquidation of Overvalued Assets: During the recession, overvalued assets and unsustainable investments are liquidated. Companies may face financial difficulties, and some projects may be abandoned.

Reallocation of Resources to Sustainable Uses: The recession phase allows for a reallocation of resources to more sustainable uses and in line with the actual preferences of consumers. Resources are redirected toward areas that are more in demand by society.

Restoration of Coordination between Saving and Investment: Market correction during the recession is seen as essential to restoring coordination between saving and investment, allowing the economy to adjust to a more solid foundation.

Austrian Perspective Summary: In summary, according to the Austrian perspective, the coordination between saving and investment during the credit expansion phase is a fundamental factor contributing to the economic cycle and requires correction to restore long-term economic health.

Boom and Bust: The phase of credit expansion is known as the "boom," during which the economy appears to be thriving. However, this phase is unsustainable in the long run. The eventual credit tightening or an increase in interest rates reveals the unsustainability of investments made during the boom, leading to the "bust" or recession phase.

Boom Phase (Credit Expansion): During the boom phase, credit expansion and artificially low-interest rates generate a significant increase in investment and spending. The economy experiences an apparent period of prosperity with apparent economic growth.

Appearance of Economic Prosperity: Credit expansion facilitates borrowing for investment and consumption. Companies increase investment in projects, and consumers take out loans to purchase durable goods. This creates an appearance of economic prosperity.

Unsustainable Investments: During the boom, investments are made in areas that, under more realistic interest rate conditions, would not be economically sustainable in the long term. Distortion in the production structure leads to an inefficient allocation of resources.

Bubbles in Specific Sectors: Easy credit availability can lead to bubbles in specific sectors of the economy, such as the real estate or financial market. Asset prices may significantly rise beyond their economic fundamentals.

Bust Phase (Recession): The bust or recession phase occurs when the unsustainability of investments made during the boom becomes evident. Credit tightening or an increase in interest rates reveals the fragility of the apparent prosperity.

Credit Tightening and Increased Interest Rates: Eventually, market conditions change. There may be credit tightening by banks or an increase in interest rates, often in response to inflationary pressures or the need to adjust expansive monetary policies.

Market Correction: Credit tightening and the increase in interest rates trigger a market correction. Unsustainable investments and misallocations of resources are revealed, and an adjustment process begins.

Liquidation of Overvalued Assets: During the recession, overvalued assets, such as properties or financial securities, may experience liquidation as investors adjust their portfolios to adapt to new market conditions.

Unemployment and Economic Contraction: The correction may be accompanied by an increase in unemployment and economic contraction. Companies may reduce production and adjust operations to adapt to new market conditions.

Restoration of Economic Stability: Although painful, the recession phase is viewed from the Austrian perspective as a necessary process to correct distortions and restore long-term economic stability.

In summary, "Boom and Bust" in the Austrian perspective represents the economic cycle characterized by a phase of credit expansion (boom) followed by a phase of credit tightening and market correction (bust). This theory emphasizes the importance of allowing the market to make natural adjustments to maintain long-term stability.

Market Correction and Cleaning Up Bad Investments: The Austrian perspective argues that the recession is a necessary process to correct bad investments and restore coordination between savings and investment. During this phase, unsustainable investments are liquidated, and resources are reallocated to activities more aligned with consumer preferences.

Recession as a Correction Process: From the Austrian perspective, the recession is seen as a necessary correction process in which distortions generated during the credit expansion phase (boom) are adjusted. During this phase, the goal is to restore coordination between savings and investment.

Liquidation of Unsustainable Investments: During the recession, investments made during the boom that proved unsustainable in the long term are liquidated. This may include scaling back investment projects, the bankruptcy of overleveraged companies, and the fall of overvalued asset prices.

Resource Reallocation: The recession allows for the reallocation of resources to more sustainable uses aligned with the real preferences of consumers. Resources that were directed to unsustainable investments during the boom are redirected to sectors with stronger demand and in line with market conditions.

Labor Market Adjustment: The recession also involves adjustments in the labor market. Economic contraction can lead to a decrease in demand for work in certain sectors, resulting in layoffs and workforce adjustments.

Restoration of Coordination: By clearing bad investments and allowing the liquidation of unsustainable assets, the recession contributes to the restoration of coordination between savings and investment. Interest rates and market signals can adjust to reflect true economic conditions.

Role of the Market Process: The Austrian perspective emphasizes the importance of allowing the market process to naturally make these adjustments, without excessive interventions that could further distort the economy.

Discouragement of Excessive Speculation: Market correction during the recession also acts as a natural discouragement of excessive speculation and unreasonable risk-taking during boom periods. Market participants learn from the consequences of poor investment decisions.

Preparation for a New Cycle: The recession prepares the ground for a new economic cycle. As accumulated distortions are cleared, the foundation for more sustainable and balanced growth in the future is created.

According to the Austrian perspective, recession and market correction are essential components of the natural economic process. Although they may be painful in the short term, these processes are considered necessary to restore long-term health and coordination in the economy.

Avoiding Interventions that Prolong the Recession: The Austrian perspective advocates avoiding government interventions that may prolong the recession. It argues that attempts to artificially stimulate demand or keep troubled financial institutions afloat can interfere with the natural market adjustment process.

Avoiding Artificial Stimuli: The Austrian perspective argues that artificial stimuli, such as additional monetary expansion or fiscal stimulus programs during a recession, can further distort the economy. Instead of allowing natural correction, these interventions can maintain unsustainable investments and delay recovery.

Natural Market Adjustment Process: The underlying idea is that the market has the ability to naturally adjust during a recession. Allowing unsustainable investments to be liquidated and resources to be reallocated is part of the necessary process to restore coordination between savings and investment.

Learning from Consequences: The recession, according to the Austrian perspective, acts as a lesson for market participants, teaching them about the consequences of unsustainable investment decisions and excessive speculation during boom periods. Avoiding government interference allows this learning process to take place.

Bankruptcy of Financial Institutions: The Austrian perspective warns against attempts to keep financially troubled institutions afloat during the recession. Allowing these institutions to face the consequences of their poor financial decisions is part of the market correction process.

Restoring the Soundness of the Financial System: By allowing financial institutions to face the consequences of their actions, it is argued that it contributes to the restoration of the soundness of the financial system. Interventions to rescue institutions can create perverse incentives and perpetuate systemic problems.

Risks of Monetary Manipulation: The Austrian perspective warns about the risks of monetary manipulation to stimulate demand during the recession. It argues that these actions can create additional distortions in interest rates and resource allocation, prolonging the necessary adjustment process.

Emphasis on Non-Intervention: Overall, the Austrian perspective emphasizes limited government intervention in the economy. It argues that government interventions, especially those that distort market signals, can lead to unintended consequences and imbalances.

Preparation for Natural Recovery: By avoiding interventions that prolong the recession, the Austrian perspective advocates preparing the ground for a natural and sustainable recovery. Market correction and the restoration of coordination between saving and investment are considered essential for this process.

In summary, the Austrian perspective advocates allowing the market to adjust naturally during recessions, avoiding government interventions that could interfere with the necessary correction process to restore long-term economic stability.

Emphasis on Decentralization and Economic Freedom: The proposed solution from the Austrian perspective often involves an emphasis on decentralization and economic freedom. It advocates allowing the market to make adjustments without excessive interventions and fostering conditions that facilitate effective coordination between saving and investment.

Decentralization as a Principle: The Austrian perspective advocates decentralization as a fundamental principle. It proposes that economic decisions and market signals should emerge in a decentralized manner through interactions between individuals and businesses, rather than being centrally planned or directed by the government.

Economic Freedom as a Driver of Progress: Economic freedom is considered a crucial driver of progress and efficiency. The ability of individuals and businesses to make free decisions about production, investment, and consumption is seen as an essential facilitator of economic development.

Market Self-Regulation: The perspective from the Austrian school trusts in the market's ability to self-regulate. It argues that, in the absence of external interventions, prices, interest rates, and market participants' decisions will naturally adjust to reach an equilibrium.

Effective Coordination between Saving and Investment: Decentralization and economic freedom are considered conducive to facilitating effective coordination between saving and investment. When individuals have the freedom to make decisions based on undistorted market signals, a more efficient allocation of resources is expected.

Prevention of Bubbles and Bad Investments: It is argued that decentralization and economic freedom can help prevent the formation of bubbles and bad investments. Decentralized decision-making is more in tune with real market conditions, and competition among diverse entities contributes to a more disciplined process.

Limited Role of Government: From the Austrian perspective, a limited government role in the economy is advocated. It argues that government interventions, especially those distorting market signals, can lead to unintended consequences and imbalances.

Promotion of Competition: Competition is considered an essential element for economic efficiency. Decentralization and economic freedom foster an environment where diverse entities compete to meet the needs and desires of consumers, driving innovation and efficiency.

Resilience of the Decentralized System: The Austrian perspective suggests that a decentralized system is more resilient to shocks and disruptions. The diversity of local decisions and adaptations can help absorb and overcome economic challenges.

Encouragement of Creativity and Innovation: Economic freedom provides the necessary space for creativity and innovation. When individuals have the freedom to pursue their goals and undertake entrepreneurial initiatives, progress and continuous improvement are fostered.

The Austrian perspective advocates for a decentralized and free-market approach as a way to allow natural adjustments in the economy, prevent distortions, and facilitate effective coordination between saving and investment. Trust in the market's self-regulating ability and the promotion of individual freedom are key principles in this economic vision.

Critique of the Fractional Reserve System: The Austrian perspective also criticizes the fractional reserve system, which allows banks to lend more money than they have in reserves. It argues that this contributes to credit expansion and the creation of fiat money, which can exacerbate distortions in the economy.

Unbacked Credit Expansion: The Austrian critique focuses on the fact that the fractional reserve system allows banks to lend more money than they actually have in reserves. This means that the creation of new loans is not backed by an equivalent increase in real deposits or reserves.

Creation of Fiat Money: The credit expansion resulting from the fractional reserve system leads to the creation of fiat money. In other words, new money supply is created in the form of bank deposits, but this money is not backed by an equivalent amount of real assets.

Distortion in Interest Rates: The critique argues that this credit expansion distorts interest rates in the economy. With more money available for loans than would be in a full-reserve system, interest rates can be artificially low, stimulating investment and spending.

Economic Cycle and Bubbles: The Austrian perspective contends that credit expansion driven by the fractional reserve system contributes to the economic cycle, generating boom phases followed by recessions. The abundance of credit facilitates the formation of bubbles in specific sectors of the economy.

Mismatch between Saving and Investment: By allowing banks to lend more than their reserves, it is argued that the fractional reserve system disrupts the natural relationship between saving and investment. This can lead to misallocations of resources and unsustainable investments.

Risk of Banking Crises: The critique also points out that the fractional reserve system may increase the risk of banking crises. If depositors simultaneously withdraw their funds, banks may struggle to meet their obligations, potentially triggering financial crises.

Inherently Inflationary Nature: From the Austrian perspective, the fractional reserve system is seen as inherently inflationary. The creation of fiat money without real backing can lead to a depreciation of the currency's value over time.

Need for Full Reserves or Alternatives: Some advocates of the Austrian perspective suggest that, instead of the fractional reserve system, a system of full reserves or alternatives that limit the creation of fiat money would be preferable, maintaining a more direct relationship between deposits and reserves.

The Austrian critique of the fractional reserve system focuses on the perceived problems associated with unbacked credit expansion and the creation of fiat money, arguing that this contributes to distortions in the economy and the economic cycle.

The Austrian perspective is not the only way to analyze financial crises, and there are various theories and approaches in economics. However, the Austrian perspective offers a distinctive view centered on the effects of credit expansion and the importance of market processes in correcting economic imbalances.

26.Competition Theory

Economic Efficiency: Competition fosters economic efficiency by pressuring companies to use their resources more effectively. In a competitive environment, companies seek to reduce costs, enhance the quality of their products and services, and optimize their processes to gain advantages over their competitors.

Pressure to Improve Quality: In a competitive market, companies are motivated to consistently improve the quality of their products and services. Consumers have choices and tend to favor providers offering better quality, driving companies to innovate and raise standards.

Competition for Consumer Preference: Competition creates a scenario where companies vie for consumer preference. Consumers have options and tend to choose products and services that offer the best value for money. This motivates companies to stand out by improving quality.

Market Differentiation: Quality becomes a key differentiation factor in a competitive environment. Companies strive to distinguish themselves from the competition by offering products or services perceived as superior in terms of features, durability, effectiveness, or other quality attributes.

Innovation to Raise Standards: Competitive pressure drives innovation in products and processes. Companies constantly seek ways to improve quality by introducing innovations that not only meet current consumer needs but also create new expectations and standards in the market.

Immediate Market Feedback: In a competitive environment, the market provides immediate feedback. If a company succeeds in improving the quality of its products or services, it is likely to experience an increase in demand and consumer preference. Similarly, negative feedback due to quality issues can have significant consequences.

Consumer Loyalty: Quality plays a crucial role in building consumer loyalty. Companies that consistently maintain high quality standards tend to gain the trust and loyalty of customers, translating into long-term relationships and repeat business.

Continuous Improvement: The pressure to improve quality fosters a culture of continuous improvement in companies. Practices and processes are adopted to consistently identify and address areas of improvement, contributing to the constant evolution of quality.

Competition as a Catalyst for Standards: Competition not only motivates individual companies to improve quality but also acts as a catalyst to raise overall standards across the industry. When a company sets new quality standards, others seek to match or exceed those standards to stay competitive.

Responsibility to Consumers: In a competitive market, companies recognize the responsibility to provide products and services that meet or exceed consumer expectations in terms of quality. Lack of quality can have negative consequences in terms of customer loss and reputation damage.

In summary, the pressure to improve quality in a competitive market is a key driver of innovation, differentiation, and consumer satisfaction. This dynamic contributes to a constantly evolving business environment where quality is a central element for long-term success.

Incentives for Price Reduction: Competition also puts pressure on prices. Companies strive to offer products and services at competitive prices to attract consumers. This benefits consumers by providing affordable options and creating a constant incentive for production efficiency.

Competition for Consumer Preference: In a competitive environment, companies compete for consumer preference. Offering products and services at competitive prices becomes a strategy to attract customers and gain market share.

Consumer Choice Based on Price: Consumers, having choices among various providers, tend to select those offering quality products at lower prices. This dynamic encourages companies to find ways to reduce costs and offer more attractive prices to stay competitive.

Production Efficiency: The pressure to reduce prices motivates companies to improve production efficiency. They seek more efficient methods, adopt innovative technologies, and optimize processes to lower costs and, consequently, offer products at lower prices without sacrificing quality.

Stimulus for Cost Innovation: Competition creates a constant stimulus for cost management innovation. Companies look for creative ways to produce goods and services at a lower cost, whether through improving the supply chain, implementing more efficient technologies, or optimizing production processes.

Price Transparency: In competitive markets, price transparency is common, and consumers can easily compare prices of similar products offered by different companies. This intensifies competition and compels companies to maintain competitive prices to attract consumers.

Incentives for Profit Margin Reduction: Competition can also generate incentives for companies to reduce profit margins to offer more attractive prices. This approach can be strategic to gain market share and generate higher sales volumes.

Elastic Demand and Price Sensitivity: Competition is affected by the elasticity of demand, i.e., consumer sensitivity to price changes. In competitive environments, companies recognize that price reductions can lead to significant increases in demand, which can be beneficial for their market position.

Benefits for Consumers: Competition that pressures prices downward translates into tangible benefits for consumers. They can access a variety of products at more affordable prices, improving their purchasing power and providing them with broader choices.

Market Dynamism: Constant competition for lower prices contributes to market dynamism. Companies must adapt quickly to changing conditions to maintain their competitiveness, driving innovation and continuous improvement.

Competition that pressures prices benefits consumers by providing more affordable options and stimulates companies to improve production efficiency to stay competitive in the market. This dynamism fosters an environment where quality and efficiency are key factors for business success.

Entry of New Competitors: In competitive markets, the entry of new competitors is a constant possibility. This not only increases options for consumers but also keeps established companies on alert, as competition can arise at any time.

Market Dynamism: The possibility of new competitors entering the market contributes to its dynamism and vitality. This dynamism compels existing companies to stay agile and adapt to changes in market conditions.

Expanded Options for Consumers: The entry of new competitors expands options for consumers. The diversity of offerings and business approaches provides consumers with a wider range of products and services to choose from, enhancing their ability to find options that suit their needs.

Additional Pressure on Prices: The entry of new competitors puts additional pressure on prices in the market. Intensified competition can lead to price reductions as companies seek to attract and retain customers in a more competitive environment.

Stimulus for Innovation: Competition between established companies and new entrants stimulates innovation. To stand out in a competitive market, companies constantly seek to improve their products, services, and processes, leading to technological advancements and improvements for consumers.

Need for Differentiation: The presence of new competitors compels existing companies to differentiate themselves. To maintain their market position, companies must offer unique value propositions, leading to increased attention to quality, customer service, and innovation.

Adaptation to Changes in Consumer Demand: New competitors often enter the market with fresh approaches and innovative solutions. This can challenge established companies to adapt to changes in consumer preferences and demands to remain relevant.

Competitive Alertness: The possibility of new competitors entering keeps established companies constantly alert. Competition doesn't only come from existing competitors but can also emerge from new companies with disruptive ideas and approaches.

Challenge to Market Share: The entry of new competitors can pose a challenge to the market share of existing companies. Those that do not respond effectively to competition may lose market share to more agile and innovative competitors.

Market Stability and Resilience: Although the entry of new competitors can pose challenges for existing companies, it also contributes to the stability and resilience of the market as a whole. The ability to attract new participants indicates that the market is attractive and offers opportunities.

The entry of new competitors in competitive markets is a vital component that promotes competition, innovation, and dynamism. This dynamic benefits consumers by providing them with more options and pressures companies to continually improve to maintain their competitiveness.

Stimulus for Innovation:

Competition is a crucial driver of innovation. Companies seek to develop new or improved products and services to differentiate themselves and gain market share. Competitive pressure drives research and development, benefiting society in terms of technological advancements and improvements in daily life.

Differentiation and Competitive Advantage:

Competition motivates companies to find ways to differentiate themselves and gain a competitive advantage. Developing innovative products or services becomes a key strategy to stand out in the market and attract consumers.

Pressure to Improve Products and Services:

Competitive pressure compels companies to continually enhance the quality and functionality of their products and services. Innovation is essential to keeping up with changing consumer expectations and outperforming competitors.

Investment in Research and Development (R&D):

Companies compete not only in terms of existing products but also in terms of future ideas. Competition drives companies to invest in research and development (R&D) to discover and create new technologies, processes, and solutions.

Problem Solving and Customer Satisfaction:

Competition creates an environment where companies constantly seek to solve problems and meet customer needs more effectively than their competitors. Innovation becomes a means to address challenges and provide more efficient solutions.

Adaptation to Market Changes:

Innovation is also crucial for adapting to changes in the market. Companies must be agile and able to adjust their offerings in response to emerging trends, consumer preferences, and technological advances.

Competition as a Catalyst for Discoveries:

Competition acts as a catalyst for significant discoveries. Companies compete not only to improve existing products but also to find new solutions and approaches that fundamentally change how needs and problems are addressed.

Fostering Creativity and Originality:

Competition fosters an environment where creativity and originality are highly valued. Companies seek unique ideas and innovative approaches to differentiate themselves and capture market attention.

Development of Emerging Markets:

Competition can stimulate the development of emerging markets by driving the introduction of pioneering products and services. The pursuit of untapped opportunities can lead to the creation of new market segments.

Benefits for Society:

Competition-driven innovation benefits society overall by generating technological advancements, efficiency improvements, and solutions to challenges. These benefits can impact various aspects of daily life and contribute to social progress.

Competition not only drives continuous improvement but also serves as an essential engine for innovation. Competitive dynamics create an environment conducive to the development of new ideas and solutions, generating benefits for both businesses and society as a whole.

Adaptability to Change:

In a competitive environment, companies must be adaptable and respond quickly to changes in consumer preferences, technology, and market conditions. This adaptability contributes to the resilience of the economic system.

Market Dynamism:

Competitive environments are often dynamic, with constant changes in consumer preferences, technological advancements, and market conditions. Adaptability allows companies to efficiently adjust to these dynamics.

Swift Response to Emerging Trends:

Competition often involves identifying and exploiting emerging trends. Adaptable companies can quickly respond to these trends, whether by introducing new products or modifying marketing strategies.

Innovation and Continuous Development:

Adaptability is linked to the ability to innovate and continuously develop. Companies seeking to maintain their competitiveness must be willing to adopt new technologies, processes, and approaches to enhance their products and services.

Adjustment to Changes in Consumer Demand:

Consumer preferences can change rapidly. Adaptable companies can adjust their offerings to meet these new demands, ensuring that their products and services remain relevant.

Organizational Flexibility:

Adaptability involves having a flexible organizational structure. This allows companies to quickly adjust their operations, allocate resources efficiently, and make agile decisions in response to changes in the business environment.

Crisis Management:

Adaptability is tested during periods of crisis. Companies that can adjust quickly and make effective decisions are more likely to overcome economic, social, or other challenges.

Continuous Learning:

Adaptability requires a continuous learning approach. Companies must be willing to analyze and learn from their experiences, as well as incorporate market feedback to improve their practices and strategies.

Competition for Efficiency:

Adaptability is also related to competition for efficiency. Adaptable companies constantly seek ways to improve their internal processes and reduce costs to remain competitive in the market.

Long-Term Relevance Maintenance:

Adaptability contributes to the maintenance of long-term relevance. Companies that can adapt to changes in the business environment are better positioned to survive and thrive as market conditions evolve.

Adaptability to change is essential in competitive environments. Companies that cultivate this capability are better equipped to face challenges and capitalize on opportunities, contributing to the resilience of the overall economic system.

Continuous Improvement:

Competition fosters a mindset of continuous improvement. Companies that seek to constantly stand out must assess and enhance their business practices, contributing to a dynamic environment of economic progress.

Market Dynamism·

Competitive environments are often dynamic, with constant changes in consumer preferences, technological advancements, and market conditions. Adaptability allows companies to adjust to these dynamics efficiently.

Swift Response to Emerging Trends:

Competition often involves identifying and exploiting emerging trends. Adaptable companies can quickly respond to these trends, either by introducing new products or modifying marketing strategies.

Innovation and Continuous Development:

Adaptability is linked to the ability to innovate and continuously develop. Companies seeking to maintain their competitiveness must be willing to adopt new technologies, processes, and approaches to enhance their products and services.

Adjustment to Changes in Consumer Demand:

Consumer preferences can change rapidly. Adaptable companies can adjust their offerings to meet these new demands, ensuring that their products and services remain relevant.

Organizational Flexibility:

Adaptability involves having a flexible organizational structure. This allows companies to quickly adjust their operations, allocate resources efficiently, and make agile decisions in response to changes in the business environment.

Crisis Management:

The ability to adapt is tested during periods of crisis. Companies that can adjust quickly and make effective decisions are more likely to overcome economic, social, or other challenges.

Continuous Learning:

Adaptability requires a continuous learning approach. Companies must be willing to analyze and learn from their experiences, as well as incorporate market feedback to improve their practices and strategies.

Competition for Efficiency:

Adaptability is also related to competition for efficiency. Adaptable companies constantly seek ways to improve their internal processes and reduce costs to remain competitive in the market.

Maintenance of Long-Term Relevance:

Adaptability contributes to the maintenance of long-term relevance. Companies that can adapt to changes in the business environment are better positioned to survive and prosper as market conditions evolve.

Adaptability to change is essential in competitive environments. Companies that cultivate this capability are better equipped to face challenges and capitalize on opportunities, contributing to the resilience of the overall economic system.

Continuous Improvement:

Competition fosters a mindset of continuous improvement. Companies that seek to constantly stand out must assess and enhance their business practices, contributing to a dynamic environment of economic progress.

Culture of Assessment and Feedback:

Competition fosters a culture of constant assessment and feedback. Companies are constantly evaluating their performance compared to that of their competitors, seeking areas for improvement and leveraging market feedback.

Identification of Improvement Opportunities:

Competition sharpens companies' ability to identify improvement opportunities. By observing the strategies and practices of competitors, companies can pinpoint areas where they can outperform the competition and enhance their market position.

Operational Efficiency:

Competition drives the pursuit of operational efficiency. Companies are constantly looking for ways to optimize their internal processes, reduce costs, and improve efficiency to deliver products and services more cost-effectively.

Innovation in Processes and Products:

Continuous improvement often involves innovation in processes and products. Companies compete to offer more efficient solutions, technologically advanced products, and services that exceed consumer expectations.

Organizational Agility:

Competition requires organizational agility. Companies seek to adapt quickly to changes in the market, adjusting strategies and processes to stay competitive. This agility is essential for continuous improvement.

Learning from Best Practices:

Competition allows companies to learn from the best practices of their competitors and other industries. This constant learning contributes to continuous improvement by incorporating successful approaches into their own operations.

Customer Satisfaction:

Competition sharpens the focus on customer satisfaction. Companies are continuously seeking ways to improve the quality of their products and services to ensure customer loyalty and gain market share.

Adaptation to Changes in Demand:

Continuous improvement involves adapting to changes in market demand. Companies constantly assess the changing needs of consumers and adjust their offerings to meet those demands more effectively.

Results Evaluation and KPIs:

Competition drives attention to results and key performance indicators (KPIs). Companies continually evaluate their performance in relation to specific goals and seek to improve areas that are not meeting expectations.

Development of Talent and Skills:

Continuous improvement also refers to the constant development of talents and skills within the organization. Companies seek to keep employees trained and motivated to drive innovation and performance.

Competition fosters a mindset of continuous improvement, where companies are constantly looking for opportunities to optimize their operations, deliver higher-quality products and services, and adapt to changing market conditions. This constant focus on improvement contributes to economic progress and the ability of companies to excel in highly competitive environments.

Benefits for Consumers:

Ultimately, competition translates into benefits for consumers. A wide range of options, competitive prices, and innovative products improve the quality of life for consumers by providing products and services that align with their needs and preferences.

Wide Range of Options:

Competition fosters a wide range of options for consumers. Different companies compete for market attention, offering a variety of products and services that cater to diverse preferences and needs.

Competitive Prices:

Competition exerts pressure on prices, leading to more competitive pricing. Companies seek to offer their products and services at attractive prices to gain market share, benefiting consumers by providing affordable options.

Improved Quality of Products and Services:

Competition compels companies to continually improve the quality of their products and services. The pursuit of differentiation from competitors leads to innovations and enhancements, benefiting consumers with higher-quality products and services.

Continuous Innovation:

Competition stimulates continuous innovation. Companies compete to offer technologically advanced, more efficient products and services that meet changing consumer demands, resulting in innovative benefits for consumers.

Enhanced Customer Attention:

Competition also results in improved customer attention. Companies seek to differentiate through customer service, providing more positive and satisfying experiences for consumers.

Adaptation to Consumer Preferences:

Companies in a competitive environment are consistently attentive to consumer preferences. This leads to greater adaptation of products and services to the specific demands of consumers, improving customer satisfaction.

Rapid Adoption of Technology:

Competition drives the rapid adoption of technological advances. Companies aim to incorporate new technologies to stand out in the market, and consumers benefit by gaining access to more modern and efficient products and services.

Safety and Quality Standards:

Competition also contributes to the establishment and maintenance of safety and quality standards. Companies must adhere to these standards to gain consumer trust and effectively compete in the market.

Facilitation of Informed Choice:

Competition encourages transparency in information about products and services. Consumers can make more informed decisions by easily comparing offerings from different companies, allowing them to select options that best fit their needs.

Development of New Market Segments:

Competition can lead to the development of new market segments. Companies seek to identify untapped niches to differentiate themselves, resulting in the creation of products and services specific to certain consumer groups.

In summary, competition in markets brings significant benefits to consumers by providing a wide range of options, competitive prices, innovative products, and high-quality services. This dynamic process continually improves the quality of life for consumers by effectively meeting their needs and preferences.

Regulation and Competition:

The relationship between regulation and competition is an important aspect to consider. While certain regulations may be necessary to ensure fair play and protect consumers, excessive regulation can also hinder competition and innovation.

Need for Regulation:

Regulation is often necessary to ensure fair play in the market and protect consumers. It can address unfair business practices, prevent abuse of power by dominant companies, and ensure the safety and quality of products and services.

Consumer Protection:

Regulations can set standards for the safety and quality of products, thus protecting consumer interests. They can also ensure that information provided by companies is accurate and that consumers are protected against deceptive practices.

Prevention of Monopoly and Unfair Competition:

Antitrust regulations aim to prevent the formation of monopolies and promote competition. This may include restrictions on anticompetitive business practices, mergers that could reduce competition, and the abuse of dominant positions in the market.

Financial Stability:

In some cases, regulation seeks to ensure the financial stability of the market and prevent economic crises. This may include regulations for financial institutions, stock markets, and other key sectors of the economy.

Guarantee of Labor Rights:

Regulation can address issues related to labor rights, ensuring fair and safe working conditions. This may include regulations on minimum wages, working hours, and employment conditions.

Promotion of Fair Competition:

Regulations can also aim to promote fair competition by establishing rules that apply equitably to all companies. This can prevent unfair practices that could harm smaller competitors.

Innovation and Competition:

While regulation may be necessary to address specific issues, excessive regulation can also hinder innovation and competition. Too many regulatory barriers can make it difficult for new companies to enter the market and compete with established firms.

Administrative Burden:

Excessive regulation can impose a significant administrative burden on companies. Compliance with numerous regulations may require considerable resources, especially for smaller businesses, potentially affecting their ability to compete in the market.

Adaptability and Technological Change:

The rapid pace of technological change can outstrip the ability of regulations to keep up. In innovative sectors, regulations must be adaptable enough not to hinder the introduction of new technologies and business models.

Risk-Based Approach:

Some regulatory approaches advocate for a risk-based approach, where stricter regulations apply to high-risk activities, allowing greater flexibility in lower-risk areas to encourage innovation and competition.

The relationship between regulation and competition is complex and requires careful balance. While regulation is essential to address issues and protect consumers, an excessive approach can have negative consequences for competition and innovation in the economy. Policy formulation should seek to find an appropriate balance that ensures a fair and competitive market environment.

The theory of competition highlights how market competition drives efficiency, innovation, and continuous improvement, benefiting consumers and contributing to economic progress. Healthy competition creates a dynamic environment that promotes adaptability and business excellence.

27.Regulation Theory

Regulation Objectives:

The effectiveness of regulation is assessed by examining whether it achieves its stated objectives. These objectives may include consumer protection, prevention of unfair business practices, financial stability, and other related aspects.

Consumer Protection:

It is analyzed whether the regulation fulfills its objective of protecting consumers from dangerous or deceptive products and services. This involves evaluating whether established regulations ensure safety, accurate information, and fairness in commercial transactions.

Prevention of Unfair Business Practices:

Regulation aims to prevent unfair business practices such as deceptive advertising, unfair competition, or market manipulation. The evaluation involves determining whether established regulations are effective in preventing and penalizing such practices.

Financial Stability:

For regulations related to the financial sector, it is assessed whether regulatory measures contribute to the stability of the financial system. This includes evaluating the regulations' ability to prevent financial crises, protect depositors, and ensure the soundness of financial institutions.

Workplace Safety:

If the regulation aims to ensure safety and fair conditions in the workplace, the effectiveness of regulations in reducing workplace accidents, promoting safe conditions, and ensuring fundamental labor rights is evaluated.

Environmental Protection:

For environmental regulations, it is assessed whether regulatory measures succeed in protecting the environment. This involves considering the reduction of pollution, conservation of natural resources, and mitigation of negative impacts on biodiversity.

Market Efficiency:

For regulations seeking to improve market efficiency, it is evaluated whether they promote competition and prevent monopolistic practices. Effectiveness is measured by observing market dynamics and the presence of unfair barriers to entry for new competitors.

Social Equity:

In some cases, regulation aims to achieve social equity goals such as reducing economic disparities. The evaluation involves examining whether regulatory measures contribute to fair resource redistribution and reduce socio-economic gaps.

Transparency and Accountability:

It is assessed whether regulation contributes to transparency and accountability in business and government conduct. This involves checking information disclosure, access to relevant data, and accountability of stakeholders.

Regulatory effectiveness may vary depending on context, industry, and the specific nature of challenges faced. A comprehensive evaluation involves considering these factors and adjusting regulations as needed to achieve desired outcomes.

Economic Efficiency:

It is questioned whether regulation contributes to economic efficiency or, conversely, imposes administrative burdens and costs negatively affecting businesses and the economy. It is examined whether regulation achieves a proper balance between protection and efficiency.

Administrative Burdens and Costs:

Regulation may impose administrative burdens on businesses, such as the need to comply with specific reporting, record-keeping, and processes. It is evaluated whether these burdens are proportionate and justified by the regulation's benefits in terms of consumer protection, safety, or other stated objectives.

Impact on Competitiveness:

Regulation can impact the competitiveness of businesses, especially in global markets. It is examined how regulations affect companies' ability to compete and whether barriers are created that hinder new market entrants.

Flexibility and Adaptability:

Economic efficiency is influenced by the regulation's ability to adapt to changes in market conditions, technology, and other factors. It is assessed whether regulations are flexible enough to allow innovation and adaptation to new circumstances without imposing unnecessary obstacles.

Cost-Benefit:

A cost-benefit analysis is conducted to determine whether the benefits derived from regulation justify associated costs. This analysis involves comparing expected economic, social, and environmental benefits with costs, including direct costs for businesses and indirect costs for the overall economy.

Innovation and Entrepreneurship:

Regulation can have significant implications for innovation and entrepreneurship. It is examined whether regulations encourage or inhibit entrepreneurial creativity and the introduction of new technologies and business models. It is also evaluated whether regulations allow competition rather than restrict it.

Bureaucracy and Complexity:

Economic efficiency is affected by bureaucracy and complexity associated with regulatory compliance. It is assessed whether regulations are clear, easily understandable, and whether bureaucratic burdens for businesses, especially smaller ones with limited resources, are minimized.

Business Environment Stability:

It is examined how regulation contributes to the stability of the business environment. Companies value predictability and stability for long-term planning. The evaluation includes considering whether regulations change constantly and if changes are communicated transparently.

Impact on Small Businesses:

Special attention is paid to the impact of regulation on small businesses. These businesses often face greater challenges in complying with regulatory requirements. The evaluation seeks to determine if regulations are proportionate and if the capacities and limitations of small businesses are considered.

When questioning whether regulation contributes to economic efficiency, the aim is to ensure that regulations are effective in achieving their objectives without imposing an excessive burden that negatively affects economic activity and competitiveness.

Impact on Competition:

It is assessed how regulation affects competition in markets. While regulation may aim to promote competition, it is examined whether regulatory barriers could, in fact, hinder the entry of new competitors and limit competition.

Promotion of Competition:

It is analyzed whether regulation primarily aims to promote competition in markets. This involves evaluating whether regulations are designed to prevent anticompetitive practices, maintain diversity of options, and ensure fair competition among businesses.

Barriers to Entry:

The evaluation focuses on identifying whether regulation creates barriers that could hinder the entry of new competitors to the market. These barriers may include costly compliance requirements, regulations favoring established incumbents, or technological barriers.

Unfair Competition:

It is examined how regulation addresses unfair competition, such as deceptive advertising, market manipulation, and other practices that distort competition. The effectiveness of regulation is evaluated in terms of its ability to prevent and penalize such behaviors.

Market Concentration:

It is assessed whether regulation contributes to avoiding excessive market concentration, where a few companies dominate and can exert significant control. Concentration can reduce competition and limit options available to consumers.

Effects on Innovation:

The evaluation considers how regulation affects innovation in the market. Regulations that impede the entry of new ideas or technologies can limit competition and hinder progress. A balance is sought between necessary regulation and facilitating innovation.

Market Transparency:

Transparency is crucial for effective competition. It is assessed whether regulation promotes market transparency by requiring proper information disclosure, enabling consumers to make informed decisions, and allowing businesses to compete on an equal footing.

Access to Resources:

Regulation is evaluated in terms of its impact on access to resources and market opportunities. The goal is to determine whether regulations facilitate or hinder equitable access to essential resources, such as access to the supply chain or key infrastructure.

Protection against Monopolistic Practices:

The evaluation focuses on determining whether regulation is effective in protecting against monopolistic practices that could limit competition. This may include restrictions on mergers and acquisitions that could consolidate too much power in the market.

Sustainable Competition:

It is considered whether regulation contributes to the sustainability of competition over time. This involves evaluating whether regulations adapt to changes in the market and prevent situations that could harm long-term competition.

In summary, the evaluation of the impact on competition seeks to ensure that regulation fosters a healthy competitive environment, avoids anticompetitive practices, and promotes diversity of options for consumers. The effectiveness of regulation is measured in terms of how it contributes to the competitive dynamics of the market.

Adaptability to Changes:

The regulation's ability to adapt to changes in technology, the economy, and market conditions is critically evaluated. The speed of change may surpass the ability of regulations to stay updated, which could affect their effectiveness.

Continuous Monitoring:

Constant monitoring mechanisms are essential to identify significant changes in technology, the economy, and the market. This may include establishing specialized units or collaborating with experts in the field.

Quick Response:

The ability to respond quickly to changes is fundamental. Regulatory processes must be agile enough to adjust to new circumstances without losing effectiveness.

Flexibility in Regulatory Design:

Regulations must be designed flexibly to adapt to different scenarios. A more principle-based approach than specific rules may allow greater adaptability.

Interinstitutional Collaboration:

Collaboration between different regulatory entities, as well as with the private sector and other relevant actors, can facilitate the identification and management of changes. This collaboration can help avoid regulatory gaps

Periodic Evaluation:

The periodic review and update of regulations are essential. This may include scheduled reviews and assessments following significant changes in the environment.

Incorporation of Emerging Technologies:

Proactively considering the incorporation of emerging technologies into regulations can help avoid significant mismatches and ensure that regulations are relevant in a changing environment.

Training and Awareness:

Providing ongoing training to regulators on changes in technology, the economy, and the market can be crucial. Updated awareness improves adaptability.

Public Participation:

Including public participation in the regulatory process can bring diverse perspectives and help identify potential issues with existing regulations in a changing environment.

Impact Assessment:

Before implementing significant regulatory changes, conducting impact assessments can help understand implications and make adjustments before new regulations take effect.

Framework Legislation:

Establishing framework legislation allowing rapid and efficient updates to regulations can be key to ensuring long-term adaptability.

In summary, adaptability to changes in the regulatory environment involves a proactive approach, flexibility in design, and a constant capacity for evaluation and adjustment.

Costs and Benefits:

A cost-benefit analysis is conducted to determine whether the benefits of regulation justify associated costs. This involves considering economic impacts, administrative burdens for businesses, and the net effect on society.

Economic Impact:

Evaluate how regulation will affect the economy overall. This includes considering its impact on economic growth, investment, employment, and other macroeconomic indicators.

Administrative Costs:

Determine the administrative costs associated with regulatory compliance. This involves examining how regulation will affect how businesses operate and the resources they must dedicate to comply with new regulations.

Burden on Businesses:

Analyze the burden that regulation will impose on businesses, especially small and medium-sized enterprises (SMEs). Regulations that are too burdensome can affect competitiveness and the viability of businesses.

Impact on Innovation:

Considering how regulation can influence innovation is important. Balancing the need to protect the public with fostering innovation is crucial, as excessive regulations can discourage investment in research and development.

Positive and Negative Externalities: Identifying externalities associated with regulation, both positive and negative, involves considering unintended side effects that may arise from the implementation of regulation.

Social Impact: Evaluating how regulation will affect different segments of society includes considerations of equity and social justice, ensuring that regulation does not disproportionately harm specific groups.

Efficiency: Seeking ways to improve efficiency in achieving regulatory objectives involves minimizing unnecessary costs and maximizing net benefits.

Implementation Period: Considering the time needed for businesses and society to adapt to new regulations. A gradual implementation period can reduce initial costs and allow for a smoother transition.

Comparison of Alternatives: Evaluating different regulatory approaches and comparing the costs and benefits of each option can help select the most effective and efficient solution.

Continuous Monitoring: Establishing mechanisms for continuously monitoring the effects of regulation over time allows for adjustments if necessary, ensuring that regulation remains relevant and effective.

A comprehensive cost-benefit analysis provides a solid foundation for informed and balanced regulatory decision-making.

Compliance and Enforcement: The effectiveness of regulation largely depends on compliance and enforcement. Examining the government's ability to enforce regulations effectively and whether there is a proper balance between regulation and enforcement is crucial.

Clear Legal Framework: Ensuring that the legal framework is clearly defined and understandable helps prevent compliance and enforcement challenges caused by regulatory ambiguity.

Adequate Resources: Ensuring there are sufficient human and financial resources allocated to enforcement and compliance is essential. Lack of resources can limit the government's ability to enforce regulations.

Staff Training: Providing adequate training to enforcement personnel ensures a comprehensive understanding of regulations and enforcement methods.

Technology and Tools: Using efficient technology and tools to enhance enforcement effectiveness, such as monitoring systems, electronic databases, and other technologies facilitating compliance tracking.

Coordination between Agencies: Encouraging coordination between different government agencies responsible for enforcement can improve effectiveness and prevent gaps in enforcement.

Proportional Penalties: Establishing penalties proportionate to the degree of non-compliance is crucial. Excessive penalties can discourage compliance, while too lenient penalties may be ineffective.

Transparency in Enforcement: Maintaining a transparent enforcement process, clearly communicating expectations, and explaining the reasons behind enforcement decisions.

Incentives for Compliance: Establishing incentives to encourage voluntary compliance, such as tax benefits, public recognition, or additional opportunities for proactive compliance.

Risk Assessment: Conducting risk assessments to identify high-risk areas and prioritize enforcement based on these risks.

Feedback and Continuous Improvement: Collecting feedback on the enforcement process and using it for continuous improvements, including adjustments to regulations or enforcement methods based on accumulated experience.

Private Sector Participation: Involving the private sector in compliance and enforcement processes allows for effective collaboration and promotes a culture of self-regulation.

Assessing the effectiveness of compliance and enforcement is essential to ensure that regulations serve their purpose without creating unnecessary burdens for businesses and society. A proper balance between regulation and enforcement contributes to a fair and compliant environment.

Innovation and Economic Development: Regulation can have significant implications for innovation and economic development. Evaluating whether regulations promote or inhibit innovation and enable an environment conducive to sustainable economic growth is essential.

Promotion of Innovation: Assessing whether regulations encourage or hinder innovation. Regulations facilitating the entry of new technologies and approaches can drive innovation, while those imposing excessive barriers can hinder it.

Regulatory Flexibility: Checking the flexibility of regulations to adapt to technological advances. Overly rigid regulations can quickly become obsolete and limit the development of new solutions.

Incentives for Investment: Evaluating whether regulations stimulate or discourage investment in research and development. Companies may be more inclined to invest in innovation when regulations provide a stable and predictable framework.

Protection of Intellectual Property: Ensuring robust protection of intellectual property to incentivize innovation. Certainty in the ownership of ideas and the ability to benefit from innovation are key drivers for economic development.

Public-Private Collaboration: Promoting collaboration between the public and private sectors to drive innovation. Strategic partnerships can facilitate knowledge transfer and accelerate the development of new technologies.

Risk and Benefit Assessment: Carefully considering the risks and benefits associated with the implementation of regulations. Ensuring that any imposed restrictions are justified by social and environmental benefits.

Incentives for Sustainable Innovation: Establishing specific incentives for sustainable innovation, such as tax benefits, subsidies, or recognitions for companies developing solutions that positively contribute to the environment and society.

Adoption of International Standards: Considering the adoption of international standards to ensure that regulations do not create unnecessary trade barriers and allow for the global integration of innovations.

Impact Assessment: Conducting impact assessments to understand how proposed regulations will affect innovation and economic development. This can help adjust regulations as needed.

Continuous Monitoring: Implementing mechanisms for continuous monitoring to assess how regulations impact innovation and economic development over time. This allows for adjustments as needed.

In summary, regulations should be designed to foster an environment conducive to innovation and sustainable economic development. A proper balance between protecting public interests and promoting innovation can significantly contribute to long-term economic growth.

Market Conditions: Examining how specific market conditions affect the need for and effectiveness of regulation. In highly competitive markets, less regulatory intervention may be needed compared to markets showing signs of anti-competitive behavior.

Market Competition: Evaluating the level of competition in the market. In highly competitive markets with multiple players and low entry barriers, direct regulatory intervention may be less necessary.

Entry Barriers: Analyzing barriers preventing new competitors from entering the market. If barriers are high and limit competition, implementing regulations to encourage a more equitable environment may be necessary.

Market Concentration: Examining the concentration of power in the market. If a small number of companies dominate the market, implementing antitrust regulations may be necessary to prevent anti-competitive practices.

Market Transparency: Evaluating market transparency. Clear and accessible information for market participants can help maintain a competitive game and reduce the need for regulatory intervention.

Consumer Behavior: Considering consumer behavior and their ability to make informed decisions. If consumers have adequate information and significant choices, relying more on market self-regulation may be possible.

Market Externalities: Identifying market externalities that may not be efficiently addressed by the market itself. Negative externalities (such as pollution) may require regulations to internalize costs.

Incentives for Corporate Social Responsibility: Assessing whether companies have incentives for social responsibility and ethical behavior without regulatory intervention. In some cases, companies may adopt sustainable practices voluntarily.

Sector-Specific Needs: Recognizing sector-specific regulatory needs. Some sectors, such as health and safety, may require stricter regulations to protect public interests.

Systemic Risks: Analyzing systemic risks that may arise in the market. Regulatory intervention may be necessary to prevent crises and protect the stability of the financial system.

Impact Assessment: Conducting impact assessments to understand how proposed regulations will affect market conditions and adjusting them as necessary.

Continuous Monitoring: Implementing mechanisms for continuous monitoring to assess how market conditions evolve over time. This allows for adjustments to regulations in response to significant changes.

Evaluating market conditions is essential to determine the need and type of regulation required. A flexible regulatory approach tailored to the specific characteristics of each market may be key to achieving a proper balance.

Transparency and Citizen Participation: Evaluating transparency in the regulatory process and citizen participation. Inclusion of diverse perspectives and transparent disclosure of information are key aspects to ensure the legitimacy and effectiveness of regulation.

Transparency in Regulation Formulation: Ensuring that the regulation formulation process is transparent, with the disclosure of relevant and accessible information to the public. This may include consultation documents, regulatory impact analysis, and details on decision-making.

Access to Information: Facilitating access to information related to regulations. Ensuring the public has the ability to understand regulatory proposals and their potential implications.

Early Participation: Encouraging citizen participation from the early stages of the regulatory process. Allowing citizens' voices to influence regulation formulation before final decisions are made.

Public Consultations: Conducting meaningful public consultations to gather comments and opinions from various stakeholders. These consultations can help identify potential issues and improve the quality of regulations.

Online Platforms and Technology: Using online platforms and technology to facilitate citizen participation. This may include online surveys, discussion forums, and other tools to make participation more accessible.

Education and Awareness: Educating and raising awareness about the regulatory process and the importance of citizen participation. Promoting understanding of how regulations impact society and how participation can influence decisions.

Inclusion of Marginalized Groups: Ensuring the inclusion of marginalized and minority groups in the participatory process. Ensuring that the voices of all sectors of society are considered, avoiding potential biases and inequalities.

Feedback and Response: Establishing a clear and transparent feedback system to inform participants how their comments and concerns have been addressed. Responding to citizen participation reinforces the legitimacy of the process.

Whistleblower Protection: Implementing mechanisms to protect whistleblowers who disclose information about potential issues or irregularities in the regulatory process. This can promote transparency and accountability.

Compliance Reports: Publishing periodic compliance reports detailing how regulations are being implemented and enforced. This provides transparency on the actual impact of regulations on society.

Culture of Transparency: Fostering a culture of transparency within regulatory institutions and the government in general. Promoting open, ethical, and responsible practices.

Transparency and citizen participation not only strengthen the legitimacy of regulations but can also enhance the quality of regulatory decisions by incorporating a broader range of perspectives and knowledge.

Risks and Externalities: Considering how regulation addresses risks and externalities in the economy. Regulation should effectively manage these elements without creating significant distortions in the market.

Risk Identification: Identifying and evaluating potential risks associated with specific economic activities and sectors. This could include financial, security, environmental, and other risks.

Externalities Assessment: Evaluating both positive and negative externalities that may arise from economic activities. Externalities may include unintended effects on third parties not directly involved in economic transactions.

Systemic Risk Analysis: Analyzing systemic risks that could affect the economy as a whole. These risks may arise from the interconnection of various economic activities and sectors.

Incentive Design: Using regulation to create incentives that mitigate risks and reduce negative externalities. Positive incentives can encourage safer and more sustainable practices.

Policy Instruments: Selecting the most suitable policy instruments to address identified risks and externalities. This may include taxes, subsidies, performance standards, among other tools.

Compensation for Negative Externalities: Establishing mechanisms for compensating negative externalities. This could involve internalizing environmental or social costs associated with certain economic activities.

Cost-Benefit Analysis: Conducting cost-benefit analyses to assess whether proposed regulations are proportionate and effective in managing risks and externalities. This analysis helps balance expected benefits with associated costs.

Adaptability to Changes in Risks: Ensuring that regulations are flexible enough to adapt to changes in risks and externalities over time. An adaptable approach is crucial for addressing changing dynamics.

Risk Disclosure: Requiring transparent disclosure of risks by companies. This helps investors and the public make informed decisions and may reduce the likelihood of financial crises.

Monitoring and Compliance: Implementing monitoring and compliance mechanisms to ensure companies adhere to regulations aimed at managing risks and externalities. Effective enforcement is essential for regulatory effectiveness.

Prevention of Future Negative Externalities: Proactively designing regulations to prevent future negative externalities rather than merely reacting to existing problems.

Long-Term Impact Assessment: Conducting long-term impact assessments to understand how regulations affect risks and externalities as they evolve over time.

Effectively managing risks and externalities through well-designed regulations is essential for promoting a sustainable and equitable economic environment.

Critically evaluating regulatory theory involves weighing the benefits of government intervention in the market against potential costs and unintended consequences. A balanced approach seeks to optimize the effectiveness of regulation without unnecessarily sacrificing efficiency and economic competitiveness.

28.Education and Human Capital

The Austrian perspective on education and human capital is based on the Austrian School of Economics, a economic thought that emphasizes the importance of individuals, human action, and social coordination. From this viewpoint, education is considered a form of investment in human capital.

Individual Decision and Human Action: The Austrian School emphasizes the significance of individual decisions and human action in economics. From this perspective, the decision to invest in education is an individual choice based on each person's preferences and expectations.

Individual Autonomy: The Austrian School argues that individuals are autonomous actors making rational decisions based on their preferences and goals. In the context of education, this implies that the choice to invest in education is a personal decision influenced by individual preferences and goals.

Preferences and Expectations: Decision-making is influenced by subjective individual preferences, which can vary among people. Expectations regarding the future benefits of investing in education, such as increased job opportunities or personal development, also play a crucial role.

Opportunity Cost: The notion of opportunity cost is fundamental in the Austrian School. By choosing to invest in education, individuals forgo other available options. The decision is based on the subjective comparison of the expected benefits of education with the alternative benefits that could have been obtained.

Decentralized Knowledge: The Austrian School asserts that knowledge is decentralized and scattered among individuals. Each person has unique information about their circumstances and preferences. The decision to invest in education involves applying this decentralized knowledge to individual choices.

Entrepreneurship and Adaptability: Individual decision-making is linked to entrepreneurship and the ability to adapt to changing environments. The choice to invest in education can be seen as an entrepreneurial act, involving taking certain risks with the expectation of future benefits.

Outcome of Human Action: The Austrian School highlights that the economic order is the result of individual human actions. In the case of education, the education system and its outcomes are the product of choices and actions by individuals seeking to improve their skills and knowledge.

Critique of Centralized Planning: From the Austrian perspective, centralized planning tends to be inefficient because it cannot account for the diversity and complexity of individual preferences. In the case of education, decentralized decision-making is considered more effective in meeting individual needs and goals.

"Individual Decision and Human Action" in the Austrian School emphasizes autonomy, subjectivity, and decentralized knowledge in economic decision-making, including the decision to invest in education. This perspective influences how the relationship between individuals and the education system is addressed within the Austrian conceptual framework.

Investment in Human Capital: Education is viewed as an investment in human capital. By acquiring knowledge, skills, and experience, individuals enhance their productivity and ability to contribute to the labor market and society at large.

Increased Productivity: Investing in education is perceived as a means to increase individual productivity. As individuals gain knowledge, skills, and experience through education, they become more efficient and valuable in the labor market.

Development of Specific Skills: Education is not limited to acquiring general knowledge; it involves the development of specific skills. These skills can be directly applicable in work or business contexts, contributing to specialization and productivity.

Enhancement of Contribution Capacity: Investing in human capital enhances individuals' capacity to contribute to the labor market and, by extension, to society at large. Individuals are expected, through acquiring skills and knowledge, to play more significant and effective roles in their communities.

Adaptability and Continuous Learning: Education investment is also related to adaptability and continuous learning. In a changing economic environment, those with a solid educational foundation are better prepared to face new challenges and learn new skills throughout their careers.

Innovation and Entrepreneurship: The Austrian School values the capacity for innovation and entrepreneurship. Investment in education can foster these qualities by providing individuals with the ability to generate new ideas, solve problems, and take risks in the pursuit of opportunities.

Appreciation of Practical Experiences: In addition to theoretical knowledge, investment in human capital may include practical and applied experiences. These experiences can provide a deeper contextualized understanding of skills acquired during formal education.

Long-Term Return on Investment: Investing in education is considered a long-term investment with returns that accumulate over time. As individuals apply their knowledge and skills in their careers, they are expected to gain a return on investment in the form of better opportunities and higher incomes.

Contribution to Society's Wealth: From the Austrian perspective, investing in human capital not only benefits individuals but also contributes to the wealth and prosperity of society as a whole by raising the level of skills and productivity in the workforce.

The Austrian view highlights education as a strategic investment in the development and improvement of human capital, emphasizing the individual and social benefits derived from the acquisition of knowledge and skills.

Development of Entrepreneurial Skills: Education, according to the Austrian perspective, is not limited to the acquisition of technical skills but also focuses on the development of entrepreneurial skills. The ability to undertake, innovate, and adapt to changes in the economic environment is valued.

Focus on Creativity and Innovation: The Austrian perspective recognizes that education should not be limited to imparting technical knowledge but should also foster creativity and innovation. The ability to think originally and propose novel solutions to challenges is highly valued.

Entrepreneurial Spirit: The development of entrepreneurial skills involves cultivating an entrepreneurial spirit. This includes the willingness to take calculated risks, identify opportunities, and create value in various contexts, whether through traditional entrepreneurship or innovation in existing organizations.

Adaptability to Changes: The ability to adapt to changes in the economic environment is fundamental. Austrian education seeks to equip individuals with the skills necessary to face uncertainty and adjust effectively to changes in markets and economic conditions.

Promotion of Autonomy: The development of entrepreneurial skills involves promoting autonomy and independent decision-making. Individuals empowered to undertake are capable of taking the initiative and leading in the identification and pursuit of opportunities.

Experiential Learning: The Austrian perspective values experiential learning, allowing individuals to learn through practice and direct experience. This approach can strengthen entrepreneurial skills by facing real-world situations and making decisions in dynamic contexts.

Risk and Uncertainty Assessment: Entrepreneurs must be able to assess risk and uncertainty effectively. Austrian education seeks to develop analytical skills that enable individuals to make informed decisions in conditions of uncertainty.

Awareness of Market Signals: The ability of individuals to perceive and respond to market signals is valued. This involves the skill of proactively identifying opportunities and adjusting strategies based on changing market demands.

Incorporation of Tacit Knowledge: Entrepreneurial skills also involve the ability to work with tacit knowledge, knowledge that cannot be easily formalized. Entrepreneurial individuals can leverage experience and intuition to make informed decisions.

Cultivation of Networks and Collaboration: The Austrian perspective recognizes the importance of networks and collaboration in entrepreneurship. Education should encourage the building of relationships and collaboration with other actors in the economic environment.

The Austrian School's approach to the development of entrepreneurial skills emphasizes the importance of cultivating creativity, innovation, and adaptability in individuals, essential aspects for economic dynamism and efficiency.

Process of Discovery and Social Coordination: Education is considered a process of discovery, where individuals explore and develop their skills as they interact with the environment. This process contributes to social coordination, as the skills acquired by different individuals combine to create spontaneous order in society.

Individual Discovery: According to the Austrian School, education is not simply a passive transmission of knowledge but an active process of individual discovery. Individuals explore their interests, discover their abilities, and find opportunities as they engage in educational experiences.

Diversity of Skills and Knowledge: The educational discovery process contributes to the diversity of skills and knowledge in society. Each individual has unique talents, and through education, they can discover and develop those specific skills, thus contributing to the richness and complexity of the social fabric.

Spontaneous Coordination: Social coordination emerges spontaneously as individuals develop and apply their skills. It is not a centralized plan but the decentralized interaction of people pursuing their own goals and contributing to society through their talents and knowledge.

Emergent Order: Social coordination through education generates emergent order in society. This order is not imposed from above but naturally arises as individuals seek opportunities and contribute their unique skills.

Innovation and Change: The educational discovery process fosters innovation and change. As individuals discover new ideas and approaches, they contribute to the continuous evolution of society, adapting to the changing demands of the economic and social environment.

Market Feedback: Educational interaction does not occur in a vacuum. Individuals receive feedback from the market and society at large. This feedback can influence the discovery process, leading to adjustments and adaptations as individuals align their skills with the needs of the environment.

Learning Through Experience: The discovery process often involves learning through experience. Individuals can try different approaches and discover what works best for them based on the feedback obtained from their actions and choices.

Flexibility and Adaptability: Education as a discovery process encourages flexibility and adaptability. Individuals are not limited by a predetermined set of knowledge but have the ability to adjust and evolve as they discover new opportunities and challenges.

The Austrian vision highlights that education as a discovery process not only enriches individuals but also contributes to social coordination and spontaneous order in society as individual skills dynamically combine.

Diversity of Skills and Knowledge: The Austrian vision recognizes the diversity of skills and knowledge in society. Each individual has unique skills, and education adapts to this diversity, allowing people to specialize in areas where they can offer maximum value.

Unique Skills of Individuals: The Austrian School emphasizes that each individual possesses unique skills and specific talents. The diversity of skills ranges from cognitive abilities to practical and creative skills. Education is seen as a means to discover and develop those individual skills.

Adaptation to Individual Preferences: The diversity of skills and knowledge adapts to the individual preferences of students. Austrian education recognizes that each person has different interests and strengths, and the educational system should allow individuals to specialize in areas they are passionate about and where they can contribute significant value.

Specialization and Value Addition: The Austrian vision considers specialization as a source of value. By allowing individuals to specialize in specific areas, society benefits from deepened knowledge and skills in various fields. This contributes to efficiency and the generation of added value.

Contributions to Society: The diversity of skills and knowledge means that each individual can make valuable contributions to society based on their particular strengths. This fosters an environment where a multitude of perspectives and approaches enrich the social fabric.

Innovation and Creativity: Diversity fosters innovation and creativity. By providing an educational environment that allows individuals to explore their unique skills, the generation of novel ideas and innovative approaches to societal challenges is facilitated.

Respect for Individual Autonomy: Valuing the diversity of skills and knowledge is linked to respect for individual autonomy. Austrian education seeks to empower individuals to make informed decisions about their own educational paths, recognizing that each person has distinct goals and aspirations.

Knowledge Economy: In an ever-changing economic environment, the diversity of skills and knowledge aligns with the concept of a knowledge economy. The ability of individuals to adapt and contribute to diverse sectors is valued, strengthening the resilience and dynamics of society.

Decentralization of Learning: Diversity is also related to the decentralization of learning. Allowing individuals to choose diverse educational paths and adapt their learning to their specific needs contributes to a decentralized network of knowledge and skills.

The Austrian perspective highlights the importance of recognizing and celebrating the diversity of skills and knowledge in society, considering this diversity as a driver of innovation, creativity, and individual contribution to social well-being.

Competition and Decentralization: Competition among education providers and the decentralization of the education system are valued aspects according to the Austrian School. A more decentralized system is believed to allow greater adaptability and better response to individual needs.

Competition Among Providers: The Austrian School advocates for competition among education providers. This entails allowing different educational institutions to compete for students. Competition is perceived as a mechanism that drives continuous improvement, efficiency, and innovation in educational offerings.

Incentives for Quality: Competition creates incentives for quality. When educational institutions compete to attract students, they seek to offer high-quality educational programs to stand out. This approach can translate into an overall improvement in educational standards.

Variety of Educational Approaches: Competition encourages a variety of educational approaches. In a system with diverse options, students can choose programs that align better with their preferences, learning styles, and individual goals.

Adaptability to Individual Needs: A decentralized educational system allows greater adaptability to individual needs. Different institutions can offer specialized programs or specific pedagogical approaches, providing students with more personalized options.

Experimentation and Educational Innovation: Decentralization fosters experimentation and educational innovation. Various education providers have the freedom to try novel pedagogical approaches, innovative teaching methods, and alternative educational models without relying on a single central structure.

Decentralization of Decision-Making Power: Decentralization not only refers to educational offerings but also to the decentralization of decision-making power. Autonomy for educational institutions, teachers, and students to make decisions that fit their specific contexts is valued.

Promotion of Responsibility: Competition and decentralization foster responsibility. Educational institutions must be accountable to students and society at large, as their success depends on their ability to effectively meet educational needs.

Consumer Choice: Competition allows students and their families to be active educational consumers. They can choose from various educational options, reflecting the importance of treating education as a service that must meet the needs and preferences of users.

Resilience and System Adaptability: A decentralized educational system is perceived as more resilient and adaptable to changes in economic, social, and technological circumstances. It can more easily adjust to changing demands in the job market and societal evolutions.

In summary, competition and decentralization in education from the Austrian perspective are associated with improved quality, adaptability to individual needs, and the promotion of innovation, creating a more dynamic and results-oriented educational environment.

Tacit Knowledge: The Austrian vision recognizes the existence of tacit knowledge, i.e., knowledge that is difficult to codify and transmit formally. Education is not limited to the transmission of explicit information but also involves the internalization of tacit knowledge through experience.

Definition of Tacit Knowledge: Tacit knowledge, according to the Austrian vision, refers to understanding and skills that cannot be easily expressed formally or transmitted explicitly. It includes wisdom accumulated through experience and intuition that cannot be easily communicated through rules or manuals.

Importance of Practical Experience: Austrian education recognizes that tacit knowledge is primarily acquired through practical experience. It's not just theoretical information that matters, but the actual application of that knowledge in real-world situations.

Experiential Learning: The Austrian vision advocates for experiential learning, where individuals are directly involved in activities and situations that allow them to internalize tacit knowledge. This can include internships, practical projects, and other forms of active participation.

Adaptability and Flexibility: Understanding tacit knowledge contributes to the adaptability and flexibility of individuals. When facing novel situations, those with a strong component of tacit knowledge can effectively apply past experiences, even when circumstances are not identical.

Development of Intuitive Skills: Austrian education seeks to develop intuitive skills through tacit knowledge. Intuition, in this context, refers to the ability to make informed decisions based on experience without relying solely on explicit rules or detailed analysis.

Valuing Creativity: The Austrian vision values creativity, often based on the ability to apply tacit knowledge innovatively. Creativity can emerge when individuals combine their practical experience uniquely to address problems or identify opportunities.

Interpersonal Transfer of Knowledge: Tacit knowledge is also transferred interpersonally. Direct interaction between individuals, such as mentors and apprentices, allows the transfer of wisdom and skills that cannot be easily communicated through manuals or formal resources.

Respect for the Complexity of Knowledge: The consideration of tacit knowledge reflects respect for the complexity of knowledge and the understanding that not all wisdom can be fully broken down and expressed exhaustively in formal terms.

Lifelong Continuous Learning: The internalization of tacit knowledge promotes a lifelong continuous learning approach. Individuals recognize that constant experience enriches their set of tacit knowledge and contributes to their ability to face new challenges.

In summary, the Austrian vision highlights that education should not only focus on the transmission of explicit information but also on the development and internalization of tacit knowledge through practical experiences and interaction with the environment.

Uncertainty and Entrepreneurship: Uncertainty is a fundamental element in the Austrian vision. Education, by preparing individuals to face uncertainty, fosters entrepreneurial spirit and the ability to make decisions in a dynamic environment.

Recognition of Uncertainty: The Austrian vision recognizes that uncertainty is an intrinsic feature of markets and economic activities. Individuals do not have complete access to future information, and education must prepare them to make decisions in an environment where outcomes are inherently uncertain.

Development of Ambiguity Tolerance: Austrian education seeks to develop tolerance for ambiguity and the ability to face uncertain situations. Successful entrepreneurs are those who can make informed decisions even when complete information is not available.

Entrepreneurial Spirit as a Response to Uncertainty: Uncertainty is perceived as an opportunity for entrepreneurial spirit in the Austrian vision. Instead of being feared, uncertainty is considered fertile ground for identifying opportunities and creating value. Education should foster an entrepreneurial mindset in this context.

Teaching Decision-Making Under Uncertainty: Austrian education not only transmits information but also teaches individuals to make informed decisions under conditions of uncertainty. This involves developing analytical skills, risk assessment, and decision-making based on available information.

Emphasis on Creativity and Innovation: Uncertainty stimulates the need for creativity and innovation. Austrian education highlights the importance of cultivating these skills, as they allow individuals to think originally and find creative solutions to challenges posed by uncertainty.

Learning Through Experience: Austrian education advocates for learning through experience, which involves directly facing uncertain situations. By engaging in practical projects, ventures, and real-world situations, individuals can develop practical skills for decision-making in uncertain environments.

Dynamic Assessment of Opportunities: Austrian entrepreneurs are seen as individuals capable of dynamically assessing opportunities as they arise. Education should prepare individuals to identify and capitalize on opportunities in changing and unpredictable environments.

Promotion of Business Resilience: Austrian education promotes business resilience by recognizing that individuals may face challenges and failures in uncertain environments. The ability to learn from experience and adapt to changing situations is essential for entrepreneurial success.

Focus on Action and Initiative: Uncertainty does not paralyze entrepreneurs according to the Austrian vision; rather, it drives them to action and initiative. Education should foster a willingness to take calculated risks and proactive measures rather than waiting for complete information.

In summary, the Austrian vision highlights that education should not only provide theoretical knowledge but also develop practical and mental skills that enable individuals to thrive in environments characterized by uncertainty.

The Austrian perspective on education and human capital emphasizes individual autonomy, diversity of skills, adaptability, and the entrepreneurial role of education in societal development. Investment in education is perceived as a means to empower human potential and contribute to the flourishing of human action in the economic context.

29.Development of Austrian Theory Over Time

The Austrian School of Economics has undergone evolution and adaptations over time, with different historical periods marked by changes in theory and approaches within the school.

Origins and Precursors (19th and early 20th centuries): The Austrian School originated in the second half of the 19th century with figures such as Carl Menger, the founder of the school, and other economists like Eugen von Böhm-Bawerk and Friedrich von Wieser. These early thinkers laid the foundations for the subjective theory of value and the theory of the margin.

Rise and Development (Early 20th Century): During the early decades of the 20th century, the Austrian School experienced significant growth, with the key contributions of Ludwig von Mises and Friedrich Hayek. Mises developed the theory of money and the business cycle, while Hayek contributed ideas on information and knowledge in economics. These thinkers influenced economic theory and political philosophy.

Period of Challenges and reinterpretations (Mid-20th Century): In the mid-20th century, the Austrian School faced challenges and criticisms, particularly in the context of the dominance of Keynesian thought. However, some Austrian economists, such as Murray Rothbard, continued to develop and expand the theory, focusing on aspects such as interventionism theory and the ethics of classical liberalism.

Resurgence and Specific Applications (Late 20th Century): Towards the end of the 20th century, there was a resurgence of interest in the Austrian School, in part due to criticisms of predominant theories. Specific applications were explored, such as public choice theory and Austrian law and economics. The connection between the Austrian School and the theory of human action was also emphasized.

Contemporary Approaches (21st Century): In the 21st century, the Austrian School continues to influence economics and political philosophy. Contemporary approaches have been developed, and Austrian economists have addressed current issues such as the global financial crisis, monetary theory, and the influence of technology on the economy.

Expansion into Other Fields (21st Century): The Austrian School has expanded its influence beyond economics, including areas such as legal theory, political philosophy, and the theory of complex systems. The connection between the Austrian School and other disciplines has been explored, leading to a broader understanding of its approach.

Diversity of Perspectives (21st Century): Currently, the Austrian School is known for its diversity of perspectives and approaches under its umbrella. While some Austrian economists adhere to more classical traditions, others have integrated new ideas and methodologies, generating internal debates and contributions to contemporary economic theory.

The Austrian Theory has undergone a rich evolution over time, adapting to challenges and developing new ideas in different historical periods. The diversity of approaches within the Austrian School has contributed to its ongoing relevance in economic theory and other related fields.